THE TRAVELLERS' LIBRARY

*

BLUE WATER

THE TRAVELLERS' LIBRARY

Some of the books now included are given below. A more complete list is given at the end of this volume.

CAN SUCH THINGS BE by Ambrose Bierce
THE BLACK DOG by A. E. Coppard
THE AUTOBIOGRAPHY OF A SUPER-TRAMP by W. H. Davies
BABBITT by Sinclair Lewis
THE CRAFT OF FICTION by Percy Lubbock
EARLHAM by Percy Lubbock
WIDE SEAS AND MANY LANDS by Arthur Mason
SELECTED PREJUDICES by H. L. Mencken
THE MIND IN THE MAKING by James Harvey Robinson
THE WAY OF ALL FLESH by Samuel Butler
EREWHON by Samuel Butler
EREWHON REVISITED by Samuel Butler
ADAM AND EVE AND PINCH ME by A. E. Coppard
DUBLINERS by James Joyce
DOG AND DUCK by Arthur Machen
ANGELS AND MINISTERS by Laurence Housman
THE WALLET OF KAI LUNG by Ernest Bramah
KAI LUNG'S GOLDEN HOURS by Ernest Bramah
TWILIGHT IN ITALY by D. H. Lawrence
THE DREAM by H. G. Wells
CLORINDA WALKS IN HEAVEN by A. E. Coppard
ROMAN PICTURES by Percy Lubbock
GRECIAN ITALY by Henry James Forman
MARIUS THE EPICUREAN by Walter Pater
THE WHITE SHIP by Aino Kallas
MULTITUDE AND SOLITUDE by John Masefield
SPRING SOWING by Liam O'Flaherty
WILLIAM by F. H. Young
WUTHERING HEIGHTS by Emily Brontë
THE COUNTRY OF THE POINTED FIRS by Sarah Orne Jewett
ON A CHINESE SCREEN by Somerset Maugham
THE CONQUERED by Naomi Mitchison

BLUE WATER

by

ARTHUR STURGES HILDEBRAND

With an Introduction by HARRISON SMITH

LONDON
JONATHAN CAPE 30 BEDFORD SQUARE

FIRST PUBLISHED 1923
RE-ISSUED IN THE TRAVELLERS' LIBRARY 1927

CONTENTS

INTRODUCTION

Portrait of a Sailor—Arthur S. Hildebrand

★

As far back as one can remember him, Arthur Hildebrand was obsessed by the sea, – although that is, perhaps, too vague an expression for the delight that his imagination found in it. It was not the beauty or the wildness of its moods, nor the magnetic power of its vast level expanse such as a poet or a painter might feel. As an artist may feel passion for only a special corner of his art, so Hildebrand was a specialist in his admiration of the sea, confining it to the sailing ships that were wafted over its horizons, to the men who sailed them, the adventures they met in battling with the elemental forces of nature, and the charm of snug harbours where at night the riding lights of moored ships reflected their moving path on the black water. For steamers of any type he had a friendly (if cold) interest. Met with outside of land, I saw him once intensely enthusiastic when a great passenger ship painted white from stem to stern came slowly toward us waving a plume of smoke and passed our idle yacht within fifty feet. But on examination it appeared that he was thinking of two things: first, of how splendid an impression we ourselves must be creating on the passengers who stared at us from round porthole and deckchair, and who, so he said, if they could obey their impulse, would leap in one body into the warm sea and board our fragile craft; and second, of the fragrant and unfamiliar Caribbean ports from which she hailed, laden with bananas, tarantulas, and human beings.

An island, any bit of land, however sterile, isolated from the mainland, had a peculiar fascination for him, as if the sea that encircled it had given its rock and earth a mysterious quality of its own. Even in his most expansive and romantic moods on those occasions—too rare, alas—when we faced each other in the smoke-laden cabin of some tiny yacht, hunched over the table to keep our heads from scraping the deck beams, inhaling the fumes dear to amateur sailors – that pungent mixture of old rope, linseed oil, pipe smoke, kerosene, burnt bacon, mouldy leather – even in these perfect and fragrant moments when conversation spouted from us as effortless as the ebb tide, Hildebrand could never explain from what limbo in his past or his ancestry this prepossession for ships had come.

We had known each other from the days when we were blithely fourteen, both of us New Englanders and already trying to forget it, both of us brought up to the comfortable and serene traditions of a middle-sized city. When first I knew him, he had already given himself over body and soul to the sea on which he was to adventure so ill prepared and to which he was to give his life. He was mildly intrigued with ordinary schoolboy interests but his heart was never in these adolescent preoccupations. A boy's schoolbooks are a sure sign of where his interest lies. 'Hilly's' schoolbooks were scribbled over with the profiles of schooners, brigs, yachts of all shapes and sizes, in harbour or at sea. His copy of Cæsar's Commentaries sported a magnificent clipper ship, house flag and all. The meticulous care he had taken with these sketches attested to the hours that should have been spent at algebra or moribund languages. And he was clever in other ways with his hands – those long, nervous fingers, a little spatulate, could handle a jack-knife with the delicacy of a woman with a darning needle. His room held neatly piled copies of the great yachting magazine of those days, *The Rudder*; and he knew by heart the designs of the latest ships, could even read those mysterious assemblages of curves and lines that will remain Greek to me to the end of my days; and could perform the miracle of transforming them into carved wooden hulls which he flattened on one side and mounted on a board.

Three years passed by like the whiz of Coleridge's cross bow, and I think that they left few shadows on his mind. For boys these years belong to reckless action and to vague day-dreaming, preparing one's self for God knows what. Sometimes we saw much of each other, and then, to my present regret, months would pass by when we exchanged no more than a nod. But I was destined to be drawn into the circle of his charm, for even then he could talk when the mood seized him as no one else I knew could talk. It is curious that I can never remember anything he said in those days, although in our last year we saw a good deal of each other. He was not a philosopher given to profound and uncomfortable analysis, but his enthusiasm was always distracted and his words caught fire at the minor subtleties of life. He was already reading widely narratives of early voyages and discoveries, and give him this for a subject or the ship that he was going to build some day when he could afford it, and he was off to a running start. By this time we had become a trio, for another lover of the sea of our own age had joined us, and between us we conspired against the peace of our families and in some measure against our own security by planning a cruise in Maine. We entered into a long (and on his part ill-spelled) correspondence with a fisherman who owned a craft called the *Helen H.*, of which we had an extraordinarily discouraging photograph and which 'Hilly' drew in pencil a thousand times until to my mind she assumed the proportions of a millionaire's yacht.

One fine day in June we boarded her, where she floated at the end of a little wharf which jutted out from a cove between two blue hills. My first night aboard her was one of horror and apprehension; indeed she was enough to have discouraged Columbus. In her cabin one man could have slept comfortably; a stove occupied half of one bunk and there was a black space forward of her mast where one could lie if one did not object to pressing one's rear against kerosene tins and wet rope. In an hour we discovered she leaked, and only 'Hilly's' incredible enthusiasm prevented us from abandoning her on the spot, for she absorbed water like a sponge. In a week we were regularly throwing overboard in pails that part of the Atlantic Ocean that flowed through her seams; in two weeks we were taking fifteen-minute shifts under way, and at night when the water from the cabin floor gurgled in our faces we took turns every sixty-five minutes, bailing her dry again. Twice before we got her back we had given her up as lost and were prepared to fling ourselves into the dinghy, with a score of miles to the nearest shore. It was Hildebrand's imperturbable optimism that induced me to risk my life for so little gain. It was a ship and he was at sea. That was enough for him.

We sailed two more summers along the Maine coast. The second summer, against all advice we had taken a sturdy sloop called the *Bonny Doone* across the menacing tides of the Bay of Fundy, and had sunk her, as we deserved to, on a reef off a miserable place called Briar Island. We had saved our lives by a good half minute, and I shall never forget the forced cheer with which 'Hilly' tried to comfort our profound depression. It was, after all, his first shipwreck, and his mind balanced the hideous fact that we had lost our ship against the thrill of a great adventure. He was certainly colder than any of us, for he was never a full-blooded man, and perhaps he was more frightened than any of us; but if he was, not a tremor of his voice betrayed it. It was on this occasion that I really discovered his merit, an indomitable will, a glowing mind, set in a body that refused to behave, (that alas was often weak with seasickness and exhaustion).

I took still another cruise with him before we finished forever with college. In three weeks we covered almost a thousand miles in a yawl that was so perfect that I have almost forgotten her. 'Hilly' said that one loved boats for their faults, and I suppose that is the reason.

Then came a lapse of years when only rumours kept

me in touch with him. He had become engaged to a girl whose only attribute seemed to be her red hair; it was broken off; he was studying architecture and was somewhere in New York, to which haven of unrest I had come myself. I saw him only once at this stage, in a room messed up with drawing tools which he shared with a stranger. And behold, this man also had been caught by his fascination. He admired him, perhaps even more than I ever had. 'Hilly' was engaged in creating a fantastic opera house which would never, and perhaps could never, be built in any land. He had learned to draw with ease and fluency and he pulled out from a drawer a series of projects for model cities and billionaires' palaces on which he had been fooling away his time. And amongst them schooners and a magnificent ketch which he was certain just then was the ultimate type of yacht.

Years passed, and 'Hilly' had given up architecture for the arduous pursuit of literature. To save himself from starving he was librarian at the Yale Club, which, like everything else in America, is the largest club in the world. For that noble refuge of bachelors and fugitives from matrimony 'Hilly' organised an extraordinarily fine library, with as many books of the sea as he could persuade the committee to buy. But once this was done he was frankly bored, and he came to live at my tiny house in lower New York, where I sheltered him with joy and with profound gratitude at the opportunity, for certainly no man ever had a more useful or accomplished guest.

Then he met one of the heroes of this book – Duncan

McGlashan Spencer. Spencer, or 'Pat', as you will know him, had spent the last two years of the War dashing about in an aeroplane, and I think that the slow progress of a sailing yacht would have appeared to him at that time tame if its adventure had not been so incredibly embellished by the nights in which 'Hilly's' imagination flew in a colourful stream over this great project, which was to include the whole stretch of the Mediterranean and the long voyage across the Atlantic to New York. The yacht was to be bought in Scotland, and 'Hilly' trusted 'Pat' to get a good one, for he knew by this time that there was plenty of salt water in this young Scotchman's veins. 'Pat' left for home, and after his cable announcing that he had bought the *Caltha* I lived for weeks with a feverishly excited man until 'Pat' had come back to us again. But of the cruise of the *Caltha* I need say nothing, for you have only to read *Blue Water*, where it is inimitably set down. Unhappily I was not to go with them, except for the first ten days of storm, which you will find catalogued in the early chapters of this book. I came back to my work in New York and waited for them to return. Now and then I worried a little. In the last months 'Hilly' had seemed to me to grow gaunter and paler; his skin seemed to stretch too tightly over his face; and certainly at his age his hair had no business to become so thin. I missed his companionship, and indeed no man who had lived with him as long as I could have helped it.

Finally, as you will read in the last chapter, they sold the *Caltha* in Marseilles. 'Hilly' was not destined to cross the Atlantic by any southern route.

He came back to us miserably on an Italian steamer on which he had been vilely seasick, settled down in a little room in New York and wrote *Blue Water*. He finished it and then wrote another book, a romantic life of Magellan which showed his increasing ability in the use of words. In a year *Blue Water* had become a classic of the sea on this side of the Atlantic, and with the appearance of Hildebrand's second book the critics awoke to his real worth. His path was clear before him, his venture already won, though he was as poor as any church mouse. If he had lived to write two or three more books I am confident that he would have left a lasting mark on the romantic literature of the sea.

Unhappily, that fine optimism of which I have spoken, that untrammelled imagination, overcame his common sense. He would not admit that he was no longer strong. During that winter before his fatal adventure he had kept his room so hot that another man entering from the crisp air of New York gasped for breath. He ate little and had to select his food carefully or else he regretted it for a week. But the frost was barely out of the ground before we found, to our consternation, that 'Hilly' was planning a voyage that would have daunted a Norseman. He had met 'Bill' Nutting, an amateur yachtsman who had crossed the Atlantic in his own boat and had twice almost lost her by holding on too long in a gale. 'Bill' had become enamoured with the type of boat they build in Norway, a shallow-draught sloop which from 'Hilly's' sketches filled uswith apprehension. The *Leif Ericcson* would sail, of course, with the wind astern or abeam, but what if she were caught with a gale ahead and mountainous seas? One night we four dined in New York and 'Hilly' talked of this mad adventure as he had never talked before. There was a map on the floor of the living room and he charted for us the incredible course that was to be his in the *Leif Ericcson*. My friend is mad, I thought, when he described the gap of eight hundred miles across some of the stormiest waters in the world, when he pointed out with a forefinger trembling with eagerness that grim and terrible shore, the coast of Greenland, when he described the icebergs they would meet beyond Cape Fear.

Well, the long and short of it is we let him go. Perhaps no power could have stopped him. But that night, after they had left, the man who had never known sickness and who had to pull tenderly on an ordinary rope lest he break it, and our friend who had spoken gaily of icebergs and who to keep warm had worn all winter a flannel dressing-gown in a room at a temperature of 80 – after 'Hilly' had gone, 'Pat' and I, his old shipmates, faced each other and one of us said, 'He'll never come back.' Should we have spoken to him? It was beyond our courage, and why it was I cannot explain. Should we have said anything to the other man? We could not betray our friend. I think often of that night, for the vital issues of life rarely take form so instantaneously and so dramatically. But, as I have said, we let him go. Perhaps the War has something to do with it. It seems so important now that a man should live his life and fulfil his desire, whether it is to die comfortably in bed, or storming one of the Poles. After all, death is not so important, nor indeed so rare, and heroism is both.

I heard from him from Copenhagen, where they had tried the boat out in sheltered seas, and from Iceland, which they reached after a laborious and delayed passage. They should have wintered there and started again in the spring of the next year. It was already too late. That brief season before ice begins to form in Davis Strait was drawing to a close. Or, after reaching Greenland, they might have sailed straight South for warmer water. Weeks passed, and there was no word. The autumn came. A Government cutter sailed North and returned baffled. Fishermen combed the distant harbours of the Labrador and Greenland coasts. At last we gave up hope. We knew that 'Hilly' was lost somewhere in those icy waters, along that desolate and barren coast which is the very antithesis of his romantic and colourful soul.

New York, May, 1927. HARRISON SMITH

CHAPTER ONE

In Which We Make a Beginning

*

It was in May, 1920, that Pat Spencer came into the garret of Hal Smith's house in New York and found me sitting on a saw-horse, looking at the stars that were shining through the rafters where the shingles had been ripped off to make a dormer window for the nursery.

'There's too much fuss in the world about going to work,' he said, without more preliminary than lighting a cigarette. 'I'd like to cut loose and go on a cruise – a real cruise, say for about a year.'

'There's something I've always wanted to do,' I answered. 'I've always wanted to go for a cruise in the Mediterranean.'

'We could do it!' he said. 'We could get a boat in Scotland, and come right around down – Penzance is the Jumping-off Place – and go all the way to Cyprus.'

This was a bit more than I had intended. I was dazzled by the promptness with which a whole year was being dedicated.

'Well,' I said, 'I'm not so sure about . . .'

'How big a boat would we need?' Pat cut in, taking a seat on the other saw-horse.

We concluded that fifteen tons would be right, big enough to live aboard in comfort, and not too big to handle easily when the weather was bad; a strong and able little ship, willing to go to windward in heavy weather, not frightened at a few tons of green water on deck; a ship built right to start with, and kept right, with legs under her for offshore work, and a long keel, so that she would sail herself; yawl rigged – since it was probable that we could get nothing else – with short spars, and the canvas well inboard. . . . Within twenty minutes we saw her, plain before our eyes, coming into some still harbour, thousands of miles away, in the warm sunshine of a blue and gold summer morning, or hove to in a black night of shouting windy weather, with the anchor light lashed in the mizzen rigging, and the crests of the big waves growling past her in the dark. We saw the purple headlands of the Balearic Isles, and the stars above the palm trees in Algeria; we saw the snow-capped mountains in Corsica, and 'Cyprus set in the Sea.' . . .

'Alexandria,' said Pat.

'Antioch the Glorious . . .'

'Constantinople . . .'

'And the Isles of Greece . . .'

'Look here,' said Pat suddenly, changing his tone. 'Are you in on this?'

'Yes,' I said. 'With the proviso of the Cup and the Lip.'

We shook hands on it and went downstairs to tell the family.

A few days after this, Mr. MacGlashan, Pat's grandfather, an old man, with years of yachting traditions behind him, came back from a visit in Cleveland, and Pat asked him if he thought this a good time to find an able cruising boat on the Clyde.

'And when I say able,' he explained, ' I mean able to go anywhere.'

'Hoots, man!' said Mr. MacGlashan. 'What the Deil's going to hurt her?'

In June, Pat went to Scotland.

All things have a beginning, and it was thus that we made a beginning of this one.

Now cruising is more than a sport; it is a means of travel, a manner of living, an attitude towards life.

I mean cruising under sail. Steam, or petrol, is preferred by some: these have engine-rooms, very neat and shining, and they listen to the hum and rhythmic thump with great delight; they stand on their bridges and steer their ships, and make their port at dawn of the day they have predicted, on the tide they selected a week before. But they miss Romance.

The liner comes and goes, blow high, blow low; she leaves her dock when the flag goes up and arrives four thousand miles away as the clock is striking – she has a certain share of the romantic, because of that very precision. But if she's late, by 'stress of weather,' she has failed, and loses credit. The sailing ship never fails. Late or early, blown off, hove to, battered, stripped, sunk, or missing, she is always romantic. She has it ; it's in her, and nothing can take it away. Her virtue is that she exists, and you have but to look at her to know it.

When you set out, in a sailing ship, the effort, and the rewards of it, are yours. It is you, with your two hands and your courage, that make her go. Your windward-open eye, your judgments of the shifts of weather and the rules the clouds are following, your imagination, interpretive, sea-taught, that knows the lights at night, the promise of the dawn, the rocks and the currents and the shallow water; your knowledge of what the ship will do, and how she likes her headsails trimmed – these things are vital to the enterprise. When you arrive, the land is yours, since you have done something to deserve it; the headland you have weathered is like a feather in your cap, and the harbour to which you ran back, that day when it blew so hard, holds always, after that, some portion of your heart. The old explorers, the wind-jammers who opened up the world – when they set up their standards on a coast, and claimed it, with all lands adjacent thereunto, they spoke no more than simple truth.

Cruising, you are at once a wanderer, and a stay-at-home; you carry your house with you everywhere, and it carries you. It is the best of houses – a snug, trim habitation, weather-tight, sheltered and secluded, although the weather itself, wind, rain, and sea, is just outside. It is compact and complete – large enough, yet not too large – neatly kept, since there is no room to have it otherwise, convenient, since disorder and a ship do not agree, resourceful, since you are cut off from all the world. To live aboard a ship is the best of lives.

And, then, the ship. She has her temperament, that calls for sympathetic understanding, and there exists between you the mutual dependence which is the foundation of all intimacy. You resent abuses to her; you feel the strains that she feels, and try to ease them; you have a generous regard for her labour in a seaway, and shorten sail to spare her. Yet you will drive her, rail roaring under, when the mood is on you, without mercy or tenderness or any thought beyond your own exhilaration – and she responds. She is willing, and demurely obedient. You may ask her to do the impossible, and she will try. No ship, ever, in any situation, in living gales or mill-race currents or shoals or breakers or Things to Come, feeble as she may be, bulged with age, incompetent as a tub, leaking or rotten, with her rig tottering over the side, ever refuses, when asked to try. However, she is no slave – she has a will of her own, and whims for you to study; she takes charge at times, and goes her own sweet way, seeming to forget you. But she comes back, in the end, into your guiding hands, with every confidence. There is something wonderful about a ship. We speak of her 'behaviour,' as if she were alive. Wood and iron and hemp – and yet, somehow, a soul.

Cruising is more than a sport. The mood of it comes over you at times, and you can neither work nor rest nor heed another call until you have a deck beneath your feet and point a bowsprit out to sea.

And I was waiting for word from Pat. I imagined him visiting, in turn, and in growing discouragement, the yards on the Clyde, steaming in and out of the doors of all the brokers' offices in Glasgow – and finding nothing. I saw possibilities of failure. I argued, reluctantly, that 1921 would be the first big yachting season since the war: all the available boats would be in use, the market would be tight, and new construction very expensive. And in our favour, on the other side of the argument, there was nothing – except our desire to go.

But on the twenty-seventh of August, I got a cablegram:

'Her name is *Caltha*. I sail to-morrow.'

Fairly skipping in my excitement, I went to the Library and got out Lloyd's List of Yachts. I did not expect to find her there, really. But she was there. Her signal letters were H. C. P. L.; she was of nineteen tons, Thames Measure, and fourteen and forty-seven hundredths tons Registry, fifty-four feet long on the deck, forty-seven on the water-line, ten feet beam, and seven feet six inches draught of water; she was designed by H. P. Blake, and built by White Brothers, at Southampton, in 1900. This was everything that I could learn of her until Pat returned. It was meagre, as to details, and there were a thousand questions that I wanted to ask, but it was something, and gave me material for thought.

When he came back, he brought a blue-print of the ship, and showed me the pictures of many of the others that he had considered; we agreed that he had found exactly what was wanted – a strong and able little ship, big enough to live aboard in comfort, and not too big to handle easily when the weather was bad. Then he went to Philadelphia for the winter, and we both settled down to wait, as best we could. It was a very long winter.

But everything happens, if only you can wait. On the seventh of June Pat came bursting in upon me – I was working on a model of Henry Hudson's *Half Moon* – a ship only four feet longer than the *Caltha* – he thumped the butt of a rifle on the floor – a gun which he had brought to kill pirates, if we should meet any – and shouted that the time had come. On the ninth, we sailed, with twenty-two thousands ton of steel under us, and four big turbines cheering for us, and on the evening of the eighth day out of New York we were walking in the gloaming down along the banks of Clyde.

CHAPTER TWO

The Bonny Banks of Clyde

★

THIS was in the days of the coal strike, and the air was unusually clear, everyone said, so that Glasgow had lost something of its characteristic atmosphere, and the Highlands across the river were very sharp in outline and dark against the pale sky. As I watched the rain squalls sweep across the face of Ben Lomond I wondered if I should be able to endure this hardy Scotch climate; I had a cold already, from merely breathing the air, and it seemed likely that all the enthusiasm would soon be frozen out of me. We got off the train at Greenock – the towns are so close together that exactness in the choice of stations is of no importance – and went to what must surely be the best hotel in the world, where the waitress recommended to me a local climatical counter-irritant which made me feel better. We were starting the Blue Water Cruise with a contrast.

We set out at once along the Esplanade, walking very fast; beside us the Clyde was rolling down to the sea, and the water was lapping loudly at our feet; a wet and blustering wind flapped the skirts of our coats. We were passing long rows of dreary villas, all resolutely shut against the bleak weather, and we could see nothing ahead of us but a continuation of them, and the misty mountains down the Firth. We came into the next town, but saw no yachts. At the end of a mile, we met a man coming in the other direction, and Pat stopped him and asked where Paul Jones' Yacht Yard was.

'Ye ken the Torpedo Factory?' the man asked.

'Oh, aye,' said Pat, quite naturally falling back to a Glasgow accent. In fact, it is difficult to avoid doing this; even I, years before in Edinboro', had unconsciously insulted people because they thought my imitation of them was an attempt at being funny.

'It's just beyond,' the man said. 'Across the park a bit.'

When we rounded the corner of the Factory fence a great bare field opened up before us, and on the far side of it, at the edge of the bay, was a group of huddled buildings, with masts sticking up into the sky above them. In bold letters across the end of the nearest shed was painted 'Paul Jones, Son, and Company.'

We ran across that blasted heath. We considered all the masts in turn, and eliminated all but two, which must, then, be the *Caltha's*. We were vastly reassured, for though Pat had seen her before, had, actually, been aboard of her, we had not been able to free ourselves from the idea that something terrible had happened, and that there was no such ship in the world.

There was a gate in the fence, but neither of us saw it, or would have spent the time to open it; we squeezed through a narrow gap and went stumbling over the timbers and chain and bits of blocking with which the yard was littered. A moment afterwards we stood under the *Caltha's* bilge, looking up at her gray sides. There she was. She was real. We reached up our hands and touched her.

There was a ladder lying near, and we put it up against her rail and climbed aboard. Her sides were streaked with dirt, and her deck was bare. The skylights stared blankly;

there was not even a bit of rigging, to give an air of vitality, but only a few frayed streamers of marline on the hoops, whipping in the wind. The two naked masts rose up, with a gantline on each, and nothing else. There was an abandoned, deserted look about her. But it seemed to do her good to have men walking on her deck again.

We opened the after skylight and wriggled in. Some cork fenders, the accommodation ladder, a bundle of spare blocks, the rudder for the dinghy, and two or three coils of line, were piled in the berths. The floor had been taken up, and the pigs of ballast were spotted with candle drippings where the motor engineers had been at work. In the saloon, the floor boards were piled on one transom, and the table and companion steps on the other. The place was cold, and a wan pale twilight shone down from above. We stepped across on the floor beams and sat down, with our feet on the ballast, leaning back against the piled-up encumbrances.

We were delighted. We jumped up to feel the solid deck beams overhead, to open the lockers, to thump the mast with our fists. We scrambled all over her and looked at everything. We kept telling each other that she didn't yet know she was alive. 'She's a lady,' we said, jubilantly, 'and she's got guts!'

We left a package of cigarettes, and a box of matches in one of the lockers – after a year, we were still keeping matches in that same locker – and went on deck again.

It was after eight o'clock on a Saturday night, and the yard was shut up and deserted by everyone except the watchman. Him we sought out and interviewed; though we knew it was useless, we were eager to make a start. We had come in regard to the *Caltha*. Aye? Aye. Could we see Mr. Jones?

'It's no Mr. Jones you'll want to see,' he said.

Pat asked why not.

'He's dead,' said the watchman, cocking a shaggy eyebrow at us. 'Aye. Dead long ago. It's Mr. Agnew you'll be wanting. Old Man Jones was a different sort of a man altogether. . . .'

In the bay, just beyond the yard, a small steamer was ashore, driven up high and dry on the weed-covered rocks by the storm of the week before; Mr. Agnew was aboard of her, and all the men from the yard, trying to float her by digging under her stern, by lashing casks to her bilge, by pulling at her valiantly and vainly with the towboat *Flying Elf*. They worked for the greater part of the night; they took out of her everything that could be moved, and piled all her coal on the shore beside her. Late Sunday night, on the flood tide, she came off.

It was eleven o'clock when we got back to our room at the hotel, but it was still light, and I stood for a time looking out at the hills across the Clyde, watching the clouds and the tumbling mists that rolled down and filled the valleys. The clear cold glow from the Western sky fell across that steaming tumult and haunted it with a wild and magical sort of beauty. The river caught the reflections of it, and carried them out to sea.

I tried, and failed, to imagine the lands that lay before us; I could not picture the *Caltha* under the hot summer sunlight, and could not believe, even, that the broad river was a part of the Great Road that goes all over the world.

I fell to thinking of Old Man Jones, 'over eighty when he died, and that was in 1910.' He had been known to all Clydeside as a 'character.' He claimed to be the first man who had hauled out boats in an upright position, on their keels; before his time they had always been dragged from the water on their bilges, like careened frigates – indeed, the fishing boats are so handled, even now, in remote harbours where there are no runways.

When he was a young man he had shipped as a sailor, and had spent the earlier years of his life walloping up and down the Seven Seas, looking at the world. Then, in the fifties, he had enlisted in the United States Navy, following the lead of his namesake. I like to think of him as a gunner, a rough, hairy lad, called 'Scotty' by his mates, and cursing cordially in thick Gourock as he dumped down the round shot beside his gun. Though whom he found to fire at, in 1850, I can't imagine. Perhaps it was this lack of any enemy that made him give up his post. At any rate, he left the navy when his time was up. He had no liking for a quiet life.

He went to sea in a Yankee whaler – in a ponderous lurching barque, out of New Bedford, probably, on one of those soul-shaking voyages that girdles the world and fights with whales and lives to tell of it – and he was shipwrecked in the South Pacific. Precisely where this happened, no one seems to know, for though he told the story often enough, 'he was a poor one to remember names.' Perhaps he was the Scotchman whom Herman Melville met, in 'Typee.' At any rate, he lived naked among the savages for a year and a-half.

Then he found a way to come back to Gourock, and he started a boat yard – a startling project, when you stop to think of it, seeing that it was evolved by a naked man in a cocoanut grove – and the boys and girls used to get him to open his shirt, when he was in a good humour – which wasn't often – so that they could admire the fantastic tattooing with which he was covered – so it was said – from the top of his collar to the tops of his shoes. He was over eighty when he died, and the neighbours remember him for his temper and his tattooing and the tales he used to tell. His name is still on the buoys that lie at the moorings off in front of the yard.

It is not supposed that Romance runs North of Fifty-three, and Gourock is two whole degrees on the wrong side of the line; but the narrative of Old Man Jones seems to open a way for adventure. Evidently, it is possible to reach Blue Water from the Firth of Clyde.

With that we went to bed, in sudden panic lest the night should be over before the daylight had faded from the hills.

CHAPTER THREE

The Yacht Yard

*

On Monday, as we were crossing the blasted heath, we passed two greasy-faced scoundrels – that is, motor engineers – who were carrying on their shoulders a section of shafting. Pat asked them if they were taking it to the *Caltha*, and they said that they were. It had already been arranged, by letter, that the bent shaft – someone had stood on it, having taken up the floor for the purpose – should be replaced, and that the motor should be put in order; this was the first sign of activity, and cheered us, although the slow passage of the shaft across the heath was not in itself encouraging.

We saw Mr. Agnew, and started. The yard was to scrub the decks, paint the topsides and the bottom, varnish, rig, bend sail, and launch. In this, of course, we helped, and the miscellaneous work, the domestic arrangements, were our sole concern. We started, but there was something wrong. Things moved with a slowness that was very irritating, and there were days together when there were no workmen, save ourselves, aboard the ship.

There was in the yard an old gentleman who wore a festive red-and-white striped cap. This man and a friend were fitting out a wee sloop, messing about with paint and putty and bits of rope, often quarrelling fiercely with each other in a choking rage at the sluggishness of events. At first we were faintly amused by it, but later we began to understand.

I invited Mr. Agnew aboard. We had told him, of course, that we were in a great hurry, and impatient of delay, but everyone who is getting a ship ready for sea feels so, and he had seen us simply as normal clients. When he came below, there were about a hundred charts piled on the table, and as soon as I saw that he had noticed the thickness of the stack, and the foreign look that there was about them, I tried my experiment.

'We're going on a long cruise,' I said.

'So it seems,' he remarked, glancing at the table. We had American charts, and the one at the top of the pile, of course, was of the Firth of Clyde.

'Fitting out is rather a special problem for us,' I said. 'This may be the last chance we'll get.'

He looked up questioningly, and I went on.

'We're going from here down through the Irish Sea, and around Land's End.'

'Yes?'

'And then we're going across the Bay of Biscay to Portugal, and down to Gibraltar.'

'Are you really?'

'Yes. And then we're going through to the other end of the Mediterranean.'

'Oh, I say!' he cried. 'In this ship? In the *Caltha?* Oh, I want to give you something. I want to give you an ash-tray.' It was the first thing that occurred to him, a remarkable tray, of his own invention, which wouldn't spill its contents, even if it were wrong side up, or rolled about like a football. His face was lighted up with his pleasure; he wanted to do something for us. It had been the same at home, before we started; everyone had given us something: something of use or ornament, or a cordial 'God Speed' to prove that, though they couldn't go themselves, they were glad that their friends were going.

The news spread through the yard. Peter the shipwright took special care with the seams of the deck; Archie the rigger, with a critical eye on the shape of the ship's body as she lay on the stocks, declared that she was 'fit to go round the world'; White the foreman painter spent an entire morning on the lettering on the stern.

The schooner *Cambria* was in harbour, just back from a cruise; she had made many voyages to the Mediterranean, and the Bay of Biscay was familiar water to her. We met one of her crew in the yard office.

'They tell me you're going to the Meddy,' he said. 'I wish you'd come out aboard the *Cambria;* she's well worth seeing, and we might be able to give you some tips, having been through it ourselves.'

Everyone took an enthusiastic interest and stopped at nothing that they thought would help us or make our voyage a pleasant one.

The fitting of a ship for sea – even so small a ship as the *Caltha* – is a complicated business, and a long one. The detail is enormous, and things must be done in proper order, to avoid interference. For us, it was chiefly a problem in assembling, for the elements were ready prepared for us; starting with the shell of the ship, we had to fit together all the loose bits of equipment to create a workable machine, calculated to endure the greatest strains that any human fabric must endure, and certain of working smoothly under any conditions, in the dark, under water, or wrong side up. When you haul a rope, whether you can see what is happening, or not, the proper thing must happen. And the moment when the rope breaks, you know is the moment most unsuitable for repairing it. Everything about a ship wears out with astonishing rapidity, and we had to think ahead for more than a year to foresee the necessary replacements, and to provide for them. Moreover, the ship was to be our home; the ink-bottle and the tea-kettle had a place in our calculations, the lamp chimneys and the teaspoons, the books and the blankets and the oilcloth for the pantry shelves.

We took a room with the Thompsons, in a 'close' quite near the yard – a strange place, filled with hard-working lodgers and discourteous dogs, where there were no sheets on the beds, and we used the same ratty old towels for two weeks. Mrs. Thompson was a bright little body with a cheery smile, gaily going about her work in spite of everything; Mr. Thompson, who had picked up something of what he liked to think was French before he was wounded and sent back, was rather fond of his little quarrel when there was opportunity for it; Annabelle, who used sometimes to come over to the yard to call us when we were late for supper, was charming, with her merry laugh and mischievous black eyes. Breakfast was in the kitchen, and dinner and supper, and another meal at the very end of the day, were served in our own room, which was a badly-over-furnished parlour that looked out towards the river. Annabelle would watch for us from the front window, and run to wet the tea for us when she saw us push through the gap in the fence. 'You put me in mind o' Mutt and Jeff,' she said once, noticing our difference in stature. Sometimes we went into the kitchen to make a call, of an evening, and sat and talked of the neighbours, or workmen's wages in America, and Mr. Thompson would fight with Annabelle about French pronunciation, basing his claims to accuracy on the fact that 'A've been where they spik th' languidge, ye ken,' whereas his daughter's school, being merely 'up the street a bit' couldn't, obviously, have the benefit of any first-hand information. But usually we would come stumbling in and up the stairs in the midnight twilight and at once sit down to our tea, dirty as we were. Indeed, if the place had been better we would not have been allowed to enter it. But if it had been worse we couldn't have stood it.

Once we took an evening off to go to the pictures, and the Favourite, in a drama of the Blue Grass Country, charmed us as she was to charm us again, long afterwards, in countries more remote, by far, than this. Sometimes we stopped work to watch the cricket in the park, and in Fair Week, when there were field sports and crowds and crowds and pipers an' a', we took reserved seats on the top of the shed and spent the whole afternoon in pleasant idleness. A man will always work better if he can hear the skirl of pipes, especially if he's working on a ship, and smells the salt in the air, and feels the keen wind blowing in from the sea. There was the Clyde, with the ships going up and down. The hills were brown and green in the sunlight, or dark heather-purple against a sky of cloud. Men sailed boats across and back again, and the big racing cutters, among which was the King's wonderful old *Britannia*, came up and rounded the upper mark over against the farther shore – and still the *Caltha's* mast rose up immovable and upright above the roof of the shed, and still we worked, and seemed to get nothing done.

From time to time the engineers dropped in to see us, and squatted on their heels over the motor. They made almost no noise at their work, and we could overhear their conversation, the burden of which was that steam was a grand power, being reliable, and easy to start. They had not yet started the *Caltha's* motor. But everything was all right, they told us; as they left, they said that there was no reason why the motor shouldn't run. A steam engine needs a reason for not running, but with petrol of course, it's another matter.

We laid the floors and put down the linoleum, we cleaned the brass and brightened up the iron-work and scraped the decks. The topsides were finished, and the first coat of anti-fouling paint was on the bottom – and each morning when we came to work we looked at that naked mast above the shed.

Then, one evening, Pat felt a sudden interest in the motor, and attacked it. There it sat, a glum lump, half submerged in the galley floor, with a look of whimsical sulkiness, like a mischievous hippopotamus that refuses to do a trick. We turned on the gas, adjusted everything carefully, and Pat ground at the heavy flywheel for half an hour. At times the motor would cough and gag in an encouraging manner. 'She's going to go!' Pat said. Just as he spoke, she went. She started off like a cyclone. The ship, being high and dry, acted like a sounding board; the beast danced and banged and fell over herself, and the echoes of the explosions came shattering back from the hill beyond the railway. There was no water to circulate in the jacket, of course, and we shut down immediately, to avoid overheating. This was a significant occasion, and a solemn one, for the motor never ran again.

The next morning, when we looked out across the yard from our window, we saw a man at the *Caltha's* mainmast head. We dressed hurriedly, and raced through breakfast. When we reached the yard Archie was at work fitting the topping-lifts; the rigging had begun. The world brightened up. We turned to and worked, carrying down all the rigging from the locker upstairs, and setting out the coils in their proper places. After the men had gone home we rigged the bowsprit and the mizzen and got the topmast on deck. We brought the anchors aboard, and stowed the chain. With the crosstrees aloft and some of the running rigging rove and the spars aboard, the *Caltha* began to look more like a ship.

We discovered a leak in the after deck, but we could not find Peter, the shipwright, and went up to the office to ask about him.

'Haven't you heard, then?' Mr. Agnew said. 'There was a race yesterday, for working-men's boats, for a cup offered by the King, and Peter went in and won. That is, he didn't exactly win; he finished second. But the silly ass that came in first had put a new suit of sails on his boat the night before the race and had neglected to inform the committee, in writing, of what he'd done. So he was disqualified, and the King's cup went to Peter. We shan't see him for a week."

A day or two later we learned that the man had informed the committee, after all. So Peter had lost. We were hopeful of getting him back again.

'Bless you, no!' said Agnew. 'They'll be at it as hard as ever, now, out of consolation.'

'Harder,' said Pat, 'because they won't have to stop to cheer.'

Sure enough, that evening after supper, Peter passed down the river. He was sitting in the stern-sheets of a little power dinghy that was skidding over the glassy water with her head up in the air; he flew the blue ensign, his feet were cocked up on the gunwale, and he was smoking a cigar.

'Hooray, *Caltha!*' he shouted.

'Our deck leaks, Peter!'

'Pleasant voyage!' Peter yelled, and sheered dangerously to avoid running down an anchored boat.

The gentleman with the red and white cap was very angry at not being launched. He had chartered his boat, but the days were going by, and men were coming to work on the *Caltha*, and he was forgotten. On Saturday the *Caltha* was moved over on to the slip. Sunday morning found him hopping about the yard, alternately swearing and wringing his hands, for with another boat on the runway, his chance was gone. 'The biggest idiot God ever made!' he cried. 'What am I to do? What *am* I to do?' His boat went into the water a week late; he missed his charter party and he sued the yard.

I seem to see two old men, one in a red and white striped cowl, and the other in a battered yachting cap, working over a wee sloop in the corner of a yacht yard. They are very fussy workers, and quarrel peevishly in vigorous yet half kindly profanity. But they always have a pleasant smile for the casual passer-by, and they are always ready to stop work for a moment to talk of the wonderful days that are to come. 'We're to go into the water to-morrow,' they say, and then, in sudden fright, they begin to scrape and paint and hammer with renewed energy. 'To-morrow' passes, and they are still at work, still wrangling. 'On Friday,' they say, 'with the morning tide.' And the tide comes up and recedes again, and the rocks are wet, and the children go wading at the foot of the runway . . . this was thirty years ago, and they are old men now, and irritable . . . and the sea is blue in the sunlight.

We brought the sails aboard, and the last odd bits that had been waiting their turn in the corner of the locker. We filled the water casks and hoisted them up. The hamper came from the laundry. We packed our bags at the Thompsons', and moved down aboard the ship.

At the very top of high water Mr. Agnew came out of the office and sent a man to the winch. We climbed aboard, and took the ladder away from the rail. As the carriage rolled down, Pat lay on the after deck, looking under the stern to watch her take the water, and I held the tiller, to keep her straight when once she was afloat. Imperceptibly she lifted from the carriage and floated away.

We felt the old familiar rise and fall of heaving water under us. We were separated from the land, cut off from everything. We could not step off, now, to any scaffolding beside the rail; and there was no ladder to clamber up and down. We were self-sufficient, of necessity.

This is what the *Caltha* was like, when she was ready for the voyage:

She is of the cutter type of design – that is, she is narrow for her length, and deep, with a bow like a clipper ship, and an easy turn to the bilge. The extreme of the type is the plank-on-edge, just as the extreme of the opposite type is the skimming dish. Her length is 5.4 times her breadth. When she was built, her model was the popular one; but there are not so many now. It is urged against her type that she is wet, and that she has too little initial stability, and sails with her ear in the water. She is wet and very lively; in a seaway she takes it aboard solid – but she slices through it, and her forward progress is barely checked. A ship with a broad bow, though she keeps her head up, hits a head sea as she would hit a snowdrift, stops dead in her tracks, and throws white water over her crosstrees. It is true that the *Caltha* heels easily, and a breeze of wind puts half her freeboard under – once there, however, she will roll no further; a broad ship with a hard bilge, though she keeps her decks more nearly level in all ordinary sailing, will reach a point in heeling where it is more natural for her to turn over than to return again to normal. You can't have everything.

The *Caltha* carries eleven tons of lead ballast; five tons in a block on her keel, and six tons in pigs below the floor.

Her mainmast is short, and is stepped well back from the bows; the topmast is very long. She has a short bowsprit, on which the jib sets flying, with an outhaul, in the usual British manner. The mizzen is small, with the mast set far out on the counter, so that the lack of space between the step and the deck provides it insufficient support – a feature which caused us trouble from the very start. This is one of the great troubles with the yawl rig – an eighteen foot mast, with eighteen inches to hold it up, is unstable; there are shrouds for lateral support, of course, but when the ship is pitching into a head sea the spar switches fore and aft like a sapling, and wears its step and heel by compound interest, so to speak, so that with each hour it has more room to shift. Moreover, most of the sail is out over the stern, where it is out of reach to furl or reef – not that it is ever reefed. The yawl used to be the great favourite with cruising men. 'If it comes on to blow,' they said, 'lower your mainsail, and there you are.' They didn't know that, with the mainsail down, all the driving power was gone out of the rig, and the ship was left with canvas that would serve her only in a tornado. 'You never have to reef a yawl,' they said. My experience is that a yawl is reefed as often as a sloop would be. The best cruising rig has short booms, with the canvas inboard – in short, the ketch. If the ship is more than sixty or seventy feet long, she had best be a schooner. And the main boom is often much too long in a two-masted schooner, even. These matters are controversial.

We found the *Caltha* smart and handy on any point of sailing. In particular, she would heave to in a manner that did a man good to watch; she kept dry, made no fuss, and ate up to windward. We had tough weather, now and again, but we never had a moment's uneasiness in respect to the capabilities of the ship.

She has a flush deck – that is, there is no cabin 'house.' The main companionway is amidships; before it, and aft of it, are the two skylights. There is a small lead-lined, self-draining cockpit aft, and behind it a circular hatch leads down to the sail room in the stern. Before the mast, to starboard, is a square hatch that leads down to the galley; opposite it, to port, is a capstan which handles the chain of the large anchor. The main halliards belay on a fife rail just aft of the mast, and on the foot of the spar itself is a double-drum winch. She steers with a tiller, as most European ships do. On the port side there were davits for the small boat, but they were very much in the way, and would not keep the dinghy up out of the water when on the starboard tack; after experience, we stowed them below, and carried the boat on deck.

When you come down the companionway you arrive in a steerage; opening from it, to starboard, is a toilet room; to port there is a berth, set high up, with drawers and lockers under it.

From the steerage a door leads aft to the cabin. On either side is a berth, with a cushioned seat before it and drawers under it. In the centre of the after wall, under the cockpit, which projects down through the deck, is a wash-stand; on either side, above the feet of the berths, are bookshelves. At the heads of the berths there are clothes lockers and cupboards. There is carpet on the floor.

From the steerage a door leads forward, opposite the

cabin door, to the saloon. There are sofas on either side, with lockers under them; at the forward ends, in the corners of the room, are sideboards, with lockers over them. Above the sofas, as above all the berths, are net racks, like railway parcel racks, running along the walls close to the deck. In the centre of the room is a drop-leaf table, ballasted, and hung on pivots, so that it remains level when the ship heels.

The walls throughout are teak panels, varnished; the deck overhead is painted white; the floors are covered with linoleum, brown in the steerage, blue in the saloon, and blue and white squares in the galley.

In the saloon forward wall, to port of the mast, a door leads to the fo'c's'le and galley, a triangular cave, twelve feet long, running into the eyes of the ship. On the starboard side is the motor, covered with a box which serves also as a table; the motor is set off-centre, with the shaft carried through under the floor to the starboard run. The stove, which is a 'Clyde Cooker,' with two 'Primus' burners, is set on a shelf above the motor. On the port side is a pantry, with drawers and lockers below and racks for dishes above. The anchor chain is stowed under the floor. Forward, in the angle of the bow, are two wooden seats, and above each of them is a folding berth, made of iron pipe with a laced canvas bottom.

In general outline, this was the *Caltha*, as she lay at Paul Jones' mooring off Gourock, on the twelfth of July, 1921.

We were beginning, now, to see an end of this preparatory stage. We sent the topmast aloft, and set up the rigging; we spent the rest of that day, and the greater part of the next, in bending sail and varnishing the rails and covering boards and king-plank. In the evening, we sat on deck in the long sunset, and tried, once more, to realise the long voyage that lay before us. It is so usual a thing to be bewildered at setting out on a long journey to remote and unfamiliar places, and to feel that it cannot, after all, be true. But we – we had thought of it so much, and had made so many plans, and were so certain that every step of it would be real to us. We could not account for the vagueness of it all. It seemed as if we had always worked in the yard, as if we could never cast off and go. . . . Then, all at once, we saw what the trouble was. We jumped up, both together, and made sail.

We put the jibs in stops, and set the mizzen and the main. Pat took the tiller, and I hauled out the jib, and dropped the mooring line. The breeze was light, but steady and confident, and we watched the railway wharf slipping past us, and the altering aspect of the shore as we receded from it, and saw that we were bound to nothing, and could go. The ship herself seemed to be eager to show us what she could do; she skipped gaily along, as if she knew that there were hundreds of ships, in other harbours all over the world, starting out, as she was, at just that moment of time, and that there was a place for her among the company. She was touched by the common spirit of all ships everywhere.

And we watched her go. We paced up and down the deck. We left the tiller and went below, to feel her sail herself. We could not let the rigging alone, but went from rope to rope in a dazed sort of satisfaction. Things had come right side out once more, and it all seemed natural.

We ran down below the Cloch light, far enough to see the entrance of the Firth, and the hills of Arran, where the sea begins, and then eased sheets and ran back to the mooring.

There remained the new suit of sails to get from Ratsey and Lapthorne, and there were enough last errands to occupy a whole day in town. Accordingly, we went up to Glasgow, and, while there, sent a telegram to our guests, who were to go with us for the first two weeks of the cruise, telling them that we were ready to start. As we were coming back to Gourock we looked out over the Firth from the train windows, and saw a breeze rippling the surface of the water. It was impossible to resist this; we piled aboard, we and our packages, and got under way again.

It was our intention to go through the Kyles of Bute and return on the other side of the island, by Tarbert, but off Rothesay the wind left us, and we lay idle on water as still as a sheet of glass, watching the fading light in the sky and listening to the sound of people talking on the shore three miles away. At last, about midnight, it began to get dark in earnest, and we thought of the motor.

In no great mood of confidence, but resolutely, Pat fell upon it. After twenty minutes' work something happened, and the cylinders filled up with water. When he took out a spark-plug to investigate, a jet, straight from the sea, spouted up nearly to the deck overhead.

This was discouraging. We had told our guests that we were ready to start. Now, should we start without a motor? Was it feasible?

'Well,' I said, 'there are plenty of ships that have gone so far without power. Look at the *Lloyd*. . . .'

'Hell,' said Pat. 'Look at Columbus!'

We went into Rothesay under sail, though it took us the rest of the night to do it.

When we came back to the yard in the morning there was a message waiting for us. Hal Smith and his wife Claire, who is Pat's sister, and Beatrice Sorchan and Evelyn Curtis, were in Glasgow, and they wanted us to join them and spend the day in Edinboro'. Of course we went.

There's no city in the world like Edinboro'. The big gray stone buildings and the streets filled with mist and the Castle rising up in the midst of it. . . . One feels that if he could live for a year in Herriot Row his whole outlook on life would be altered forever. I know that this isn't true, but it indicates the atmosphere of the place. And there was Tusitala, the Teller of Tales, living at the very centre of the South Pacific, remembering, and thinking back to the old house in Herriot Row – I wonder if it had a green door then? – and being inevitably and hopelessly homesick! If ever a spot on earth would make a wanderer long to come home again, it's Herriot Row.

We came back all together to the *Caltha*. That was our last night on the Clyde.

CHAPTER FOUR

Dune the Watter

*

In the morning we rowed in to the landing to take delivery of the new sails, and stopped for a time in the loft to talk with Mr. Lapthorn. It is a pleasure to watch such sails being made, as it is to see them when they are done, and to use them. Mr. Lapthorn talked of his work with all the enthusiasm of an artist for his art, launching out, with amorous precision, into all the details of the processes, of cutting and measurement, of the rope and canvas which he uses as if they were silk and satin. When we left – for he knew where we were going – he wished us luck, and a pleasant voyage.

There were still some things to do, but we tried to forget about them. 'We haven't everything,' we said, 'but we have enough.'

At noon on the fifteenth of July, in the rain, with a shifty wind from the northward, we got under way from the old mooring, and started dune the watter. Dune the watter for Ailsa Craig, beyond which is the sea.

Still it did not seem like a veritable jumping-off; inland waters, with familiar harbours, lay for many miles ahead of us, and the presence of our friends, who brought with them so much of the atmosphere of home, made tangible connections with the past. People who were not going all the way with us made this portion of the trip seem tentative and preliminary. We seemed to have a thirst for loneliness, and to be content only with the idea of utter isolation.

Below the Cloch the rain stopped; the water was still, and the clouds hung motionless, aground on the tops of the hills. With the last puff of the wind we ran into Millport, on Great Cumbrae Island. The little town is built along the shore of the bay in a half circle, with the manor house of the Earl of Glasgow in the centre. There are four church spires, through the belfries of which you can see the green fields on the slopes of the hills beyond.

There was once an old sea captain here, Claire told me, who had voyaged all over the world, and when his house was torn down to make room for some other buildings great chests of pieces-of-eight and bars of yellow gold were found concealed in the thickness of the walls. And there was a lady who had married a Spanish gentleman, also of the sea, and she went on a voyage with him, and was cast away on some distant island, and lived for a long time among cannibals, 'or at least, coloured people.'

And once upon a time there was a family of eight who lived in a lonely farm in a misty hollow in the hills behind the town; they all died, of consumption, except the last, a girl who had a baby; she killed herself, and her body was found in the woods. This suggested the story of the boy who was drowned while bathing, and of how a certain Davie, beside himself with grief and disappointment, confessed, then, that the boy was his son, though he was unmarried, and no one had previously suspected the relationship.

Now although things like this can happen in Millport,

the woman who used to deliver groceries to Mrs. MacGlashan refused to come near the house, on one occasion, because beside the front gate there was a man, 'and he was smoking a cigar.' This was no more than fifteen years ago, and when I asked how it was that people who were shocked at cigars were not killed outright by the other tragic irregularities of conduct, Claire said that the cigar was plain evidence of wickedness, but that the other things happened, essentially, in the secrecy of certain individuals' minds, and no one could so readily believe in them.

Indeed, times have changed in Millport. Even the yachting fleet – which once included the famous *Bloodhound* – goes elsewhere now, and the little harbour seems very spacious and still.

It was completely calm for forty-eight hours. We had, by this time, gotten much of the water out of the motor, and we took the muffler ashore to the plumber's for re-soldering. The motor might be disposed to run now, at any time, and we did not care to discourage it with a defective muffler. While we were waiting for it, standing in the doorway of the plumber's shop, we felt a breath of air pass through the little street, and looked out between the houses to find the water blue and rippling with the breeze.

At half-past four in the afternoon we hove anchor and got away, running for Holy Island, under the dark hills of Arran. While we were close to the shore, in the smooth water, we had dinner, and when we came on deck again we jibed over and set a course south-west, for Ailsa Craig.

South, for blue water. There will be an 'S' in all our courses now until we sight the flying fish and watch the dolphins play. The breeze was behind us, and we went along merrily, singing all the songs we knew, to express our satisfaction, watching the hills of Arran grow darker, and more and more like cardboard cut-outs and clearer and sharper against the light in the sky. Ailsa Craig was ahead – a pinnacle in the sea, a thousand feet in height, with thirty fathoms of water all around it. It was our first milestone.

At midnight it was abeam. The tide was running strongly against us, as if reluctant to let us go, but the breeze held on astern, and the dim spire of rock faded and vanished in the darkness, and before dawn the last loom of the light had gone down into the sea.

When Hal called me, at sunrise, it was calm, with no land; only a shining gray sea, with flocks of lonely ducks, who cried plaintively, as if they felt lost so far from shore, yet dived, when they saw us, as if to demonstrate that they were really in the midst of all the resources of home. Many steamers were passing in the distance, and their smoke hung low over the waters, looking like distant hills.

When the wind came, it was ahead, and very light. During that day we took three great tacks over towards the coast of Ireland, and at nine in the evening, when the breeze grew stronger, we settled down to fight the tide-rips off the Mull of Galloway. This was the last of Scotland and our second milestone.

The wind was north-west after dark, very keen and clear. During my watch on deck we passed a schooner, also reaching around the Mull, her sidelights glaring indignantly at us as we crossed her bows, and later a trawler kept us company for a time, her sails very black against the dawn. I took in the lights and hauled the boat up to the very top of the davits in an attempt to keep it out of the waves on the lee bow; as I came back aft again, under the boom, I was thinking how poor a time it would be to fall overboard: there was the lee rail, close down to the rushing water, and the *Caltha*, with everybody asleep, roaring along on her course with the helm lashed.

At six I went down and called Pat. He had slept all night on the sofa in the saloon, and couldn't believe it. Yet there it was, morning.

When I was called again, at breakfast time, we were flying along under the high shores of the Isle of Man. The coast was rocky, with cliffs, and the farmhouses seemed to grip the ground and hang on, against the force of the wind. But the cows were grazing contentedly, not suspecting the danger they were in. It blew in solid gusts down over the flat-topped hills, and made the water smoke. We raced along with our rail in the water, heading for Douglas Harbour.

The wind was whistling out of Douglas Bay, taking the tops off the waves. We took in the staysail and got the anchor ready, and reached across the Bay towards the entrance. On the pierhead was a confused mass of people and objects – we couldn't tell what was there. When we were no more than fifty yards away from the harbour mouth, out of the tangle a man appeared with a megaphone.

'Yawl, ahoy!' he yelled.

We straightened up and tried to listen. He shouted

something else, but the noise of the wind was too loud, and the spray too thick, for us to catch a word of it. He waved his arms, seeming to motion us off. Perhaps the harbour was too small for us to enter in safety at that steamboat speed; perhaps the tide had not yet covered the shoals at the entrance – we never knew. We came about, in a mad scrimmage of banging sails and whipping ropes, and put her off before it, straight down the path of the sun, away from the pier. High rollers and a whistling wind, and the land receding swiftly like a rolling curtain . . .

Then a hard gust struck us, and rolled us down. The dinghy on the davits dipped and touched the water, and the forward tackle unhooked like grease. She hung giddily in the belly-bands – one more wave, and she was gone. Hal was up, struggling with the tackle; I ran to help him, and we got her fast, and moused the hook, before the next one came. Then we furled the mizzen, trimmed sheets, and let her roar for Holyhead.

I went below and got out the chart and the parallel rule.

'South south-east,' I shouted up to Pat. 'Fifty miles.'

That was all we saw of the Isle of Man.

It was amazingly rough during the night, because of the tide-rips. Pat picked up the light on the Skerries, and stood off and on to wait for daylight. At seven o'clock we ran in and anchored behind the breakwater. There was another yawl there, larger than we were, bound around Land's End for the Cowes Regatta. We thought to get away together, when the weather permitted it, and looked forward to racing her, being bound south ourselves, though there was no doubt that she could beat us.

Holyhead is a small place, filled with docks and railway yards, of importance only because it is a port for the Irish mails, but the raw bleak tone of the place shows through its commercial aspect – rather, surrounds it and swallows it up. Wind and rain, on a headland in the sea. . . . The windows of the houses are small, to keep the weather out; the sea-mist swirls through the narrow streets. When a west wind shakes the chimneys, and the glass goes down, people look to see the harbour fill up with sailing vessels, some with torn sails, some with pumps going, beating up for shelter, or running, wallowing in the seas, past the savage ledges off the Skerries. There are pictures of wrecks on the walls of the hotel parlours. A frontier town of the ocean, set on a salient of the Western Front.

We remained in Holyhead while the west wind blew itself out. The term of our imprisonment was seven days. We walked over the hills in the rain; we sat at home in the cabin and played bridge, endlessly. We took the train to Carnarvon, and visited the castle, amusing ourselves on the way with the delightful Welsh names: 'Pen Cw' on a sign beside the road, and 'Lnwr' on the trainmen's caps. We crossed to Ireland in the mail packet, running twenty-five knots into a head sea and a howling wind, jumping and crashing and flinging water like a flurried whale. We went to the pictures, and were reminded of home by the Canadian Mounted Police, who are as much a feature of North Wales as they are of Broadway. At the close of the seventh day it was present in all our minds that we wanted no more than half a chance to get away.

During the night I was awakened by the grating of the chain on the bobstay, and went up to quiet it with a wrapping of canvas. It was an amazingly beautiful morning; the moonlight very bright, throwing the shadows of the rigging across the deck, the stars shining, the coming dawn dull orange over the breakwater. But it was very cold, and I worked fast. Back in my berth, I went instantly to sleep, and in the morning, when I told them that I had dreamed that the stars were shining, they could not believe that I could dream anything so foreign to experience. So I showed them the canvas on the chain.

But indeed the weather had changed; it was bright and sunny, and the wind was from the south-east. We asked the advice of a boatman on the beach, and he said that it was no time to get away, since all the signs were for a return of a mean south-wester; but when, out of impatience and eagerness, we questioned his findings, he reversed his opinion, seeing, I suppose, that we would go anyway. Immediately after breakfast we made sail, and got away. We went alone.

Off the South Stack the wind dropped and shifted, coming up again, stronger, from the north-east. We bowled along merrily, looking ahead for Bardsey Island, which was our next mark; everything was in our favour, and Fishguard seemed as good as won.

We never even saw Fishguard.

After dinner, I was on deck alone. There was lightning in the southern sky – a thunderstorm was coming up against the wind. The north-easter held right up to the storm, and into it, and through it. It rained white. Then, after the centre of the storm had passed, the wind whipped around into the south. Although we had been expecting this, enthusiasm at being on our road again, or, perhaps, mere indifference, kept us from shortening sail until the last moment. Before we could touch a rope, it hit us.

We were carrying the four lower sails and a big club-topsail. If we should slack the topsail sheet, in that squall, the sail would blow out over the gaff instantly, and simply leave us. So we hung onto everything. We tightened the preventers, and tried to make things snug, and rushed off to the westward – away from the land – in a smother of boiling foam.

In a quarter of an hour it moderated, and we put her on her course again. When I went below, about ten o'clock, Bardsey Island light was in sight.

Later, shortly after midnight, I was awakened by the flapping of the jib. We were heeled down, and going fast, and the ship was jumping into a head sea. Claire called to me that I was wanted on deck, and at the same time I heard Pat shouting from the tiller. In my haste and excitement I did a very foolish thing. I went on deck as I was, in my pyjamas.

It was bitterly cold, and the wind was screaming in the rigging, driving the spray like spindrift. Over my head the jib, with its sheet gone adrift and wrapped about it in a hundred turns, was struggling in the sky. I crawled aft on my hands and knees till I reached the tiller. 'What do you want done?' I yelled to Pat. 'Get the jib,' he shouted.

I crawled back to the bow, standing astride the forestay and made a clutch at the whipping sheet. It was as stiff as wire, twisted tight, and yanking savagely. The sail jabbered and jumped, and time after time tore the tangle from my hands. In the end I cleared it and brought it inboard. I was crossing the forward deck when another squall came yelling down on us; the ship dived into a deep hollow, flung me up, and dropped me on my face. I put some sort of hitch in the sheet. I was dazed and soaked and shaking, but I managed to crawl below. The sheet tore loose again as soon as my back was turned.

It was light by that time. They called for me to come up and help take in the mainsail. I tried several times, and at last made the deck, crawling aft to consult with the others as to a plan of operations. The sea was very heavy, roaring down on us, and the wind had settled to a steady blow. We were hove to under the whole mainsail and jib – the main was torn at the leach and streamed out in rags across the sky. We were well clear of the land. It seemed best to keep her as she was.

During the next three days I was unable to come on deck at all. I was humiliated at my failure, but try as I would, I had no strength left to call upon, and the whole work of the ship fell to the other two.

They kept her hove to all during that day, and during a lull towards evening took in the mainsail and hove her to again under mizzen and headsails. During a part of another day they let her sail herself, with no one on deck, and she spent a night alone, also, riding to a sea-anchor. At the end of this they ran back sixty miles to Holyhead, and were unable to beat into the bay against the wind and sea. They took a long leg offshore, and reached back in again at night, sighting the Skerries, and getting some shelter from the Anglesey shore. At noon of the fifth day they were off Point Lynus, which is the outer station of the Liverpool pilots.

Having recovered, I was able to lend a hand. They set the International 'P.T.' in the rigging, and waited. In half an hour a small steamer came out from under the coast, rounded up ahead of us, lowered a boat, and put a pilot aboard. His name was Peterson.

It had been our plan to take our guests to France, or, at least, to some of the down-channel ports, so that we might all go together for a holiday in Paris. But this was out of the question now. The time remaining to them was too short, and we should have to go to Paris from whatever port was within reach.

'Is there a harbour near,' Pat asked the pilot, 'where we can get shelter, and where we can safely leave the ship for a week?'

'Liverpool,' said the pilot.

We put her east, for the Bar light-vessel at the entrance to the Mersey, and Hal and Pat had an opportunity for rest. They piled below, as they were, in oilskins, and slept.

At nightfall we could see, through the rain, the lights of the city. We passed the light-vessel, and cut across the shoals. At four o'clock in the morning we anchored, in the rain, over towards the Birkenhead shore, across from the landing stage where the liners tie up to take their passengers.

I rowed Mr. Peterson ashore to Birkenhead. He set off towards the rows of dingy red brick houses that lined the miles of deserted streets, hopping across the puddles on the flats, his shoulders hunched, to bring his collar up about his ears – for he was very wet. I came back aboard, and, from the forward deck, watched the dawn come over Liverpool.

There is always a charm in arriving in a city before its inhabitants are awake – it is like being up first in the morning, and having the tranquil house to yourself. You seem to be the only one who knows that the day has come, and thus you have gained an enormous advantage over those who are still in their beds. The streets are free to take whatever colour you choose to give them; you may create your own atmosphere for the place, and give it whatever name your fancy may select.

A wan pale light gleamed in the sky – a cold, colourless light, like dull silver; it spread through the rainy streets and over the high towers on the hill and the black shipping in the docks, and was reflected in a wavering sheen from the brown and foaming river. People began to appear in the streets; the trams went grittily along the quays; ferries came out, crossing and recrossing between the piers; the smoke from the factory chimneys spread and settled like black fog. There was a sense of returning life, but without cordiality or cheer. It was a cold and pallid resurrection.

At nine o'clock Mr. Peterson returned with the tow-boat *Silver Foam.* We hove our anchors, passed her a line, and she took us up the river, past the landing stage, and shot us into the open gates for the Albert Dock.

Our guests took the train for Paris.

CHAPTER FIVE

The Deep-Water Men

*

The Albert Dock is a square pit, surrounded on all sides by the towering walls of vast and gloomy warehouses with iron shutters at their windows, and the iron sky set down upon the top of it like a lid on a pot. It is a shadowy region between death and life; the ships that lie there are either well on their way to the end of their days, or else they are waiting, in a pathetic sort of hopefulness, for the coming of better times. They lie there on the quiet, mossy water breathlessly, as if frightened at the impending turn of fate that shall send them out to sea again, or to the wrecker's yard. As you look at them, caught in a humiliating and wretched phase of their existence, you will come to believe that they realise their position.

A band of aged ship-keepers presides over this disillusioned, but still hopeful gathering. Dismasted steamers, half-rigged ships, superannuated packets, coal-hulks that had once been living vessels and are now no more than skeletal remains. . . . And yet just beyond the dock gates is the swarming activity of the whole port.

Standing at the rail of the trawler alongside which we were moored was a man in a blue jersey – a big-chested lad, with keen eyes, and a chin that stuck out like the prow of a Roman galley. This one addressed us, and asked if we wanted our mainsail mended.

'Are you a sailmaker?' Pat asked him.

'Ho!' He laughed scornfully. 'I'm used to sails. I've spent my life on the sea. If it's anything to do with ships, I can do it.'

We exchanged glances; this might be the man we were looking for. His quick eye caught the glance.

'Were you wanting a hand, sir?' he asked.

'Perhaps,' Pat said. 'What have you done? What experience have you had?'

'Twenty-nine years I've been to sea in sailing ships,' he said. 'There's not many places I haven't been to. Aye. Across every ocean, and all around the world . . . under sail.' He paused for a moment. 'If you're wanting a hand, sir,' he added very simply, 'I should be pleased to ship.'

'We'll talk it over and let you know.'

'Very good, sir. I hope we can come to some arrangement. You'll find I know my work. There's few ships here now; only them damned steamers. And I've seen this port full – full of sailing ships. That one over there, now; you can see the royal yards of her over the roof of the building. She's from the End of the World, from the Other Side of Nowhere – from South Georgia, with a cargo of whale oil. I was over to her before she'd got into the dock. She's going to lay up. It's the same everywhere you look. There was the *County of Inverness*, a four-masted barque; aye, and a proud ship she was, too! I made two voyages in her. And where is she now? You see that steamer there at the other end of the dock? The *Carmen?* With that ugly stack on her, sticking up like a standpipe? And the bridge, that don't fit her? Look at that big clipper bow she's got, and the flare in the rails up forward.

And if you look close you can see the sheave hole in the quarter rail where the main brace used to lead aft. Aye. That's what's happened to the old *County of Inverness.*

'Well, I'll be down again in the morning, sir. And I hope we can come to some arrangement.'

This was one of the deep-water men, out of Liverpool, who go all over the earth; a representative of 'that now nearly-vanished sea-life under sail.' Nearly vanished; yes. Within memory.

So many proud ships, coming in around the Skerries, under a press of sail, laying a course for the Bar lightship at the entrance to the Mersey, roaring up the river sixteen miles an hour when they had half a gale of wind behind them. Standing up the river, taller than the church spires, with the big ensign at the monkey-gaff, and the signal flags standing out stiff in the wind. As they reached up past the pierhead opposite the pilots' office the men would lay aloft to take in sail, and look down from the royal yards at the dawn stealing through the rainy streets and the smoke that spread and settled like black fog. Deep-water men, out of Liverpool, home from a voyage. And where are they now? The ships are gone, or are chopped up into steamers, and the men are keeping moribund hulks in the Albert Dock, or walking the streets looking for work – any work, so long as it has to do with ships.

The shipkeepers sit by their galley fires, or step out, between rain storms, for a turn on deck. They are old men, for the most part; they have a ship's deck under them, at the least, to keep their memories fresh, and they look back over the past, not regretfully, and tell long rambling yarns of ships and voyages and foreign ports and lost companions. I think they did not look forward to such an ending for their lives – except, perhaps, in moments of despondency – rather, each of them imagined himself in a small snug house in a quiet street, with lace curtains at the windows and curious corals and polished sea-shells as ornaments on the parlour mantelpiece. There he would sit and think. But it is only the fortunate ones who have this. The rest are glad of a chance to keep a ship.

There is a column in the Liverpool *Post* called the Log Book, wherein sailors set down their reminiscences. 'Dannie' writes to recall the record passage home in the old *Mexico*, in '68, when they carried a roaring quarterly wind all the way from Saint Helena to the South Stack. Another, who signs himself 'Charlie,' remembers very well the incident referred to; but does Dannie know of the run the *Mexico* made in the winter of '65, coming home from the Columbia River, when they never had the reefs out of the topsails from the Line to Fifty-three South? Frank Cook was bo'sun of her then, and where is Frank now? 'Donald' knows; he saw Frank himself, not three years back, in the Solomon Islands, running a trading schooner up and down Indispensable Strait. The ship-keepers toddle off uptown to buy the *Post*, and read it on deck in the evenings, pausing between the paragraphs. Nowhere but in Liverpool could a paper have such a column.

In Liverpool, one never gets completely away from the sea. Even from the top of Bold Street hill you can hear the steamer whistles. Over behind the Customs House there is a street called the Mariners' Parade. And I know where there is an inn called the Flying Dutchman; you turn off at the foot of South Castle Street.

When our man came back in the morning we questioned him again, and learned that he had had some yachting experience, which is a rare thing in a Liverpool sailor.

'One more question,' Pat said. 'We're going to the Mediterranean. Would you go there?'

'I certainly would, sir. Or Tierra del Fuego – it's all the same to me.'

That settled it. 'Signed on Robert Ball as Able Seaman,' is the entry in the log.

Pat and I packed our bags and went to Paris. He stayed for ten days, but I returned a week sooner, because I had important business in Liverpool.

As soon as I reached the Lyme Street Station I felt a sense of welcome, and my progress down to the Albert Dock was like a journey home. The *Caltha* was all shipshape and Bristol fashion, and Ball was bending the mainsail, which was back, mended, from the shop.

As I was going back over the Salthouse bridge I stepped in at the ship chandler's to order a set of preventer forestays for the mizzen, for the spar was like a horsewhip now, and something must be done to keep it in the ship.

'I say,' said the young man in the office. 'That man of yours tells me you're going south.'

'South; yes,' I said.

'He says you're going to the Mediterranean.' He seemed incredulous, and hopeful of being convinced that he was wrong.

'We are,' I said. 'Why not?'

'Oh, nothing. But I shouldn't care to go so far in so small a boat. Just at this time of year.'

I could think of nothing against this, and remained silent.

'The Bay of Biscay, you know . . .' he went on. 'I shouldn't like to try it.'

For a moment I thought that he might know of some secret danger of the sea that he was going to reveal to me. But he had said all that he had to say; he wouldn't care to go.

I went away vaguely puzzled.

I made my way over the dry-dock gates to the pier-head and went to the Pilots' Office, where I asked the young man at the desk if I might speak with one of the pilots. He went into another room for a moment and came back with a man who introduced himself as Captain Meyers.

I told him that I was from the *Caltha*, in the Albert, and that I knew Mr. Peterson, who had brought us in. To this he merely nodded. He seemed to know all about us.

'I've come to ask you,' I said, 'if you can tell me of someone who will give me some instruction in navigation. I want to be crammed, in as short a time as possible. I haven't got to take any examinations, and I'm not going near the Board of Trade. I simply want to know how to run the ship.'

He considered for a moment. 'You won't be going out of sight of land?' he asked.

'Oh, yes,' I said. 'We're going to the Mediterranean.'

Captain Meyers looked up at this, as if it put the matter in an entirely new light. But my announcement was too much altogether for the young clerk.

'Are you going through France, or around it?' he asked.

'Around,' I said.

'Good God!' exclaimed the young clerk. His tone implied that I was going to catch it now. As if we had been caught in some schoolboy prank together.

Captain Meyers said, 'You'd best go up to Cleavor and Hutchinson's in Faulkner Street. It's a good school. They can shoot enough into you in a week, or at least I think they can, to take you through. And get them to tell you something of the currents off the coast of Portugal, too, because in a small ship you'll be set – you'll be lost, sure as Hell. . . .'

I thanked him, and as I went out I saw the young clerk turn to him with something like indignant surprise. Clearly he thought that I had been sent to certain death.

I kept thinking of this. How could I be sure that only the ignorant were pessimistic?

The police helped me to find Faulkner Street. It was empty when I turned into it, and as I walked along, looking at the numbers of the houses, I had a feeling of futility. It seemed likely that I should be told that what I wanted was impossible of attainment, and that the Bay of Biscay – well, the Bay of Biscay, you know – was no place for me. Some pessimist of authority was going to tell me that it was folly to think of taking the *Caltha* – such a small ship – to the Mediterranean, across the Bay, or anywhere.

I pushed open the door in all the embarrassment of

a new schoolboy. A long line of hats and coats hung in the hall. There was a bulletin board, with notices of the lectures in seamanship and signalling, and a notice concerning smoking in the schoolrooms. Behind a door marked 'Second Mates' I could hear someone lecturing. I turned away and ventured to the second floor, looking for the office. Here there was a door marked 'Mates and Masters'. 'This is what I want,' I thought, arrogantly, and opened it and went in.

A solitary student on a high stool was at work before a long table that ran the length of the room, and beside him was an instructor, who rose to meet me as I came forward, and introduced himself as Captain Hutchinson. He took me down to an office on the first floor, which had been there all the time, of course, only I was too flustered to see it.

He listened attentively while I told him what it was that I wanted. At the end, I asked him to give me some idea of how long it would take.

'Well,' he said, smiling, 'it isn't possible to make a navigator in a week, is it?'

'I'm sorry to hear that,' I said, 'because that's exactly what I want. I don't need any seamanship or piloting – all the coastwise work is familiar enough. I don't want any formal knowledge; I don't care if I don't know what I'm doing, so long as I can get an intelligible result. I suppose that is displeasing to you, as a teacher.'

'It is, in a way,' he admitted. 'We prepare men here for the Board of Trade examinations.'

'Well, instead of the approval of the Board of Trade,

I'll ask you for your own. Will you tell me when you think I'm competent to take the ship out?'

'I shouldn't care to take that responsibility.'

'Then I'll take it. I'll tell you when I think I know enough, and the power of veto will rest with you.'

'Leave it that way, if you like,' he said. 'Will you come in on Monday, and we'll begin. The hours are from nine to four-thirty, with as long as you like for lunch.'

There it was, you see. No admonitions, no talk of the Perils of the Deep, no hints of wandering for years at sea, unable to find the continent of Europe. I came back to the ship in a mood of simple happiness. The riggers were aboard, taking measurements, and fussing about with the mizzen. In the evening, I went to the theatre, to celebrate.

On Monday morning, I began a week of hard work. Navigation is a simple thing if you have time to go at it patiently, so as to understand it a little at a time; it is simple, even, when you cut corners and take into consideration only the essentials, if you have someone beside you to tell you what corners you may cut, and what the essentials are. The astronomy of it, the spherical trigonometry, the bewildering question of Mean and Apparent Time – let them go. Nothing remains but arithmetic. But it is fatally easy to make a mistake in arithmetic, and a wrong addition may put you a hundred miles out of the way, or, for that matter, on the opposite side of the earth. And the knowledge of the consequences of such an error does not tend to make you avoid it.

All day, and every day, I sat on my high stool at the

long table in the front room, and did arithmetic. By Dead Reckoning you compute the distance you have come, and the direction of your progress. There are no celestial bodies involved; there is no more to it than simple addition and subtraction – except, of course, that you must be careful to make no errors, and must perform your operations in the proper order. There may be a high percentage of error inherent in the method, and this may accumulate from day to day, so that at the end of a week your Dead Reckoning may be worse than useless. You can depend upon it only when you are forced to do so – which, with a perversity that is typical of life, is just when you need it most keenly. For if you cannot see the sun, Dead Reckoning is all you have.

The Noon Observation for latitude, and the Time Sight for longitude, are other matters; you observe the sun, and have more positive information. Experts do not hesitate to ask their questions of the stars or planets, but the sun is more dependable, and comes more within the scope of a week's intensive cultivation. A lunar observation means nothing to me, and when I am face to face with Venus, as occasionally happens, I am helpless.

I was surrounded as I worked by a number of ambitious young men who were preparing to face the Board of Trade. Seven years' experience is the minimum preliminary requisite for the various examinations leading to the Masters' Certificate. You may judge, then, how great were the corners I was cutting, and what a piece of impudence it was for me to sit in the Masters' schoolroom and do seven days' arithmetic!

Yet I was very busy, even so. When I came home from school at night Ball had supper ready for me, and as soon as the table was cleared I sat down to work problems. I could hear the steamers hooting in the river outside, and the soft patter of the rain on deck. 'At 4 p.m. on Feb. 11, a ship in latitude 36 S . . . . .' So the problem would begin. And my mind would wander off to Thirty-six South, picturing the sea, and the ship in the midst of it, and the man who sat in his cabin, sucking his pencil, trying not to make mistakes in arithmetic. He must have had fair success, since his ship reached port – the answer to his problem is given in the back of the book. To get away to sea. I was possessed by a longing for it, a hope of it, greater than I had known in all my life; I was tired of the rain and the smoke and the dull gray sky; I wanted to get south, into the blue water. I bent over my problems again. 'A ship in 121 E Long. . . .' Dear, dear, that'll be off the coast of Borneo!

Every day Ball asked me when Mr. Spencer was coming back, and every day I told him I didn't know. But on Saturday he did come, clambering over the ships that lay between us and the quay, and asked me, almost as soon as his feet touched the deck, when I should be ready. I answered that I thought I should leave school on Monday night. We got out the almanac and found that the dock gates would be opened at two-thirty on Tuesday morning.

On Monday morning I told Captain Cleavor that we were to sail on Tuesday morning. I was very uncertain as to the result of this announcement; I imagined that he would want me to spend another week at school, and I pictured the failure of confidence that I should experience if I went to sea in defiance of his advice.

'Very well,' he said, in his dry, precise manner. 'We will spend the day, if you please, on the Sumner Line problem.'

Once upon a time there was an American ship, Captain Thomas H. Sumner, master, which sailed from Charleston for Gourock on the Clyde. After a hard passage, he arrived off the entrance to St. George's Channel. Tuskar Rock lies on one side, and the Smalls on the other. Now there had been no opportunity for an observation of the sun for several days, so that the Dead Reckoning had been carried forward far beyond the limits of probable accuracy; it was in December, and blowing a gale of wind; he had a dangerous rocky shore somewhere under his lee; he didn't know where he was. Surely it was time to do something. Captain Sumner took a guess at three possible latitudes, and computed his longitude on the basis of each of them, in the hope of finding, at least, the extreme range of all his possible positions. These three points, so determined, he marked on his chart, and sat down to study them. Here was a discovery. They lay in a straight line! Obviously, whatever latitudes he might assume, within reason, his resulting position would lie on this line. It happened that the line ran east-north-east, and passed through the Smalls light. Captain Sumner didn't wait to consider the theory, which is now set forth in all the text-books as if they had known about it from the beginning; he went on deck, sent a man aloft, and put her east-north-east. In less than an hour he made the Smalls light, dead ahead.

Captain Cleavor set me several problems – leaving out the lee shore and the December gale – and I sat down to study them. The perfected process is somewhat different now from what it was when Captain Sumner discovered it, in 1837. Now, you work the data twice, and get two lines, on both of which, of course, your ship must lie. The intersection is your position.

There is a beautiful exactness about this. I was glad that it came last in my course.

It was after school hours when I had finished, and everyone else had gone. I went to Captain Cleavor and thanked him for his patience and for the iconoclastic methods that I had asked him to adopt.

'I should like to send you a postcard from Gibraltar,' I said.

'I should be very pleased,' he said. 'A pleasant voyage to you. Good-bye.'

So I left school, graduated, feeling very detached and excited as I hurried down Lord Street, clutching my exercise books and my sextant.

Pat had made a busy day of it. Stores and water were aboard, and everything was ready. We had supper, and then cast off our lines from the trawler beside which we had been moored, and towed across to the dock gates. 'This is worth a pint of any man's money,' said Ball, pulling at his oars. Aye, so it is.

We tied up against the dock wall, close to the gates, waiting for them to open. The stern of the *Carmen* towered up above us. And a proud ship she used to be, too. The *Caltha* is one of the lucky ones; she is getting away from the Albert, away to sea. The moon is up, stars are visible, the wind is from the west, blowing up the river, and the glass is rising. The dock is very still. The other ships that are to go out on this tide are lying near us, clustered about the gates, waiting drowsily.

At midnight I was sitting on a bollard on the dock wall, smoking, watching the moon on the water, thinking of the peace of it all, the security, the freedom. Away to sea. The course is west by north for a position two miles off the Skerries. Once around the Skerries. . . .

A Bobby stepped up beside me.

'Going out to-night, are you?' he asked.

'Yes. With the morning tide, if the breeze holds.'

'That's fine, isn't it?' he said. 'And when will you be coming back?'

'Oh, we're not coming back,' I said.

CHAPTER SIX

The Jumping-Off Place

*

But we didn't get away on that tide, for all our feeling of finality. There was no wind. 'Not a breath!' the dock-master said, standing on the quay above us, and his voice sounded very loud and positive in the stillness of the dock. The other ships went out, and the gates were closed. We went to bed and I dreamed that the *Caltha* was caught in this Purgatory of Forgotten Ships, and would never see open water again. When I awoke I reassured myself with the reflection that hundreds of ships, in the old days when there was no steam and no towboat, had waited over a tide because there was no fair wind to take them down the river. There was no meaning in my superstitions, surely. But it was a disquieting feeling, none the less.

On the afternoon tide we had a better chance. With the steam-trawler *Shamrock* and the smack *Mable* we hauled through to the outer basin, and after a great deal of shouting and confusion and contradictory orders from the dockmen and all hands on the trawler and the smack, we passed a hawser to the *Mable*, and the *Shamrock* yanked us both out into the stream.

As soon as we were well out into the current, a man came aft on the *Shamrock* and shouted something. 'Tell the yacht . . . ' was all we could hear of it. Word was passed aft along the deck, and the skipper of the *Mable*, heaving one leg up on to his quarter rail as a prop, shouted to us to 'get your mains'l up; we're going to drop you off,' and all the crew made hoisting motions with their arms. We got canvas on her and cast off. Soon afterwards the *Mable* made sail, too, and the *Shamrock* went sputtering away alone.

It seemed as if every ship in the port was going out on this tide; the river was as crowded as a busy street, and the stagnation which had been clutching at us from behind seemed quite unreal. The smack *Confidence* was astern of us, and we two fought a very pretty race down channel; we were the faster, but she knew the water better and was able to cut outside the buoys on the corners and take advantage of all the tricks of the tide. For four or five miles it was very close; she picked up till we could see her crew grinning at us and waving their hands, and then, when we caught a more favourable slant of wind, we pulled ahead again. But down where the channel was wider and the breeze grew stronger, we definitely left her, and when she tacked north across the sands towards St. Bee's, she was half a mile astern.

Off the Bar light-vessel we hove to and pulled the boat up, put up our sidelights, and settled down for the run to the Skerries. Behind us the lights from the city shone up on the clouds, the channel buoys winked and twinkled and blew faint, and the running lights of hundreds of ships, on all sides, heading in all directions, swung up, and passed, and went glimmering away in the distance. By midnight, the shore lights and the ships were gone, and the sea was empty.

At dawn we were off Mouse Island, with Point Lynus under our lee and the Skerries in sight ahead. But here the breeze dropped and the tide turned against us, and it was noon before we passed the Mouse again, and nearly dark when we opened up Holyhead Bay. We thought we could see the topmast of the big yawl, showing over the breakwater; she had missed the Cowes Regatta, and there was a discouraged look about her spars. There was an air of old times about Holyhead; it was as if we had once lived there for years on end. The South Stack was familiar, and Bardsey Island recognised us and glared amicably as we passed. But the Smalls stared coldly over the rim of the horizon, and seemed perplexed at our entry into new seas.

'If there's a man aboard that writes books,' Ball had said, 'I can spin him some yarns that will turn his head.' Now he began to put this threat into execution. Whenever an opportunity offered, day or night, he would squat on deck beside the tiller, or stand in his galley door, and tell his tales.

They were long, rambling, loose-hung yarns, without beginning, and ending nowhere; stories of the old 'hard ships,' with weevils in the biscuits and living slime in the water casks, of 'longshore fights in foreign ports and desperate times at sea; the story of the Norwegian bo'sun who went mad and drove all the men from the stokehold with a red-hot shovel; of the old sailmaker who died in his bunk, the second night of the voyage, and came back to haunt the ship; of a Greek named Tony who unwittingly signed on for a voyage out of New York with a skipper that had sworn to kill him if he ever set eyes on him again; of that time in the Marquesas when the man from Pittsburg staked his native wife on a throw of the dice, and lost, and wouldn't pay.

'I'm no great hand at expressing these things, but I've often thought I'd like to have a go at setting them down. People don't know what goes on in the world, sir, that's a fact. I always say, truth is stranger than fiction.'

But truth is easier than fiction too, and this Ball would not believe. The impression of his stories, as a whole, was of a fascinating manner of life, but the vividness of each yarn, and the point of it, lay in the fact that he, who was speaking, had been on the spot when it happened. When I attempted to weave a pattern, to put causes before effects and find some consequential conclusions, he kept interrupting me to say that – so far as he had been able to discover – 'it did not happen so.' Ball was an artist of the old school: fiction, he thought, was but a poor substitute for truth.

At sunrise of the second day we passed the Smalls. To the east was Lundy Island and the mouth of the Bristol Channel; westward ho was the broad Atlantic. There are phantom ships in this sea; sleek tea-clippers and brave East Indiamen, frigates and seventy-fours and galleons, and even dim images of coracles, paddled by shock-headed, foolhardy pioneers whose bright eyes saw far, but did not understand.

It was only ninety miles to Land's End. This was good progress. Bill Sisson was to join us at Penzance, and we began to think that we would have to wait for him, instead of his waiting for us – an unpleasant prospect for him, this latter, since he didn't know where we were, nor when we were coming, nor from where.

But that night the sun set in a bank of black cloud, and the wind hauled south-west. It came in puffs at first, and then in heavier squalls, darkening the water. We knew, now, the nature of a south-wester on this coast, and at the very first wail of the wind in the rigging we made all snug. We took the boat in on deck, set the storm jib in place of the big one, tucked a reef in the mainsail, and furled the mizzen.

At half-past eleven we made our landfall, and picked up the light on Pendeen Head, a point on the lee bow. This was just right. We roared along, and by two o'clock the Head was abeam, and the Longships was in sight. But there was a heavy sea against us. Somewhere offshore a gale was blowing, and though we never felt the force of it, the great rollers were charging in before it, outrunning it, silent, ominous, lifting up tremendous crests, sharp and black against the black sky. In the hollows we were becalmed; on the ridges the wind caught us and sent us skidding down the slopes like a coasting sled. And every wave set us in towards the shore.

Several steamers passed, some very close. Ball was steering, and I was sitting in the companion, watching the lights. All at once I felt something near us, as a man will sometimes become aware of a person standing over him while he sleeps. I looked astern, and saw the masts and funnel of a steamer in the sky. No hull was visible; only the bare masts and the stack, rolling out black smoke. Then the hill of water between us rolled away, and she rose up, as if spewed forth from the bottom of the sea, black, blind, silent and threatening. Her red and green eyes glared at us. Then she sank, without a sound, and the lights went out. She plunged again, and came up nearer. We had a stern light in the mizzen rigging, and a dozen times I blinked at it, asking myself if it was really there, burning brightly, plainly visible. Did she see us? Was she blind and dumb? Did it matter to her? That iron cliff, staggering ahead through the dark, lifting up and swooping down, so insensible, so unaware. . . . At the very last moment, when she was separated from us by the length of only one wave, she put up her helm, and passed under our lee. Her bow went down, and her propeller pounded the water; it rose again, streaming cascades of foam. Ball flung a cordial curse at her as she passed.

The Longships appeared on our lee bow. Then, though we kept our course, it showed ahead; in an hour, we were heading for the dark land to the eastward of it. Each wave swung us in, dropped us, and left us for the next. We came about, and painfully, inch by inch, crept back to the westward. But when we had our offing, and came over on to the other tack again, the light at once began sweeping across our bows, and seemed to rush up to meet us. A dozen times we tacked, thrown sidewise while we were heading south, eating our way out to windward, but getting no nearer the corner, while we were heading west.

It was maddening work, endless and hopeless. By four o'clock we had had enough of it. We set the big jib, yanked up the mizzen, shook the reef out of the mainsail, and drove her. The seas couldn't stop us then. Yet we had no more than a hundred yards to spare when we turned the corner. At daybreak we eased our sheets and started up the Channel. As soon as we were clear of the rocks the wind went down.

We came slipping into Mount's Bay through a thick fog. On the port hand we could make out the rough outline of the land, and the wreck of a large steamer, lying in a crumpled heap at the foot of the cliffs. Here under the shore the big waves were tamed to long and gentle undulations, pale and coldly gleaming. We came lapping through the white silence like a ghost.

Then, all at once, the fog split, and we sailed out of it into the clear warm sunshine. Penzance breakwaters, the town behind them, the green trees on the slopes of the hills, appeared before us. There was St. Michael's Mount, and the lovely outline of Godolphin Hill. The sun shone on the church tower and the gray roofs of the houses. All was serene and still, like a Sunday morning.

We tied up just inside the head of the mole, scrambled ashore, and went uptown to look for Bill.

We visited all the hotels in turn, and found no trace of him. In one, the landlord said he had an American there – yes, a fairly tall man, with a brown hat, he thought – no, he didn't know his name. He was out at the moment, but when he returned he would ask him. We went to the post-office, and found neither mail nor wire. Back at the hotel where the American was, the landlord said that his name was – well, he'd forgotten it again. But it wasn't Sisson.

Down at the harbour, the trippers and the summer-people were standing in rows along the quay, looking down at the *Caltha*. The men were explaining, pointing aloft with their canes, calling attention to this or that detail of the rigging; the women and girls listened absently and nodded, and stood on tiptoe to try to look down the companion. Among the feet of the crowd the small boys whispered excitedly, and bet one another that 'she could go!'

It was very natural and understandable. So often had we ourselves shown a similar enthusiasm, standing for long wondering hours at the edge of a wharf, looking down at a ship. But now the conditions were reversed, and it was we who looked up from the deck, incurious and indifferent. For we knew how the *Caltha* had looked in the big seas off the Longships that morning, and they did not. And we knew that off to the south, over that clear straight horizon, five hundred and forty-seven miles away, was Porto, on the Douro River, and that we were going there.

In the morning a telegram came from Bill, who was in Nevers, where, he said, he had been 'unavoidably detained,' and asked us to wait for him. What could have detained him? With the ship ready for sea? We gave it up. We would wait, of course. We knew, at least, that he was in Europe. But – Nevers? How could he have been detained at Nevers? We kept thinking of the bitter orations we would deliver to him, and wondering what he could possibly find to say in reply.

But at least we could get everything ready, so as to be ready to leave as soon as he should come. We got out the new sails and bent them. We looked over the rigging carefully, and made repairs where we found weak places. We confessed that the *Caltha* was too small to carry a boat in davits; we had found a way to lash it so that it was secure, but every third wave hit the bottom of it, with a terrifying crash, and there was no comfort in it. We took the davits out entirely, and lashed them on deck. We found an old sail which might have been designed for almost anything; by some contriving, we made a working topsail of it, though it fitted like washing on the line. We hunted up a sailmaker – an old man, with only one eye, who, Ball said, had only two speeds, Dead Slow, and Stop – but he was a marvellous man with a needle, and he made us an excellent cover for the boat.

In the ship-chandler's shop where we went on errands – a pleasant place, with boots and oilskins hanging from the ceiling, filled with the tarry smell of rope – there was an amiable man with a passionate enthusiasm for football. He was manager of a local team. While he told us the scores of every game that had been played for the last dozen years, and showed us pictures of the men who had played in them, the cat, lying in a pile of fishermen's caps on the counter, blinked reprovingly at him, and yawned elaborately, to give him a hint.

'You going north from here, or east ? ' he asked.

'South,' we said.

'South ? Why, there's nothing . . . you ain't going to sea in that little yawl?'

'Yes,' we said. 'To Gibraltar.'

'Well, now!' he exclaimed admiringly. 'To think of that! We had some boys here one time that took one of our luggers out to Australia. Yes. Five of 'em. Going to the gold diggings, they were. In '48, it was. They took the mails for Melbourne, and, do you believe it, they beat the regular mail packet. Beat her to Melbourne – oh, I forget how much. And you saw that little pilot boat in the harbour? The little cutter? Well, one of our men took the sister to that one down to South Africa. No more than forty feet long, she wasn't. And he took her right down to the Cape.'

The cat brightened up at this, and yawned no more. Yet I thought she looked reproachful: 'Here I've been living with you for seven years, and you knew this all the time, and never said a word about it!' Indeed, this was better. No mention of 'the Bay of Biscay, you know,' or the grim Disaster that stalks the seas – but men making long voyages in small ships, and thinking of nothing but the joy of it. Englishmen are always doing such things; they have able boats, and they will take them anywhere.

And yet, one of the Liverpool pilots told me that he admired American yachting, saying that we had better boats, and did more real offshore cruising than they themselves did. I told him that the admiration was mutual. He was judging, I suppose, by the *Typhoon* and the *Lloyd W. Berry* and the *Diablesse.* And he had never seen Long Island Sound in August.

We came last, and reluctantly, to a consideration of the motor. What was to be done about it? We opened the cage and peered in at the rusted, sodden mass of junk, and saw that there was no hope for it, ever. We took off the propeller and stowed it under the cabin floor. The matter was settled. The motor might recover, now, or disintegrate, as it felt inclined. But it had lost its chance for usefulness.

Every night we went to the theatre, or the pictures, coming back down to the ship afterwards through the delightful winding streets where the candlelight was shining in the windows of the little houses. On the quay in the blue darkness Ball would be sitting with a group of fishermen or loafers, telling them tales of the other half of the world. Life, it seemed, might go on for ever in this same serenity, and the *Caltha* might end her days there in harbour, watching her reflection in the water.

On Saturday morning Pat had gone uptown to do some errands. I heard a step on the deck, and went to the companion. There was Bill Sisson. He had arrived in town late the night before, and had come down now, before breakfast, to join the ship. He had lost his trunk somewhere, but as soon as he could buy some oil pants he would be ready to go. We met Pat, and romped off gaily to the ship-chandler's, singing and laughing gaily about nothing.

You, I suppose, have dreamed of an ideal inn. 'Somewhere, there's an inn,' you have said; an inn of all the perfection that your imagination has given it; bright with Romance, and yet remote and dim, like an appealing memory. That inn is near the harbour at Penzance. We had been so fortunate as to discover it, and had saved it for one important day.

We went in and ordered ale. We tried to talk of winds

and Sailing Directions and the chances of gales, but the inn itself simply would not let us be practical. There is a crest on the glasses: the name of the inn in a circle, with a ship in the centre. There *are* no such inns.

It faces the water, and there is a bay window, just large enough to hold a table and three chairs, which looks out over Mount's Bay across a pebbled beach. There are neat curtains at the windows, and the panes are very bright and clean. In the gray granite lintel above the door, which is so low that a tall man must stoop to enter it, is cut the date '1717'; the mossy roof sags with the weight of the years.

The sitting-room floor is worn hollow around the knots in the planks; the beams of the ceiling are black with smoke, because a south-west wind, which is from the sea, sends draughts down the chimney. It seems specially selected, of all inns in the world, for an inspiration of romantic tales, and a starting point for high adventures. For two hundred years mariners have sat in the bay window, with their glasses on the shining table before them, telling long yarns of voyages and ships and intricate escapes, of stupid accidents that turn to adventures in the telling, of living bloody gales of wind.

'He seen Ushant, he did, for he told me so. He seen Creac'h light, and was trying to beat up for it, and split his blooming mainsail, by God, from luff to leach. All in a mess, he was, and leaking like a basket. He run for home. I don't know what else he could do, by that time. I remember how it blew; you wouldn't think no vessel could live in it. He came right across, a-roarin', in nine hours, and run her on to the beach there, between we and the Mount.' For two hundred years.

We sat there. And we talked of all the adventures that must have had their beginnings at such an inn.

At such an inn were the smugglers caught; before that door the magistrate and his men went galloping down the frozen road in the moonlight. It was at such an inn that the highwayman rapped with the butt of his pistol on the window-shutters. The lovely lady was carried across just such a pebbled beach and put in the waiting boat, that red dawn when so much happened under the beech trees behind the church.

The 'Admiral Benbow,' where Bill Bones died, was such an inn; Pew and his gang turned the place upside down, looking for Flint's Fist. It was at such an inn that the Squire stopped, in Bristol, while the *Hispaneola* was fitting out for her voyage. We remembered how he came to the door to meet Jim Hawkins and Tom Redruth.

'Here you are,' he cried, 'and the doctor came last night from London. Bravo! the ship's company complete!'

'Oh, sir,' cried Jim, 'when do we sail?'

'Sail!' says he. 'We sail to-morrow!'

Now this was on Saturday, the third of September. On Sunday we sailed.

CHAPTER SEVEN

Biscay

*

THE sun came up very hot over the top of Godolphin Hill as we warped out of the dock. The surface of the bay was like polished copper. But a ripple on the water at the foot of St. Michael's Mount promised a north-east wind. We had hoped for this; it was just what we wanted. We made sail as we dropped down the bay, and before Wolf Rock was abeam the breeze was blowing merrily. There never was such luck; the glass was high and steady, after a week of fluctuation, and the sky was settled and serene; we kept that north-easter astern of us for a week.

The coast behind us shimmered and gleamed in the misty sunlight like gold. Smoke was rising from the chimneys, and we could see a few people passing up and down the quiet little streets. The sound of the church bells grew faint. In three hours the last of Cornwall, the last of England, had faded out of sight astern, and we were at sea. The next land that we would sight would be of a very different sort from England, and in the streets of the next town on our route we should see no little mullioned windows set close up under the eaves of gray slate roofs, no chimney-pots nor mossy thatch nor inn signs swinging in the wind. Our course was south-thirty-seven west, for Cape Finisterre, the north-west corner of Spain.

In the afternoon the horizon ahead of us was notched by the topsails of a ship. At ten miles' distance Ball pronounced her to be Norwegian, and so it turned out; a big barque, on the opposite course to us, close-hauled on the starboard tack, reaching up across the entrance of the Channel for Land's End. We passed close to her, being on the same road. She towered up, seeming to fill half the sky with that tremendous rig of hers; we could hear the water swishing in her wake, and the faint booming of her upper canvas, just lifting in the wind. The ropes were slatting gently, tapping against the spars, and somewhere far up in her rigging a block was chirping with a plaintive bird-like cry. The sunlight gleamed on her spars and on the polished rail about her poop, and the bright brass of the binnacle glinted and sparkled. Three sailors in the waist, standing against the rail under the gray arch of the big mainsail, and the man at the wheel, gazed at us as we passed. Perhaps at supper that night they spoke – in Norwegian – of 'that little yawl,' saying that we had found the best of all possible ways to go to sea. We spoke often of her; there is a certain impression of capability, a noble sort of assurance, about a big ship, that a small one can never attain.

There was something very pleasant about passing this ship, out there in the new world that we had entered. We were not merely men who were passing through the country, men who would be out of it again by nightfall, in some harbour of the land – we were inhabitants. The sea is very big and lonely, brutally indifferent, utterly unexcited – but it is not uninhabited. There is always someone out there.

We were headed south, for blue water; before we had gone a hundred miles we noticed a new purity on the face of the sea, a clear serenity in the air, that grew up about us as we progressed. The water lost the cold gray look of the Narrow Seas, and took on a fresh blue colour, reflected from the sky. When the sun went down there were no more than scattered clouds, and the stars came out, and shone as never before. After all the black nights through which we had passed, stars were only a distant memory; but now they shone out again, faithfully, and fairly blazed in heaven. As I watched them, sweeping along just above our topmast head, I wondered if they could gleam more brightly, even in the south. I might have known. It was seven hundred miles to Cape St. Vincent, of which it is said, 'beyond this cape lies Summer.'

A dozen times, during that first night, I was sure that I saw the light on Creac'h Point, on Ushant, shining up over the edge of the sea, though I knew that it could not be true. We were more than eighty miles from Ushant.

It was impossible to be entirely trustful of the weather, for all the glass was high, and the wind held so strong and steady. We kept a watchful eye on the behaviour of the clouds, and tapped the barometer whenever we passed it, for when the wind should shift, and how we ought to steer to take advantage of it, was our chief concern. Because this was the Bay of Biscay.

A gale, if it came, would probably strike us from the north-west, or, more doubtfully, but worse, if it should happen, from the south-west. And then we should have to get out to the westward – out of the Bay, away from the land – as fast and as far as the wind and sea would let us, for, to put it no more elaborately, it often blows hard in the Bay of Biscay, and often the sea is very rough. It would not be too much to stand out to Eleven, or even Twelve, West Longitude, to counteract the set of the sea and the drive of the gale. If once a ship is driven in behind Ushant, among the rocks and the shallow water, it's all up with her, and on the southern portion of the coast of France there is a line of wicked beaches, with the mouth of Garonne for shelter, which she couldn't hit – not to save her life.

As for the north-west corner of Spain, it has a reputation. The coast is bold and rocky, many of the lights are weak, placed so high on the cliffs that they are easily obscured in thick weather, and the currents run like demons. In the very centre of the Biscay chart appears the word 'Caution' in large capitals, with a notice to that effect. If a ship falls in with the land at night, or in fog, or with a gale blowing, she may call herself foolish, but there is little else that she can do. There are harbours, hidden away behind the walls of rock, but they are of little use if it blows too hard to carry sail, or if the sea is too big to run before it into shelter.

If it should come on to blow from the east, which was unlikely at this season of the year, but still possible, we must reverse the directions, and stand up into the Bay, for when we had passed the corner we should need a lee, and the closer we were to the cliffs, the better. If no gale came at all, then Seven West was far enough, and we were best off where we were.

But nothing happened. We had an easy following sea, a steady wind on the port quarter, and during the whole passage, day and night, we never even had the skylights closed. There was no way of knowing this in advance, however. Every night, after supper, when we put up the running lights, we took in the spinnaker and the big club-topsail, because we could not make it seem prudent, considering the circumstances, to carry everything. On the third night out from Penzance, however, we did carry everything, and during that twenty-four hours we made a hundred and thirty-two miles. We would have done better if the wind had been stronger, but we were happy to make so much. Good luck couldn't last forever, and speed was of first importance.

Ball called me at midnight, and I steered for two hours and a-half. He and I were always very formal and punctilious; he would give me the course, and I would repeat it to him, and then he would report the ships that he had seen, or call my attention to anything that happened to be in sight at the moment. He said 'Good-night' and went shambling forward; I always saw the black silhouette of his head and shoulders, against the starry sky, as he stopped, halfway down the hatch, for a last look about him. Then he folded his elbows against his chest and sank out of sight.

When I came on deck on that third night we were running seven knots, rolling deeply, so that the boom trailed in the water from time to time with a spout of faintly phosphorescent spray; the sails were steady and quiet, and the *Caltha's* long thin bow was cutting the water with a steady roar. The port light, shining into the hollow of the spinnaker, made the sail glow ruby red; to starboard, under the boom, I could see the faint spectral green of the starboard light on the tumbling bow wave. We carried a riding light in the mizzen rigging, with a tin shield on the forward side of it, and it lighted the quarterdeck. The dew had tightened the boat cover, and I drummed on it. Before me was the compass card, the most important point in the world, a yellow disk, floating in space.

At two-thirty I thumped on the deck for Pat. Through the skylight I could see his shadow on the floor as he moved about, and then I could hear the creak of the companion steps as he started up. His head and shoulders emerged into the starlight. He looked first at the water beside the rail, and then around at the empty sea. 'Hi!' he would say. 'How are we doing?' The answer was always the same. He came aft and took my place, wrapping the square of canvas about his knees, and I went below.

After the endless waves and the rush of the wind through space it was pleasant to stand for a moment in the saloon doorway and feel the security of the four protecting walls. The lamplight filled the room and glinted cheerfully on the panels. The swing table, with its brown cloth, dizzily balanced the chart and the Light List that lay on it. The yellow oilskin coats were piled in a corner of the sofa. After the squeal of blocks, far up in the dark, and the gnawing noise of the water beside the ship, the ticking of the saloon clock was a small, comfortable, domestic sound.

In the cabin, the dim starlight, reflected from the mainsail, shone down through the skylight, showing the backs of the books in the shelves, and the white pillows in the berths. It seemed very strange that there should be a bed here, in the very centre of the sea, a warm bed, with a mile of cold sea-water under it. The noise of the wind outside was like a faint memory of things that happened long ago, and could not happen now.

Bill had the morning watch, and it was he who saw the sunrise. When the day came, it showed us the same surrounding sea, the same clear sky overhead, the same tireless wind. We began each day in the centre of the circle, as if we had taken the Universe with us during the night.

To tell of the daily details . . . those who know these things will complain of tiresome repetition, and those who depend upon imagination will find more in the imagining. Yet the old sailors of history, for whose manner of life we are entirely dependent on what they were willing to set down on paper – it is impossible to think of them aboard their ships, because they never told us how they lived. With startling lack of foresight, as strange as it is hard to forgive, they fancied that the sea would never change, and that whoever was curious about the cabin of a galleon had but to step aboard and look about him.

What did we do, from hour to hour, in all that time? Why, we worked the ship and watched the weather and admired the round world; we slept and ate and read books and talked, not exactly as if we were on shore, but as nearly so as the circumstances would allow.

We had the ordinary breakfast – oatmeal and bacon and eggs and very bad coffee – for which Ball apologises by saying that he does no better than his best – but the circumstances of it are very different from those of a similar meal ashore. The whole cabin is on a slant, and rolls from side to side, so that the lamps in their gimbals seem strangely tilted, and the coats on the hook beside the doorway hang out from the wall in grotesque rigidity. The doorway, which is wide enough for easy passage when normally vertical, becomes contracted, and one pushes himself through it as if he were dropping into a sloping slot. In the galley, the tea-kettle hangs above the stove in a system of wires, like a spider in the centre of a web. When a cupboard is opened, all the articles within are crowded around the exit, waiting to leap out and pour down in a shower. The table capers; the dish of oatmeal swings down to the level of one's knees, and up again to one's chin. Except on the table, things are never set down, but are wedged in, for inanimate objects, such as books, or tins of tobacco, have a crazy tendency to move off sidewise, as if by their own perverse accord. The whole ship is alive with a thousand little noises, and the water rushes past the planking in growls and gurgles; the mainmast, which comes down through the saloon, hums with the strain of the sails.

It is all very different, and hard to accept completely. Yet up on deck, with the slanting sails above and the broad tumbling ocean all about, it seems natural enough.

There was – relatively speaking – no lack of company in the Bay. A topsail schooner came up from the westward, early one morning, and crossed our stern. The first light of the sunrise shone on her spars and turned them champagne-colour against the blue of the sky. There was something of the exhilaration of champagne in the sight of her. A French trawler – from la Rochelle, perhaps – stood out near to us one afternoon, and as we watched her brown sails and black hull dipping in and out of sight between the waves we marvelled that a ship so small should dare to venture three hundred miles from the land. Yet she was twice our tonnage. So firm a feeling of confidence emanates from the ship one's self is in! We sighted steamers, prosaic and unlovely, but endowed with new qualities now that they were seen offshore, at work. As we proceeded south they came in increasing numbers; some hull down over the edge of the world, with only their masts and funnels showing; some so close that we could see the faces of the men.

We sighted sailing ships at night. The aspect of a tall ship, at sea under the stars, is a thing no one can hope to state. She passes as an inspiration passes through the mind. . . . Ball, who had spent his life in such ships, grew reminiscent and sentimental at sight of them, and talked as a man would talk who had had his youth given back to him.

On the fourth morning we saw a whale. He blew first at a distance, in the classical position of 'Weather bow' and later came close, to look at us. We brought a rifle up on deck and fired at him when he came to the surface under our stern. The bullet struck the water near him; he sounded, and did not come back.

For the navigation, I had prepared a note-book of the passage, with tabular arrangements for the data, exactly as I had been taught in school. The problems were no more difficult than others that I had solved. But the answers were not in the back of the book; they were in that corner of Spain for which we were heading. It was in a very humble and deferential attitude of mind that I brought the sextant out on deck, that first day, off the entrance to the Channel, and took the altitude of the sun.

St. Michael's Mount, from which we took our departure, lies in 50° 7′ North and 5° 28′ 40″ West. The position for which we were bound, off the Spanish coast, is 43° 4′ North, 9° 28′ 15″ West.

At noon of the first day we were in 49° 51′ North, 5° 45′ 10″ West. Thereafter, our daily latitude decreased as follows: 48° 28′ – 46° 49′ 42″ – 45° 5′ 18″ – 43° 23′ 12″. Our successive longitudes were: 6° 30′ 10″ – 7° 10′ 10″ – 9° 43′ 30″ – 9° 33′ 30″.

At noon on the fourth day I had marked our position on the chart with an insolent cross. 'Here,' I said, 'we are. And Finisterre lies east south-east of us, distant twenty-six miles.' We looked at one another, and went trooping solemnly up on deck, where Ball was steering.

'Put her east south-east,' Pat said.

'East south-east, sir,' said Ball, and hauled the tiller over.

This was at noon. At twenty minutes before two we made out a luminous cloud on the horizon ahead, and an hour later we saw the sun shining on a high red cliff. This was the north-west corner of Spain. It seemed incredible. Yet there it was.

There is always something miraculous about a landfall. That a man should be able to find his way across the 'trackless ocean' – about which one hears so much – when his guides are the Magnetic Pole, the Observatory at Greenwich, a pair of printed books, and the sun in the sky – all of which are fantastically remote from his immediate question – seems nothing less than magical. And the magic increases with the inexperience of the navigator. In our case, the wonder was supreme.

There was little enough in the aspect of the coast itself to evoke enthusiasm. Bare mountains, brown and dry, rose up from the sea, and there was white surf at their feet. Here and there a farmhouse clutched at the side of the hill, and in some of the ravines, where the slope was less steep, were meagre villages, seeming pitifully conscious of their isolation. Mule-trails went wandering up over the jagged crest of the range. It was all very barren and forlorn and compromisingly lonely. But it looked as we felt Spain should look. And we ourselves had discovered it.

We passed a fisherman – a long, lean, double-ended boat, carrying an enormous lateen sail set on a great yard that bent like a whip. Ball cried, 'Buenas dias, señor!' as she went swooping past, and the man at the tiller raised his arm in greeting and shouted something in reply. There could no longer be any doubt of it.

That night, we had dim land on our left, and the moon came up behind the hills. We were around the corner; we had passed the Cape at the World's End, and were running down the coast of romantic Spain. This is the boundary and sea-wall of the Old World. Men came this far, and then turned back. In the later adventurous age the explorers stood on their reeling quarter-decks and watched this rampart of dreary hills drop away behind them, and their lookouts found a welcome in it when they came home again.

In the afternoon we passed the mouth of the Mino

River, which marks the boundary between Spain and Portugal. An island in the centre of it is strongly fortified. There was something absurd about it; here was the whole clean sea, with the wind and the waves to fight, and on the boundary lines of countries little-minded and wrangling men erected forts!

At sunset we altered the course half a point offshore, and hove to, at midnight, estimating that we had arrived opposite to Leixoes. The entrance to the Douro River, on which Porto lies, is impeded by a formidable bar, where the breakers roll incessantly. Leixoes is an artificial harbour. The Pilot Book said that Leixoes should be pronounced 'Layshowings,' but we did not believe it.

At dawn we were in a world of still white fog. We stood in towards the east, wondering just where the land might be, and how we were to recognise it when we saw it, for there was no way of telling how far we had come during the night. The Pilot Book said that there was an eighty-ton crane on the breakwater at Leixoes, plainly visible to vessels standing along the coast.

After an hour of gentle progress – for the wind had fallen very light – a steam trawler came out of the fog ahead and circled around us; a crew of at least thirty men stared at us, and the man in the pilot-house leaned doubled up over his window-sill in frank amazement. We hoisted our ensign, to help his incredulity.

'Vous allez à Layshoings?' he asked finally, as if he had waited long for courage to address us.

We answered that we were, and asked the distance.

He held up three fingers, and clanged his engine-room

bell for full speed ahead. Some of the crew shouted something in what we believed to be Portuguese, and waved their arms in the direction of the open sea. We looked, but could see nothing but fog. Perhaps this was what they meant. The trawler vanished again in the direction from which she had first come, as if she were going home to report our coming. Her name was *Christina.*

We followed the direction she had taken, which was a little more southerly than the course we had been steering. The sky, and the air, were white, and the translucent sea caught the reflection of it; there was no land, no sound of surf on the shore, no faintest indication of the presence of a continent. And then, suddenly, out of the whiteness before us, detached from earth and sea – an apparition in the east, like the ghost of the Old Man who haunted Sindbad – appeared the dim outline of an eighty-ton crane.

We hoisted the 'P.T.' The breakwaters appeared, lines of dull gray, the masts of the ships, the red tile roofs of the houses in the town, the palm trees on the ridges of the hills.

At the entrance of the harbour the pilot's boat came out to meet us.

CHAPTER EIGHT

'A Small Country, Once Great'

*

None of us had been in Portugal before, excepting Ball, who has been everywhere.

The first person we saw – after the pilot and the health officer had left us – was a sleepy Republican soldier in a sentry-box on the quay. He was very hot and desperately bored with life, and though he would have liked, plainly, to honour us with a gesture of salute or of defiance, he remembered – we saw him – the weight of his rifle, and remained immovable.

Indeed, everything in Portugal is beautifully Portuguese.

Leixoes is an odd, anomalous place. Although it is a mere village, a loose collection of rude huts, yet there are some large modern buildings, cleanly and solidly built. Although the harbour has been constructed at enormous expense and has recently been appropriated three million English pounds for improvements, yet the few streets of the town are half-finished, littered with refuse, and ankle deep in dust, so that the place seems haunted by an ancient curse of poverty. It faces the sea in a flinty, desperate manner, as if it felt danger at its back.

The houses are white or pale yellow or salmon-colour, plastered, or faced with tiles; the roofs are deep russet red; the sky above is blue – a deep, endless, aching, inevitable blue. The women, selling fruit or carrying great balanced loads on their heads, are festooned with rags and gay scarves; the swarming children wear one simple garment each and stare through their tangled hair with great dark eyes that seem mostly white in comparison with dirty faces. The shops in the streets are dingy and barren, the goods for sale piled on rough counters or stacked against the wall or hung beside the doors, with no attempt to make them look saleable, so that one never knows whether he is in a shop or a private storeroom. The windows of most of the houses are tightly shuttered against the heat, and the doorways are hung with heavy curtains.

Along the shore beyond Leixoes we passed villas, spotless and crudely new – heroines of moving-pictures seemed moving about under the deep shadows of the palmtrees among the blazing flowers, and the villains of the plots, stealthy, 'faultlessly attired,' though somewhat frayed, and with a self-conscious air of grandeur, tiptoed across the gravel walks and through the tall iron gates.

What else could Portugal be like?

The Douro River is narrow, and flows between high banks. It was crowded with sailing ships – ships painted white, kept very neat, exotic, romantic, with a graceful air of poetry about them. They lack the iron nerve that ships should have, and they lie tucked away there in that close sheltered valley as if they were hiding from the sea. The tradition of Prince Henry the Navigator has passed, these many years, and Vasco de Gama died in 1525.

The tram set us down in the principal square of Porto, in front of the ship-chandler's, and when we had bought a log – for ours had been lost in the Bay – we asked him where we should go to find the sights of the city.

We found two very fine churches, one with a beautiful slender tower like a minaret, set on a hill, dominating the city, and one with walls of tiles. The contrast between the gray granite of the window frames and cornices and the deep blue of the pictured tiles was admirable. There were several parks, in which the deep cool shade of the palms was most grateful after the dazzling sunlight shining on the white walls of houses. The largest square is paved with cobbles set in a mosaic pattern of wavy lines, giving a horrible, dizzy feeling of earthquakes. There is a quaint sort of facetiousness about this, as if the designer fancied himself smart.

We could find no attractive café and no interesting restaurant. We looked for a theatre, but could discover nothing but a play, which it would have been foolish to see, since we should not have been able to understand a word of it.

In the end, we went back to Leixoes in a Ford.

In the next morning's paper there appeared the following notice, which I translate literally enough to preserve something of the flavour of the original:

'SHALLOP OF RECREATION ENGLISH AT LEIXOES

'Proceeding from Glasgow entered our port of Leixoes yesterday, about twelve o'clock, a shallop of recreation English *Caltha*, of the command of the Captain Spencer.

'The shallop, which is very elegant, is of fourteen tons, and pertains to an English nautical club, conducting three young members of the said club on a voyage of recreation.

'The three voyagers disembarked and visited various points of this city.

'After dropping in at Lisbon, goes later to Gibraltar.'

It was not long before the results of this publicity began to be evident. We had dozens of visitors, who stood in groups on the quay or rowed out across the harbour in boats. One party of four men, who spoke French, we invited aboard. They were greatly interested in the ship, our experiences in the past, and our plans for the future; they gathered, perhaps from something we said, that we were not greatly pleased with Porto, and in a generous spirit of hospitality they took us ashore with them, in order that they might correct our impression.

This was the beginning of a very long day. They showed us places that we had been unable to find for ourselves; they took us to call on an artist, a splendid, grave, massive man, whose house was filled with wonderful and lovely things: they went to dinner with us at a gorgeous restaurant, which was, however, deserted except for ourselves; they told us of everything we should see and do in Lisbon, which was, 'after all, the capital.' It was after one o'clock when we returned to the harbour.

They were eager that we should have a favourable impression of Porto. They, themselves, were our impression.

Ball was not aboard. The lamp was burning in the cabin, and Bill's army revolver – one of these tremendous hand-cannons, designed to frighten animals now extinct – lay on the table.

After we had gone to bed, Ball came back, continuing some long, elaborate, and complicated argument in English and in Spanish, and about five o'clock we heard him laughing heartily to himself.

At breakfast time we noticed that most of the cups and saucers were missing from the pantry shelves. We asked what had happened.

There had been a party in the fo'c's'le of an American ship anchored near us. The topic for discussion was the Rights of Small Nations in general, and of Norway in particular. This did not hold Ball's attention. He was drinking and passing the time with a 'Russian Finn' as he called him; the meeting was noisy, and it was with difficulty that they could carry on their conversation. After a time it happened that something was said which touched the sensibilities of the Russian Finn; he seemed to think that a speech would help matters, and started one accordingly. 'Now,' said Ball, 'I liked that Russian Finn; I was on his side from the very beginning.' The Norwegians were of the opposite persuasion.

The account becomes confused at this point. At any rate, Ball admitted that he was 'not quite quick enough.' and, in explanation, pointed to his eye. Indeed, his left eye was horribly bunged, and looked like a doughnut. The party seems then to have adjourned aboard the *Caltha*, whence Ball had great difficulty in dislodging them with the blooming gun. 'I couldn't *get* rid of 'em,' he said.

We asked what had become of the dishes.

'Aye, that's just it,' Ball said, with an air of deep cleverness. 'What's become of the dishes?'

Soon after this he slipped ashore again, where Pat found him later, in the corner grog-shop with the Russian Finn. He brought him out aboard, sent him below, and we got under way.

We left with our same faithful north-easter blowing – though it was blowing harder, and there was a feel of purpose behind it – and set a course down along the coast to pass inside Burling's Island on our way to Lisbon.

In the afternoon a schooner loomed over the northern horizon and came roaring down on us before the wind, passing so close that we could read her name, and the 'Grand Bank' on her stern. She was a Newfoundlander, from St. John's, and she brought her own sort of weather with her; before dark the wind hauled to the westward, and it shut in thick with Grand Bank fog. The land and the sea were hidden, and every rope dripped with moisture.

I went to bed at my usual hour, and it seemed that I had slept but a very short time when Ball thumped on the deck for me. I went up.

'I've called you a bit early, sir,' Ball said. 'I hope you won't mind it. But I'm awful sick.'

I took his place at the tiller, and as he staggered forward he remarked that it was all his own fault. He paused for a moment in the hatchway, as usual, his face turned up to the sky.

'There is no Pity,' he said bitterly, and sank out of sight.

I adjusted the canvas around my knees, and looked at the clock in the binnacle. It was ten minutes past nine.

The ledges off Burling's Island are easy enough to avoid, if one can see the lighthouse, but that night, when we could not see the length of the ship, and our mainsail towered up into the sky with no visible top, the light might as well have been on the other side of the world. It was barely daylight when we heard breakers ahead. Before we could come about we saw them; ugly green waves rolling in on rocks, spouting white foam. We could not tell if this were the middle, or the end, of the shoal, nor which end it was. We ran east, for the coast. In an hour we heard the rote again, and a black cliff, with breakers at the foot of it, reared up before us. Having thus painfully discovered the middle of the passage, we squared away and ran down the coast again.

After noon it cleared, and showed us the land, high, with white buildings on the hills, very clear and lovely in the bright sunlight.

That same evening we entered the mouth of the Tagus. As we passed Lloyd's signal station on the point the agent ran up the flags that mean: 'Please show distinguishing signal,' and we set the 'H.C.P.L.' – the same letters that I had looked up in the library in New York in August, 1920. There was something very pleasing in this sort of reception – we were looked for and expected. The pilot at Leixoes had telegraphed ahead.

We came in with the dying breeze, through a fleet of hundreds of lateen-sailed fishing boats, skirting close to the shore, and anchored in Cascaes Bay. The entrance to the river is crossed by a chain of sandy bars, on which, though the sea was so smooth, the long rollers were sweeping smoothly in and breaking; sticking up through the ferment of haze and thunder were the masts of two vessels which had been lost in the attempt to find the channels. Cascaes Bay is outside all this and apart from it.

All along the shores are the houses of the winter residents – English and Swedish and German – and it is for them that the shops are kept so neat and attractive, the streets so clean, the roads in such good repair. At the head of the bay is an elaborate casino, partly finished when we were there, with a great formal garden containing pergolas and pavilions and fountains. It seems that these things are done always for foreigners.

In the morning we went ashore and hired a carriage to take us to the city. The villas along the road shone in the sun like jewels, in their settings of gardens; the dark olive trees grew on the slopes of the hills. From time to time we passed through a village that showed some traces of antiquity; a lichen-covered gateway, a crumbling fountain, a bit of ancient wall.

We knew nothing of Lisbon, except that there had once been an earthquake there, which destroyed a famous chaise. But it was, 'after all, the capital,' and we were hoping for great things.

A short distance within the city limits a wheel came off the carriage.

The commercial streets along the waterfront, lined with big warehouses and the branch offices of establishments from every country in the world, were busy and prosperous; the business streets, which came next as we progressed, were crowded and active, though nearly every article set out for sale in the shops was imported from somewhere; the squares – the principal square is the inspiration of the one in Porto, with the dizzy pavement, though I am happy to be able to say that it has now been destroyed – the parks along the boulevards, though laid out in the grand manner, were rather meagre in detail, and careless. The magnificence, which we were continually expecting, failed to appear. There was no air of decay, nor any sign of degeneracy – simply, it was as if the city had felt a great and crushing obligation to be 'the capital,' without knowing exactly what it was that was required, and, in a panic of decision, had missed the essential idea.

We went to a hotel. I passed a miserable night, being unused to so broad a bed, and continually disturbed by the noises in the streets, the cries of the news vendors especially. As I leaned on the railing of the balcony and looked down at the bright lights and the crowds, the rumbling carts and hooting automobiles, I was thinking that the external aspects of what we call Western civilisation are everywhere much the same. In Spain, I saw nothing that led me to a similar thought; Spain is Oriental, exotic, eternally unchanging; but Portugal seems obstinately determined to conform.

As we were returning to Cascaes in the train we ran into fog. Ball had shifted the *Caltha* further offshore, and she lay rolling heavily in the seas that the south-wester was sweeping into the bay. After a great deal of difficulty we got on board. As the sun went down the wind moderated, and we went to bed.

During the night it came on to blow again. I dimly

realised that we were pitching a great deal, and that I had nearly worn an ear off the side of my head, shifting back and forth on my pillow, but I fancied that the sea was growing less, and had become just the right length to toss us. But as soon as it was light Ball came into the cabin and said, 'It's time we were out of this, sir.' So we got up.

It was dirty weather, raining, with low driving clouds and a big sea. We set a signal for a pilot, and waited while the pilot boat dropped a man aboard each of three steamers that were wallowing about outside the bars. As soon as they were free to bring a man to us, we got under way, under short canvas, and went scurrying up the river. We cut through close to the point at the north side of the entrance, by a passage that was a private secret of our pilot, with rocks under our lee, roaring with surf, and the sickening breakers on the shoal. Everyone was running for shelter. We came up in the midst of a fleet of craft of every sort, which branched off at intervals to anchor in favourite coves along the shores. We brought up opposite the railway station from which we had taken the train the night before.

So we were back in the capital after all.

We determined on seeing some of the night life and gaiety of which our provincial friends had told us, and to that end hunted up a 'Club' that they had recommended. The building in which it was located was ornate and imposing, making it impossible to resist the conclusion that it had been inherited from some former régime of magnificence. But the human part of the organisation was very depressing. A thin veil of cheap festivity was thrown over it, and the enjoyment of the guests was no more spontaneous than that of the waiters, or the members of the orchestra. We were the only people present who did not understand the intention.

'Every week we come here and get drunk,' some young men told us. 'There's nothing else to do. The girls won't dance with us, because they know we won't take them home. They might dance with you; they don't know you. There are five or six English families here, yes. We call, and now and again we get up a dance. But what is that? We come here and get drunk.'

On the way back to the ship, through the dismal and echoing cañons between the warehouses, we became involved in a street fight. There was a very considerable quality of excitement in it at first, but when the gendarme drew his sword it dwindled into a mere babble of explanations. As we went down along the docks we noticed that someone was following us. We saw at once that we had interfered in the work of some gang; that this spy had been sent to follow us to see where we went; that we should be stabbed, in some dismal alleyway, and never heard of again. Just before we reached the water's edge, Pat turned suddenly on the man, who had now come quite close, and asked him if he spoke English.

'Damn right I do,' said the boy – he was no more than a boy; a pale, frightened, ragged urchin.

'What are you following us for?' Pat asked.

'Maybe I could get a job, or something. Sometimes I get a job with some of the stewards of the American ships that come in, and they give me something to eat. They'll give you a job in this place, but they don't give you no money. Never.'

'Where did you learn to speak English?'

'I'm an American. I was born in Boston. And I'd like to get back there, let me tell you. My father's in Boston – I guess he is. My mother – I don't know where the hell she is. I got a grandmother here, and her and me makes a home together. If I could get some money we'd beat it back, believe me.'

He spoke up very bravely, out of all keeping with his timid manner, and half of his speech was profanity – as if he wanted to show us that he had not learned his English in school. We talked for some time with him – though he had no more to say than he had said: that he didn't like Lisbon – and then he left us.

Ball was not aboard.

Also our boat, which we had left drawn up on a sort of levee that borders the river at that point, had disappeared. A man appeared out of the shadows and volunteered a long story of the catastrophe, in which four small boys and a lost oar seemed to be important phases. 'But where is the boat now?' we asked him. The man exploded expressively and hunched his shoulders.

A moment afterwards Ball came, carrying a package wrapped in a newspaper, and leading a small boy by the hand.

'Where's the boat?'

'Aye, there you've hit it,' he said. 'Where is the boat?'

The boy now began to speak rapidly, pointing up the

river with a vague gesture, and Ball, putting his arms about the child's shoulders, led him away in the darkness.

Meanwhile, our Portuguese informant, who had gone off in the opposite direction, found the boat, and paddled it up to where we were standing.

When Ball returned he said, 'Them little devils!' savagely, through clenched teeth, and taking a penny from his pocket turned to give it to the boy. But the boy had run like a rabbit as soon as Ball had released his hand.

On Sunday we went to a bull-fight. There was only a small audience, and there was a violent thunderstorm. It rained and hailed most amazingly, and the arena was knee-deep in water within ten minutes. There was no bull-fight. We stood around in the corridor, under a corrugated iron roof on which the rain made a shocking noise, and when the storm had passed we walked back to town, after receiving a rebate of half the sum we had paid for the tickets.

The pilot was very welcome when he came aboard on Monday morning. The wind was light, and we were the greater part of the day in getting down as far as Belem, where we lay the night. On Tuesday we made six miles more, and at half-past three in the afternoon we dropped the pilot in Cascaes Bay and set a course for Cape St. Vincent beyond which lies Summer.

CHAPTER NINE

The Western Gateway

*

It was already the twentieth of September, and the Equinox, inevitably, would have some special weather put aside for us. Indeed, one glance at the sky in the east would have served to convince even the most optimistic that the weather would never be fair again.

A great mass of black cloud was rolling down over the mountains in the interior, burying the Tagus valley. We could see the gray curtain of smoky rain sweep over the country, hiding everything. We rove off the reef-tackle as we watched it, and rearranged the contents of the sail-room so that the storm jib should be conveniently to hand, for the Portuguese coast is an evil one, and there are only two harbours on the whole length of it, both of which were then behind us, and to windward.

It happened that the wind of that storm did not come near us, though the clouds obscured the sky for days. But in Lisbon, houses were wrecked, trolley cars derailed, and many people lost their lives by being swept into the sewers by the floods. It is easy to imagine what would have happened to us if we had been caught among the big ships in that raging, swollen river that rolled down on to the shoals.

It is ninety miles to St. Vincent, and as we made our slow way towards it it seemed to retreat before us. The stars, that we had won back by carrying sail, were hidden; the sky was dark and heavy, and the wind kept shifting, and dropping, and springing up again as if it did not know what to do. It was the very day of the change of the sun, and something must happen. We must turn the corner; the cape would close a door behind us, shutting up winter on the other side; once past, we looked for some splendid change in the aspect of the world.

St. Vincent is a corner on the Great Highway; sooner or later, most ships pass within sight of it. We spent a night in the traffic. Steamers were all about us, some heading up for the channel and the gray Northern Seas we had left behind, some rounding joyfully down to the south, seeming relieved at the prospects of serener waters before them, some standing out to sea for the Western World, some coasting down along Africa for the mysterious lands below the Line. Somewhere, at the end of the trail, there was a harbour waiting for each of them. We watched their lights as they came up out of the sea ahead, passed by, and went winking and glimmering out of sight again between the dark crests of the waves.

The cape was close aboard. As we drew near the signs of summer welcomed us. The raw north-easter dropped to a gentle offshore breeze, bringing the smell of pine woods with it. The sea went down, the clouds vanished, and the sun rose, clear, brilliant, yellow, out of Cadiz Bay.

The Equinox had a strange surprise for us. For three days we were becalmed. One afternoon I read an old letter on deck and threw it overboard when I had finished; the next morning, after breakfast, the torn bits of paper were floating under the stern. We lay breathless and motionless

– for three days. To hearten us Ball told of being becalmed for seven weeks off the Western Isles – now and again they had a tearing rain-squall, and the ship would rush off, fifteen miles an hour, for two hours, and then it would fall calm again, and she would lay and slat, and drip – and of how they ground up the grain of the cargo, in a coffee mill, for food. Whales came and played about us, day and night. With the current, we drifted slowly eastward, sighting the sand hills of St. Mary's and the lights of Cadiz. On the fourth day, off Cadiz, the breeze came.

The ropes shook, the blocks rattled and thumped the deck, the water began to talk beside the ship, the sails left off their idiotic clamour and went quietly to work. We heeled over and went ahead. After three days of calm and baking sunlight and glassy blue water so clear that the ship seemed suspended in the midst of it, it was a bewildering sensation to be under way again – unreal, and rather unpleasantly exciting. We took a new interest in living; we began to count time again; we looked ahead for Cape Trafalgar as if it were the only cape we ever hoped to pass.

Then we saw flying fish. They are things that the fairies must have made for their own delight, miracles of delicacy, as fragile and elusive as dreams, of an ethereal blue, like the sky or the waves. They skip over the crests and go darting in swift swoops through the hollows; they vanish so quickly that one cannot be sure they are veritable creatures. Even the hard-eyed and sinful old mariners speak gently of them, as they would speak of saints or angels, inspired to a mystical sort of reverence.

They have deep connotations; of blue water and bright sunshine, of far seas and shimmering beaches and Trade Winds, proud ships and long voyages and endless sailing.

By mid-afternoon Trafalgar was abeam. But we were no longer counting it a corner to be passed; we checked it off our list, simply, and looked ahead for Tarifa. We realised too keenly that we were nearly there.

The wind came up ahead, through the Straits – we could see it coming, tramping along, feather-white on the water – and to avoid the short impeding sea we kept close to the shore, under the hard and naked Spanish hills. Away to the south, piled up in the sky, were the mountains of Africa. The Gateway was closing in on us, and we had a continent on either hand. It was after dark when Tarifa opened out clear before us, and we began the long beat through the Straits.

So many men, through the long ages of history – and long before – had passsed this way. Roman galley, pulling five banks of oars, booming in from sea . . . .

But the first men to pass went *out*. There is something magnificent in the insolence of it; they dared the gods to destroy them, and went out. They left the safe surrounding land, cities and harbours, home and their friends, and stared Fear out of countenance on the vast empty Atlantic. It must have seemed to them like the Gates of Death, with the experience of Eternity on the other side. For they knew – it was no more conjecture for them, no foolish disproven legend – they *knew* that some time soon there would come a last sunset, and they and their ship would slide sickeningly down a smooth cascade of green water and fall into space. The End was out there. But they wanted to see how far. . . .

Something of their courage and audacity haunts the place still, and touches all who pass. One feels presumptuous, thrilled with the consciousness of doing something splendid.

The east wind brought mist; the hills emerged, towering up black against the stars. The three flashes of Tarifa, spinning like a wheel, threw long pale arms of light out through the fog. Ships were on all sides, coming and going, crossing, turning, weaving in and out; liners with their decks bright with lights, tramps and tankers, steamers bound to the far East, or coming home from there, sailing ships, all dark, gliding silently down wind, making lanes through the traffic.

It was midnight when we brought Tarifa abeam and came about for the last long leg over towards the African shore. We made Ceuta light ahead, and steered for it, and the Spanish coast dropped away behind us. We were close up under Ape's Hill, the Southern Pillar of Hercules, when the moon came up, clear and bright, out of the sea, a dished crescent of gold.

This was the end of my watch. When I came on deck again we were reaching into Algeciras Bay.

The sun came up behind the Rock. It reared up into the sky, its summit wrapped in cloud – enormous, rising up, the sky all bright behind it. . . .

As the light grew stronger we could see the ships in the harbour and the town along the shore at the foot of the cliffs. Smoke was rising from the chimneys where people were getting breakfast. There was a feeling of home-coming, a sense of welcome.

It was just after nine o'clock when we anchored, well up in the harbour, under the North Cliff. We were six hours short of a week out of Lisbon.

CHAPTER TEN

Gibraltar

★

As soon as you enter the town of Gibraltar – through a deep and solid archway with iron doors – you feel that you are in a fortress. Though the town is so delightful and gives you so warm a welcome, it is stern, bristling with authority, and insists on a grave and serious view of life. Wherever you want to go, there is a sentry to pass, and, though he allows you to proceed, you proceed on your good behaviour. Even if you duck out of sight around a corner, there is the Rock, filling half the sky, and you know that unseen – and critical – watchers are looking down at you.

The officer on guard at the gate gives you a dated ticket as you enter; you may remain in town until 'first evening gunfire.' You feel specially privileged, at once, and become self-consciously innocent in everything you do.

When Bill and Pat went over to Linea, one evening, for a brief investigation of Spain, they stopped just outside the gate for a moment's conversation with the guard.

'If you give up your ticket,' the guard informed them, 'you can't come back into town until to-morrow morning.'

'Then we won't go out,' they said.

'But you're out now,' said the guard.

They spent the night in Linea.

The gateway through which you come in is characteristic, in its solidity, of the entire establishment. You come upon fortifications, unexpectedly, in the most ordinary streets; there are barracks wherever there is room for them to stand; batteries border the park; there are impassive and substantial buildings everywhere, tightly closed, with letters and numbers of military connotation painted on their doors. Even the houses have this same martial look about them; they stand there on their two feet, with the Rock behind them; their windows look out on the world as if they knew right well that nothing could ever shake them. There is Discipline in the air all about you; you are shut up with Permanence and Security. The 'come one, come all' spirit of the Rock dominates the atmosphere of the place, just as the actual mass of it dominates the streets.

The streets are noisy with the languages of a dozen nations, and confused with heterogeneous costumes and traffic that never elsewhere get together. The carriages are light, bouncing canopy-topped things, with white curtains looped back at the corners of their roofs, quaint and fantastic, as if they were made up to please a child; they go rattling through the crowds. There are Greeks and Spaniards and Hindus, Levantine Jews, Arabs from Mogador, Moors from Tangiers, Egyptians and Italians and wandering mariners from everywhere. And mingled with these, shoulder to shoulder with them in the narrow streets are the British residents and the native Gibraltarians, soldiers from the garrison and sailors from the Dockyard. The turmoil and clatter of all this makes the town hum with a sound like that of a metropolis.

Indeed, it is as busy and excited as if it were the very

centre of the world. It is a perpetual World's Fair. It is like that 'Everywhere' that exists in the imagination. Yet the British residents consider themselves colonists, living in an outpost, and not infrequently they spend a great deal of their time in wondering when they shall get away. If you ask a man how long he has been out, he will be likely to sigh as he answers; if you politely suppose that he 'gets back to England now and again,' he will shake his head and say, 'No such luck!' I met a boy who nearly wept at the thought that he had left home to come to Gibraltar – but then his home was in Malta. Why, you would think, until you stop to consider it carefully in the light of realism, that one could be happy for ever, simply living in Gibraltar, with no other activity in life.

The shops are filled with wonderful things from every corner of the earth. The windows glitter with glass and inlaid work and jewels, while the flaming scarves and mantillas and embroideries that hang beside the doors give the street the colour of a true Oriental bazaar. It is, in fact, a cosmopolitan bazaar. There is nothing, almost, that you can imagine, that cannot be found here – Quaker Oats or bronze Buddhas. Baghdad is represented, and Timbuctoo and Lancashire and Samarkand and Baltimore, And in the background of all this are the sedate Government buildings, with the sentries at their doors, and the Bobbies, in the familiar London uniforms, keeping order.

A Moor from Tangiers passes, in his flowing robes of white, his red fez, his yellow slippers and bare brown legs; as you are trying to recover from the surprise of it, you look up and discover that you are staring at a sign on the corner of the nearest house: 'Main Street.' Walking down Main Street, in his native costume, a Moor from Tangiers, who, perhaps, got out of bed in Africa that very morning. And you seem the only person who is surprised.

We were ten days at Gibraltar, and became accustomed to it. Gibraltar is, now, for us, that kaleidoscope.

The Commanding Officer very courteously offered us the facilities of the Dockyard to have the *Caltha* hauled out and painted. She was put on a slip between a towboat and a destroyer, and there were nine men working on her at once. In four days from the time we had requested the permission the ship was back at her mooring in the harbour.

In all this time we had had nothing but clear skies and summer winds, and we had lost all thought of the possibility of bad weather. People had told us that some wicked winds visited the Mediterranean at times, and that 'winter' was more than a mere name. And indeed, we had not been so foolish as to think that Cape St. Vincent was an impassable barrier; somewhere along the coast, we knew, winter would catch us. But we had only one thunderstorm as evidence of it.

There was a vague lightning in the south; it had an artificial look, as if someone were setting off magnesium flashes behind the African hills. We had finished supper, and were sitting in the saloon, discussing the four hundred and fifty miles that lay between us and our next port, when the first sudden squall came whistling over the moles and struck us. The chain tightened on the capstan with a crash, and we heeled over, under bare poles as we were.

We went on deck and gave her more scope. She took up the slack immediately, bracing back on her anchor like a frightened horse.

It blew very hard for half an hour, and then began to shift. The lightning was almost continuous; we could even see the top of the Rock, the ships in the harbour, and the outline of the Spanish hills. Between the flashes it was very dark and clear, and the anchor lights appeared, burning yellow. All around us ships were rattling out chain. A man in a white rowboat went careening past, hurrying home, or aboard some boat, to save her before it was too late. We could see the black inside of his boat as she rolled, and the figure of the man, his legs spread out, pulling crazily at his oars. 'Better come aboard here with us, Mister,' Bill called to him. He didn't answer – needing all his breath, I suppose – and when the next flash came he was gone.

The wind shifted rapidly from south around to northwest, and the lightning passed off behind the hills – vivid flashes that jumped from cloud to cloud like white flames. The strength of the wind was gone before the rain came.

The harbour is crowded with coal hulks, and their mooring chains lie on the bottom in a close network. We had dragged our anchor enough to hook it under one of the chains, and when we tried to lift it we had the whole pattern, hulks and all, like beads on a string.

A group of men were watching our efforts to get the anchor up, and one of their number came over to us in a rowboat and suggested that we needed a diver. He thought the matter could be arranged for twenty pounds, but this was more than the anchor was worth, and we offered five. He rowed back, and as soon as he came within shouting distance of the crew he had left we saw the whole crowd burst into activity, running back and forth along the deck of their boat, overhauling their gear, and casting off their lines.

The diver himself was a thin, dark, desperate-looking man, very fierce and nervous in his motions. His helper was a cold-spirited, sombre lad, who went about his preparations in the manner of a hardened undertaker. While the diver was being buckled into his dress he smoked continually, lighting one cigarette from the stub of the last. Under his diving dress he wore a brown knitted romper, like a child's, and his head was covered with a vivid red stocking cap. His lead shoes were strapped to his feet, the last porthole in his goggle head was closed, after emitting a faint puff of smoke, and he tucked the air-pipe under his arm and went lumbering down the ladder that hung over the stern of the boat. He floated off, paddling clumsily with his hands, until he was over the anchor; then he opened the air-valve, letting the balloon suit collapse, and disappeared. We followed his progress by the trail of bubbles.

The silent and dismal crew turned the pump handles, without a word, without an expression. The helper sat still as a statue, his empty eyes fixed vacantly on the surface of the water, holding the signal line over one extended finger, like a fisherman waiting for a bite.

After a few moments the line twitched. The helper turned his lugubrious countenance in our direction and made a rotary motion with his hand, meaning that we were to haul up. The anchor appeared, and the diver followed it, manœuvring clumsily, like a turtle, to reach the foot of the ladder. While we were making sail he removed his helmet, lighted a cigarette, and said, 'Good-bye.' These were the only words spoken during the entire operation.

The sun was setting as we slipped past the end of the mole, barely moving with the dying evening breeze. As we looked back at the lights of the town, coming out one by one, we all felt a real regret at leaving.

And now the story of Ball, like one of his own rambling yarns, trails off to an inconclusive ending.

At first, he had said that he did not want to go ashore. He was remembering Lisbon, and Porto, and other darker and more intricate adventures out of his past. He had been in trouble in most places on earth; doubtless the misfortunes grew more severe, and he felt them more, as time went on, so that his earlier years must have seemed happy and innocent. Now, he was wishing them back again. He had spent several years in Gibraltar, at one time or another in his wandering life, and he would be sure to find friends there – friends who, for him, would be worse than enemies.

While the ship was in the Dockyard he was safe enough, for he could not pass the gates, either to go or to come, without a written order. As soon as we were back at our anchorage in the harbour, however, he felt free and unrestricted. He was tired of restraint. He asked leave to go ashore for the evening, and vanished.

On the second day we had news of him. He had tried to get off to the ship without a permit, and had had trouble with the guard. On the third day his passport and sailor's papers were found in the road near Ragged Staff; how they came there, no one knew, then, or afterward. On the fourth day he found his way back to the *Caltha*, and, in shame and contrition, asked to be discharged.

It was not hard to comply with his request. He was of no further use to us, certainly. We could not keep him at sea forever, and he could not live in port.

Yet his condition was pitiable. He had sold, or bartered, everything but his shoes and coat and trousers. His pockets were empty. His papers were gone, how, or where, he didn't know, so that he had lost his identity. He had become a mere human animal. He was unshaven and unwashed; his hair hung down over his brow like a caveman's; his face was scarred with the dried blood of barroom fights. He was dizzy and tottering, and he could not speak without weeping.

Pat and Bill were aboard when he arrived. They gave him a drink of rum – he could take no food; he had had nothing to eat in all those four days. They swore at him, and he meekly admitted that they were right; they argued with him, as though he were a naughty child, and he shook his head and said that he wasn't fit to associate with decent people. They gave him a shirt, a cap, and a shilling, and sent him ashore. I was coming back to the ship, and met him on the quay. 'Well, we're parted,' he said, and shook hands. Then he went on vaguely up the street, shaking, padding uncertainly in the dust with his bare feet.

Now a seaman may not be discharged in Gibraltar. The fortress does not want a man without a job. A Spaniard or a Moor may come as he likes, because, if he becomes destitute, it is a simple matter to send him back where he came from; but a British subject is farther from home, and offers, in consequence, a more difficult problem. The Authorities make short work of it. 'You brought him here,' they say. 'Take him away again.'

We got permission to leave Ball in town until Saturday, when a home-bound P. & O. steamer was due to call.

On Friday, Ball spent his shilling, sold his cap and shirt, quarrelled with a policeman, and was sent to jail. The steamer arrived. The police were willing that we should take him out of jail to send him aboard. But the Line refused to take him as a passenger.

There was but one thing left for us to do. We gave him money for his fare to Liverpool, and put him aboard the Algeciras ferry. He would go to Huelva, he said, or Cadiz, and try to get a ship – aye, he'd walk it; he hadn't no choice, had he?

That's the end of the yarn.

And what's going to happen? Aye, that's just the point; what's going to happen? He'll set out, tramping to Huelva – and a bleeding long way it is, too – and perhaps he'll get there. And perhaps he'll get a ship . . . and turn up in a sailors' lodging-house in Yokohama, or some place . . . or meet a man he knows in Melbourne; shipmates with 'im, 'e was . . . or run into a chap as owes him money; not likely, it ain't, but truth is stranger than fiction, and that's a fact . . . or . . . perhaps in Bombay. . . .

It will end somehow. He'll walk into the little house in the side street near the Albert Dock, fling his cap into a chair, and say, 'Well, here I am, home again.'

CHAPTER ELEVEN

The Long Coast Line

*

El Dorado

EVERYONE remembers that the Roman armies, in critical situations, were always reinforced by troops of Balearic slingers, who appeared suddenly at the very fifty-ninth minute, and won the day. To perpetuate this tradition, the islands of the Balearic group are sometimes known as the Slingers' Isles. But nothing else is known of them.

Indeed, if you ask anyone to accompany you to the Balearic Isles, he will accept enthusiastically, and, in the same breath, ask you where they are. The Slippery Islands would be a better name. You will never see a picture, or read a word of description. You will be able to discover nothing but the fact that they grew slingers in the old days, and now belong to Spain. Yet once you begin to acquire knowledge of them, they will bulk large in your consciousness, and you will find news of them wherever you turn.

You will learn that the group is composed of Mallorca, Minorca, Iviza, and some lesser islands, that the capital is Palma, and that it lies one hundred and thirty miles south-east of Barcelona. This much we gathered from the chart. We held an unsupported conviction that the place was delightful. The Pilot Book says of Palma that 'the houses are well built, but the streets are narrow.' Which is exactly right.

'In five days,' we said, 'or perhaps a week if we have bad

weather, we shall be there.' We named it El Dorado, and set out for it in a mood of high enthusiasm.

When we came out of Algeciras Bay we met a heavy swell, rolling in from the east – as if a gale were blowing somewhere – and a flat calm. We rolled about all night, our sails hanging idle, the booms crashing and tearing at the sheets. Except for the current – which did, indeed, take us out of sight of land before dawn – we were motionless. The sky was thick with clouds, and the glass was falling.

In the morning we picked up a very faint breeze from the east – dead ahead – and sighted Callaburros Point, the first corner of the south-east coast of Spain. In the afternoon it blew harder – still from the East, still dead ahead – and before sunset we were reefed, bucking into a short dancing sea that broke continually. The waves, moving past the ship from ahead, gave an impression of progress, but we dipped our bowsprit into every one before us, and sat down on those behind with a jarring slam that sent the white water shooting out from under the counter, twenty feet on either side.

A big barque passed us, bound west. It was just the weather for her; she was carrying everything but staysails, roaring along down wind, pushing the seas before her. At Callaburros she shifted her course offshore, heading for the Straits, and disappeared as if she would be in Cuba by daylight. Later in the day we sighted a three-masted schooner ahead – from Nova Scotia, by the cut of her topsails – and a little barquentine. The barquentine, which could not head within seven points of the wind, was making poor work of it; she beat back and forth a dozen times over the same path, stopping her way by her heavy rolling, and thrown to leeward by the seas. We soon passed her. But it took us all night to pass the schooner.

There was a possibility of a change of wind in the morning, but when it got light – there was no dawn, nor sunrise – it blew harder. The low clouds flew like smoke. We went along by dropping into the holes between the waves; we dropped only once into each hole, but the holes were coming to meet us.

'At this rate,' we said, 'we shall be no more than tired old men when we get to El Dorado.'

We were fifteen miles off shore, directly in front of Malaga. We eased sheets and ran for harbour.

MALAGA

With the wind abeam we came roaring. Inshore, we could see the irregular outline of the hills, very dark and flat in the pale light, and below them, in a confused strip of gray and black along the shore, the moles and ships and buildings of the city, with tall factory chimneys rising up in the midst of it, and the towers of the cathedral.

Two sardine boats came through the opening of the breakwaters and stood past us out to sea; they were carrying full sail, like Vikings, for all it blew so hard, slicing into it, throwing white spray, shooting half the length of the keels out of water as they topped the crests of the waves. We passed close to them, and could see the men bending down to watch us under their bulging gray sails. It seemed strange that they should be going out in that weather, when it was too rough to fish. And, indeed, an hour later they came back. Perhaps they were just out for a sail.

We came scurrying in, the waves boiling under us and throwing us forward; the colour of the water changed suddenly from blue to brown; the moles reached out to us like arms; we shot in through the entrance and hauled our wind in the smooth water of the harbour. The spray was flying over the top of the mole like smoke.

We dropped anchor just inside, in a bad place, among the steamers. Immediately we were boarded by the pilots; the Medical Officer was with them; they swarmed over the rail. The doctor was not without humour, for even in the confusion he found time to tell me that I should shoot the leader of the pilots. I shook my head, meaning that I did not understand. 'Yes!' Yes!' he said. 'Gun! Dead!' He completed his meaning with gestures – indicating also, in a touch unconsciously characteristic, that the man ought to be shot in the back. Just then the stern of a steamer broke away from her lines and came swinging down on us, and while we slacked away handsomely on the chain to avoid having the bowsprit taken out of us the Medical Officer bowed gravely and went below to talk with Pat about our papers.

To moor us in a proper place was an intricate business. There was such a confusion of men and ropes, such a hubbub and rumpus of urgent instructions, meaningless cries, and incomprehensible laughter, that the whole Spanish world became no more than a scene of artificial unreality. But on the quay, across the harbour from us, there was a man with a donkey-cart. The sight of that plodding figure, going about his business as if nothing had happened, served, in some manner or other, to make Malaga a place of human habitation.

All cities of Southern Spain are alike in this: along the waterfront there is a park of flowers and palms; from this, at a convenient point, there branches out a principal street, always lined with cafés, and always taking the direction of the sun at noon, so as to afford a maximum of shade to both sides; there is always a hill with the ruins of a Moorish castle on it and a tangle of steep and narrow streets at the foot of it. And, of course, there is a Bull Ring. Malaga has these things.

It is a serene and complacent city; an easy, indifferent sort of happiness seems to pour down with the sunlight from the bright sky. Slow ox-carts go creaking through the streets. Convoys of mules, with jingling bells and embroidered harnesses, wind up and down the narrow alleys of the old Moorish Quarter. Flocks of goats impede the progress of the trolley-cars, for in Spain milk is not delivered in sanitary sealed bottles; it is delivered in the goat. Such things make life seem very simple. People saunter up and down, and drop suddenly into the chairs before the cafés as if they had come to the very end of their energy. There is no real reason for the occurrence of anything exciting. Is not life itself a pleasant thing, and are there not cafés?

It is in the cafés that people spend their time. Goatherds and generals sit side by side. They scan the pages of the newspapers, or write letters, or, at times, play checkers in a rapid and reckless manner that soon gets a game out of the way. They drink the sweet red Malaga wine, or tea in glass bowls with silver holders, sitting at ease, with their feet up, tipping back their flat-brimmed hats, endlessly rolling Habana cigarettes, gesturing and pattering Spanish for all the world like people hired to furnish local colour in a play. In all this there is no positive feeling of enjoyment, yet there is no evident boredom either. Simply, a Malaga day, in which bedtime comes before breakfast, is endlessly long, and there is nothing to do.

In two days the storm had blown itself out and the sky was clear and cloudless again. But instead of going to sea we hired a car and set out over the mountains to Granada.

ENTRADA

As soon as we left the city we began to climb. The hills were of red rock, bare and stony, washed by the rains into sharp ridges and hollows across which the sun threw deep shadows; the white farmhouses were scattered over the slopes at almost regular intervals, as if they were afraid of getting too close together. Up through this the road went endlessly clambering, sticking to the steep inclines, climbing at times in sharp bends up through narrow ravines or along crests of the ridges. At every turn it seemed that we must be at the top, yet when we rounded the corner there were more hills before us, and we could see the white road looping away up over them.

The high, windy ravines are desperate places, as lonely and silent as the spaces between the stars. There were no houses, no cultivated fields, no fences; nothing but rocks and sky, and the road winding through in a lost and frightened way. We passed mule trains, the drivers seated sidewise on the hindmost mule, drumming on his ribs with their bare heels in time to some tune that runs in their heads – for no one would have the courage to sing aloud in such a place. We passed waggons. They are vast lumbering ships, very heavy, without springs; they have a prairie schooner top, two seven-foot wheels, a high-backed body, and a cellar for additional cargo, slung under the floor by rope or chain. They are drawn by seven mules in tandem.

After thirty miles of steady climbing, we reached the last of the wild and heart-breaking passes, and came down – a little – into rolling country of a softer aspect. Farms appeared again, some with gardens near them; there were occasional green fields, and trees grew beside the slow, wandering streams.

Then we came to a bridge that had been undermined and ruined by a freshet. A gang of peons were at work on a coffer-dam, and their chief, a pleasant-faced rascal, without a dry stitch on him, waded across the stream to us and told us that we might easily cross in the car – but not, he explained, just where he had come – a little farther up. Our driver went ahead, and before we had reached the centre of the river the carburettor went under water, and we stopped. The chief set off at once for his oxen, which had been tethered at a convenient point in the background.

The oxen – or, more properly, an ox and a cow – were brought into position before the car, after a great deal of shouting and splashing. A tiny calf, who could not endure leaving his mother and uncle, followed into the stream, getting in everybody's way, until the water got too deep for him, and he was obliged to turn back. By ducking under water, the chief managed to fasten the chain to the front axle of the car, and we floundered across and up the bank. Pat argued about the fifty pesetas that was demanded as salvage money, but this was merely to give time for the water to run out of the carburettor.

It was dark long before we reached Granada. The last ten miles were over the worst road in the world, a road swept bare by the rains, filled with holes and loose round stones, and encumbered with the great seven-mule waggons which carried no lights, so that by the time the streets of the town shut in around us we were bored and stiff and heartily tired. We turned suddenly into a side street, buzzed noisily up a long hill in the dark, and went through a narrow Moorish gateway. Beyond this gate we were wrapped up and surrounded by a deep hush, a peaceful seclusion, as complete and beautiful as if the spirit of the Orient had never left the place. In front of the hotel a row of tall trees made a vault between us and the sky. Water bubbled up from a spring beside the road and made a pleasant noise. The simple loveliness of it was wonderful.

And just across the road, separated from us by no more than a strip of dark woods, was the Alhambra.

THE ALHAMBRA

The Moslems cared little for external appearances. The outside of the Alhambra is no more than a pile of irregular walls and towers, bare and formidable, designed wholly with a view to strength. But within – within was an Earthly Paradise, a stately pleasure-dome, decreed for the enjoyment of existence. The Gate of Justice is a mere block of brickwork, without a cornice, without even a coping on its parapet – but the gateway itself is beautifully proportioned and elaborately ornamented in intricate line and glowing colour, because this was the portion that was used. Similarly, we came through a small and simple doorway – no more than a hole in the wall, to be exact – which gave no promise of anything behind it, and stepped all at once into a glorious court.

I remember an impression of brightness. There was brilliance even in the shadows. Golden tawny walls, gay roofs of tile, sparkling ornament, glaring white sunshine, a still green pool with dark myrtles hanging over it, and a blue, blue sky. The whole is perfect. It is this fact that makes the impression so difficult to capture; there is no detail to select for special admiration, no phase of the whole to which one may consider the remainder as a setting. Like a picture with too much in it, it gives the seeing eye no point of focus, but only an ensemble of impression.

By what anachronous instinct did these outlandish barbarians arrive at beauty? Why, by no instinct at all; only a real knowledge of what is beautiful. The courts of the Alhambra are filled with beauty – and with Romance. Far away and long ago . . . one pauses in the splendour, and begins a never-finished tale of 'Once upon a Time.' Once upon a time there was a King – who also knew.

The Court of the Lions – it comes after the perfection of the first court, and before the perfection of the Halls within. There is nothing with which it may be compared – except only the hopelessness of real achievement. Mohommedans do not use animal forms in decoration. Yet there are those twelve lions that support the basin of the fountain. Well; Allah knows the court needed those lions; they are like a friendly human voice in a lonely desert – lions, set about with the intricacies of geometrical design. And besides, Allah, they don't look like lions.

There is the Hall of the Ambassadors. It was here that Isabella received Columbus; she took the jewels from her casket and gave them to him. Old Castile, Spanish treasure, a new World waiting for discovery, an explorer who sailed over the sea beyond the sunset – the Romance of the courts of the Alhambra. It crowds too fast and blindingly. One turns gratefully aside into a little room.

Yet even in a little room, the silence is so lovely, the seclusion and tranquillity so deep, that one cannot rest. The peace of the place is exciting. Through the windows of the Favourite's belvedere the view into the little garden of Lindaraxa is so beautiful that one cannot take it calmly. One may not be seated in the presence of Romance. One cannot wait with indifference face to face with Beauty.

GITANOS

In former days – a hundred years ago – the courts of the Alhambra were occupied by robbers and vagrants and gipsies. They must have given to the place an air of picturesqueness more in keeping than did the sophisticated luxury of the Spanish Kings. The Catholic monarchs brought with them their own way of life; they covered some of the Barbary ornament and built new rooms in their own manner; in the midst of the building they began the erection of a vast palace in the Renaissance style to serve them as a tolerable habitation. I suppose that the Moorish buildings were distasteful to them because of the associations of so recent a subjection; it is inconceivable, at least, that anyone could have wanted to replace so wholly beautiful a thing as the Alhambra. Where it would have stopped – this process of modernisation – one cannot guess; at last fear of earthquakes drove the Spanish Court away to Madrid, and left the Alhambra to the ruffians and the gipsies.

The gipsies, in their turn, were driven out by the tourists. Heaven knows that there is nothing congenial in the idea of tourists in the Alhambra, but at least the building is safe, now, from further alteration. By the admission fees of visitors the work of restoration and maintenance is carried on. The place is kept by, and for, those who care to see it. And the gipsies live in caves across the river.

We went into one. A brick floor, whitewashed walls, an uneven roof shaped somewhat like a vault, and electric lights. From pegs in the walls hang bright brass and copper bowls, and on the broad shelves in the corners are a few household utensils. There are two caves cut into the hillside, one behind the other, with small alcoves to serve as kitchen and storeroom; in the rear room, shut off by a red curtain at the door, was an iron bedstead, a bureau, two chairs, and a crucifix. The whole was very neat and clean, for, to tell the truth, this is a show place.

The caves in which the gipsies really live in privacy, however, are no different in general plan, except that usually there is a chimney, appearing as a hole in the field above, and the rooms are not so obviously neat. The housekeeping is more evident. An open fire on a raised hearth in the centre serves for cooking, and the roof is black with smoke. There are no windows.

We met some of the gipsies – not a difficult task, for they crowded around us, asking to dance for our entertainment. We found an interpreter and arranged that we should come back in half an hour and find them ready.

Meanwhile, we visited some Early Christian catacombs on the hill just beyond the limits of the Arab town. There is something appealing in the idea: when the Moslem kings were at the height of their power, at the climax of their zeal for slaughter of Unbelievers, no farther away than across the river, the Christians dared to build a chapel and worship there. The underground establishment is curious. The bones of saints are to be seen, together with some other impossible relics; there are the bodies of two martyred children – the actual bodies themselves, encased in lifelike wax. There is a Marriage Stone, worn smooth by the lips of girls who have kissed it to assure their being married within the year, and there is a stone of opposite virtue, also, which derives its reputation from the lady who bit a large piece out of it, to make sure.

When we returned to the caves, the gipsies had put flowers in their hair and brought out their gayest shawls, and three Hawaiians – or so they looked – were ready with guitars to furnish music. There were twelve women:

three young girls – one, only fifteen years old, had had a baby the week before – a few of difficult ages, and two elderly matrons. One of these last had danced in *Carmen*, long ago, at the Opéra Comique in Paris.

They danced without finish or formality ; there was a natural gaiety in it, but little grace, a wild kind of enthusiasm, but no real understanding. The dancers, and all the others, kept up a continual clatter with brass or wooden castanets, and there was a tambourine in the orchestra; the little cave was humming with noise, for a part of every dance was sung, and shouts of encouragement came from the side lines in the manner of a crap game.

It was suggested to us that we provide some wine to increase the joyousness of the occasion. We bought six bottles, and the bowl was circulated. Later, they asked for dried fish. Then, another six bottles of wine, to go with the fish. We began to see the nature of the party.

As time went on, the intervals between the dances became longer, and there was less spontaneous enthusiasm. We saw that it was time to go. We couldn't have stayed forever, at any rate; but leaving was a mistake.

As soon as we declared our intention, by getting to our feet, they rushed for us. They crowded around us like dogs around a stag. We were driven back into our chairs again. A girl asked me for a cigarette; I passed her the box, naturally; it went into the bosom of her dress. They all wanted to tell our fortunes. An elderly lady with an evil look clutched my hand, and told me that I was lucky. I didn't see it so. If I would put three pieces of silver in my palm – her palm, she meant – she would open the portals of Futurity and reveal the Plan. I said I had no silver. She confessed that paper would do. Foolishly, I took out a fifty-peseta note, explaining to her, through the interpreter, that she was to consider it merely as a loan, for the purpose of working the charm, and not as a gift.

Well, I was lucky. By the same side on which I put my head in, I took it out again. A 'brown girl' was weeping for me at home. Something was implied about a wife, already existing as such. I was to have two children; one, a son, was to achieve a title. There was more rubbish of the same sort. I never saw which way the fifty pesetas went.

Pat was involved in similar difficulties; Bill was fighting them off with his back to the wall. I broke through to the door, and stood shouting 'Hey, caballeros!' trying to be heard above the noise. The old dragon of the Opéra Comique asked me if I was pleased with them. 'Yes,' I said, giving a rose to a girl while I gestured with the other hand to indicate that I had no money. 'I am glad,' she said, in broken French, 'because we are pleased with you.' It was the only attempt at a human remark in the entire battle. Our picturesque band of gipsies had turned into a pack of wolves.

We pushed out to the car, finally, and got away, ripping through a crowd of children and tearing away the clutching hands that reached in at us.

On the way down the hill Bill told the interpreter that he was going to kill him.

SALIDA

We returned to Malaga by a different route, across the plains of Granada, first, and then up a long stony road between the hills that soon shut out the last sight of the sunlight on the towers of the Alhambra. We left the pleasant valley country and emerged among a range of dismal mountains where quail and grouse were wandering in the road like chickens, and where the wind was rustling over the rough gorse and whining between the boulders. There were no mule trains, nor so much as a hoof-print in the dust of the road. In fifty miles we passed two villages, mournful and insignificant places, where the inhabitants ran to the doorways to see us pass.

Descending from this we came into flat prairie lands, shut in on all sides by steep and lofty mountains; the road ran straight across it and stopped abruptly at the foot of the cliffs. The valley walls came together, like the entrance to a trap. Then, suddenly, we turned a high spur of naked granite, and saw the sky below us.

A tremendous valley, miles wide, sloped down and down from the narrow pass, seeming to descend to the very bottom of the world. The plain behind us, which had seemed the natural level of the earth while we were on it, was in reality a thousand feet above the sea, and now the horizon ahead of us, lost in the mists of distance, was below our very feet.

The road went winding dizzily down the valley. We passed muleteers, camping by the roadside, gathered about a fire, with their mules hobbled behind them, and saw the whole country as a stage on which the natural lives of the inhabitants made a perpetual pageant of picturesqueness. We passed ruins of Roman walls and thought of the legions, tramping wearily up, watching that notch in the sky-line. The old Moorish watch-towers on the summits of the hills showed that this was the road by which one came from Bagdad, or anywhere, to go to Granada.

The farms were closer together now, and there were towns. The air grew warm and moist again. In the evening, we came through a grove of bamboo trees growing in sandy soil, and saw the moonlight shining on the sea.

The sea is the road to El Dorado.

TOROSE

But there was another interruption before we could take to the road again. There were posters in the shop windows, flags were flying, and everybody in Malaga was excited. The ship-chandler told us that we should not miss it. There was something to do in Malaga at last.

The Bull Ring was crowded. In the boxes were ladies with high combs and mantillas, and they hung their brilliant shawls over the balcony railings, making a ring of colour; there was a flutter of bright fans from the seats on the sunny side of the arena; yelling boys went through the crowds selling peanuts and bottled lemonade; strips of coloured paper, with advertisements printed on them, were showered down, like confetti, from the galleries.

There were groups of wounded soldiers here and there in the audience, and people rose to their feet from time to time to cheer and applaud them, for this fight was for their benefit, and in their honour. The bands were playing, and everybody was in a state of happy expectancy. Behind the gates on the opposite side of the arena we could see the heads of the picadors, mounted for the opening procession.

Some sort of signal was made from the Governor's box; the official across the ring touched his cap, and opened the gates. A girl on a fiery horse came dashing in, straight across the arena, making a sweeping bow to the Governor. Some personage of note tossed down to her the key to the bull pen. The band struck up, exactly in the manner of a circus band at the entrance of the elephants, and the procession began.

The principal performers were on foot, in gorgeous embroidered cloaks and splendid uniforms that glittered with gold and silver; the picadors followed, mounted on aged cab-horses which were to end their lives in one crowded hour of glorious combat. They came marching up, in stately array, and saluted. There was something depressingly solemn about it; an air of *Morituri te salutamus*. But the applause never ceased for an instant, and every one was gleefully enthusiastic.

The performers circled back and took their places at the sides of the ring. The girl on horseback retired, after losing her hat in one tooth-loosening buck in the centre of the ring, and the gates were closed.

A bugle blew. The official touched his cap. Another pair of gates were opened, by a man who peered anxiously into the darkness within. There was a moment of tense silence. One matador stood out alone in the centre of the arena.

The Bull Himself.

Bull-necked, in truth, dark and shaggy, ominously strong, staring about him with dazzled eyes, bewildered, but with a fixed, though unformulated, plan of malign destruction. He stood for a moment, turning this way and that in indecision. Then he fixed his eyes on that lone and isolated matador, and charged. He gathered speed like a battleship, lunging forward, snorting, throwing up the sand behind him. The matador flipped his cloak. Then he ran for it.

The bull stopped dead against the fence. But he seemed to shrug his shoulders. Almost one could hear him say, 'Better luck next time.' Almost he said, 'You wait till I get the hang of this.' With that he charged the rest.

They received him one after another, and played with him. This was a phase where a greater knowledge of the fine points of the game would have helped us to appreciate, for the flip of the cloaks was so graceful and sure, the avoiding of the rushes so easy, so confident, so slight, that it seemed quite effortless. The crowd cheered the man and taunted the bull. One would think that the bull was playing the game too. It was impossible to believe – just then – that he would kill those men if he could.

The next stage of the combat is horrible. One of the grooms leads out a mounted picador, his lance held ready; the horse is blindfolded on the near side; the bull's attention is drawn to this new contest to which he is invited;

the matadors stand ready with their cloaks to see what will come of it.

The bull hesitates. He sees the horse and rider plainly enough, but clearly he doesn't know if they will vanish before his charges as those swift red cloaks have vanished. Still, he makes up his mind to it. He charges, feeling his strength, knowing nothing of his weakness. His horns thrust into the horse's side; the picador thrusts him in the shoulder with the lance.

The horse and man are lifted into the air. The man is thrown, sometimes under the horse, sometimes beneath the very feet of the bull. The horse's bowels pour out – he struggles to his feet and goes stumbling blindly forward, trying to get away, somewhere, his entrails dragging on the ground between his feet. One can hardly realise what is happening.

The bull is forced away – usually – by the prick of the lance. The matadors play him again with their cloaks. Some one kills the horse, or, if it is not a 'fatal' injury – that is, if the creature's whole insides are not spilled out of him – he is sewn up, or a handful of straw is stuffed in the hole. Then another picador tries a hand at it. The net result is blood on the sand, and three dead horses. The worst is over.

The bugle sounds. One of the matadors puts aside his cloak and advances to the centre of the ring, carrying a pair of small wooden darts, about two feet long, wound with ribbon. After some difficulty, he induces the bull to charge him; he reaches over the lowered horns and jabs the darts into the bull's shoulders. It is cleverly done –

so cleverly that there seems to be no danger in it. Three pairs are so fixed. The bull is raging mad, but is tempered somewhat by his fatigue; his rushes are still full of savage energy, but they lack the fire and dash of his first ones.

The bugle goes again. A toreador advances and bows to the Governor's box, or to some group of wounded soldiers – 'I kill this bull for you.' He takes a small red cloth, like a banner, and a sword; he tries the point of the blade on the palm of his hand, shouts angrily to the others to leave this bull to *him*, and goes in for the killing.

He plays him for a time – very cleverly, and with much applause-provoking trickery – and then, when the time comes, he adopts the tactics of the bull, and makes a charge himself, driving the whole length of the sword down between the shoulder-blades into the lungs. Usually, that finishes it. There are a few more rushes at the cloaks, with periods of uncertainty between them ; then the bull seems to decide that he will lie down for a time before he has another try at it. He never gets up.

Eight bulls, one after another, with time enough between only to drag out the dead. Then the band plays again, and the crowd, in a glow of delight, cheering its favourites, discussing the fine points of the afternoon's game, drives back to town to dinner.

'And you enjoyed the fight?' asked the ship-chandler. '. . . . Ah, yes, the poor horses. But what would you have?'

True; what would you have? One's sympathy is with

the bull, who has the odds so greatly against him. He has so little chance . . . except against the horses.

THE ROAD TO EL DORADO

It is said of the wandering gipsies that they always travel towards the east. Yet, after all these centuries, they are still scattered over the face of the earth in a fairly even distribution, and it must be that the east is unattainable, and the road lengthens under their feet as they progress. There is a melancholy sort of witchcraft about it, calculated to discourage the hopeful. In consequence of reflection on these facts, we saw the unwisdom of swearing an oath to achieve or perish. We were bound east. 'We will go as far as we can,' we said, 'and will stop at Cartagena if we have to.'

But it was calm when we left Malaga, and we began our journey to the east by drifting fifteen miles to the westward during the night. When the breeze came, in the morning, it was light, and ahead; at sunset of the second day we were opposite Malaga again. During the following night it improved, and we began to leave the familiar hills behind us. But the weather is never satisfied; the next day it blew too hard, raising the same steep, inconvenient sea. We crashed into it, mile after mile, hour after hour. The waves were all alike.

Away to the seaward we saw a sail – a small vessel. She came running in, with the wind abeam, and passed three miles ahead of us, heading for a part of the coast where there is no town nor harbour. 'A smuggler,' we said, and watched for the signals. Sure enough, at nightfall a fire blazed up on the beach ahead of her; blazed, and went down, and blazed again, as if it were alternately smothered and released. In the gathering darkness we saw her heave to, a mile offshore, opposite the spot where the fire had been. There is a romantic air about a smuggler, and no vessel is more in keeping with the character of the tale than a Spanish schooner.

We moved an inch at a time, but each inshore tack brought us further along the coast; at sunset of our third day we were in front of the town of Adra, where we might have run in. But we were under the lee of the Plains of Almería, a great flat projection from the coast that barred our way; it was dead to windward, and a cape to windward is a challenge. We kept on.

All night we beat back and forth, watching the lights on the capes that form the two seaward corners of the Plains. It was dreary work, and lonely. As I sat at the tiller I was thinking ahead to Almería, which seemed a million miles away; there would be people passing up and down the streets, I was thinking, and lights in the windows of the friendly houses, and inside, well-worn rooms, with familiar household things that had been in their same places always, and always would be. People would be sitting around the old table together, comfortable and warm and shut in – exactly the environment, I reflected, a moment later, that produces unbearable unrest, and a longing for adventure. There they would be, passionately wishing that something would happen. They would have no appreciation for the things they had. They would not be able to be satisfied with the present moment. And yet there I was, sitting at the tiller of an able little ship, working her to windward, in a night of windy weather, around a cape in Spain, sentimentally envying the people in the lamplight, with their old familiar things about them. Why couldn't *I* be satisfied with the present moment?

Then it was Bill's watch, but I stayed up on deck for a time, to watch progress. Our sidelights were out – had been out for hours – the weather one destroyed by the wind, the lee one shaken to death by the slatting of the slack rigging. We had an anchor light in the cockpit at our feet.

For some time we had seen a green light ahead. It seemed to be the starboard light of a steamer, which would cross our bows, but it changed its bearing hardly at all, and acted queerly. All at once it seemed to get very near. We jumped up and stared. There was a black shape in the darkness, very close. It lurched, and a red light showed. The sidelights of a sailing vessel, heading straight for us, reaching in behind the cape. Some of these square-riggers carry their sidelights aft on the quarter rail, where they can be seen, but this one hung his forward, in the old traditional place on the rigging, and his fore course covered his port light like a blanket. Bill snatched up the anchor light and held it so that a glare from it fell on our sail. Just in time the brigantine saw us, put down her helm, and went under our stern. She was scudding down wind, roaring, trampling thundering white water; she leaned above us like a tower.

At sunrise the last cape of the Plains was behind us.

We eased sheets and ran up the bay. But the wind came ahead, and we beat into the harbour.

We were ninety-three hours out of Malaga. And Cartagena, even, was ninety-five miles away, and to windward.

LORD NELSON AND THE COOKS

The ship-chandler at Almería is a man with one eye, very talkative and persistent ; he was alongside before our anchor was down, and all the time we were stowing sail and putting away gear his boat was nosing about the gangway. He kept asking what he could do for us. In the end we told him, and as he left he handed up his card, which, when we had time to examine it, we found to bear the name of 'Lord Nelson.'

Subsequently we asked Mr. Henderson, the British Consul, if Lord Nelson was a reliable man, because we wanted him to help us find a cook.

'He's about as good as the general run of them,' Mr. Henderson said. 'He's about the only ship-chandler here, at any rate. Some of the others, younger men for the most part, have tried to break into his game from time to time, but he has money enough to undersell them, and he doesn't hesitate to give away supplies, even, for the sake of freezing out his competitors.'

Accordingly we asked Lord Nelson to recommend us a cook. He thought for a moment, pretending to search his memory, and at last he muttered, 'Pepe!'

'There's man for you,' he said. 'Good cook, good sailor.

For six month he cook on Norway salvage ship; he go way, because ship no go to sea. Always he want go to sea. He marry my little girl. You see? And I try make him go into ship-chandler business with me But no. No, no. He love sea. Always sea. Good sailor? Whoof! Go up mast like' – he hesitated – 'like goldfinch! Bad weather? More bad weather, better he like!'

The wind was still in the east, and we stayed three days in Almería, and Pepe came and cooked for us. He was a good cook, and neat and pleasant, but he was so fat that it was impossible to imagine him going aloft in any manner even remotely resembling the flight of the goldfinch. We asked him if he was willing to stay with us.

'Yes; I go,' he said. 'For six months I try get into ship-chandler business here in Almería, but damn Lord Nelson he give away meat, figs, wine, eggs, everything, to ships that come. So I lose three thousand pesetas, and give up. No got more money. I go. Where you go?'

When we told him, his eyes grew wide with astonishment. He reflected for a moment, and then, saying that he thought the ship too small for safety, resigned.

We sent for Lord Nelson again, and asked for another cook.

'I know very man,' he said, without a moment's hesitation. 'Speak English same as you; better than me. Name Martini. Good cook, good sailor. Been ten years at sea, American ship. Yes. Fine man. I tell him. You see.'

Martini was quick and clever in the galley, and had once made a voyage in a steamer to Newport News. But he was no goldfinch for going aloft, and it was hard to understand Lord Nelson's enthusiasm for him, unless – sure enough, it developed, on investigation, that Martini had been trying to break into the ship-chandler business, and that Lord Nelson had been obliged to give away supplies to defeat him.

The wind came westerly on the fourth day, and as we were making sail, Martini came on deck with his bundle under his arm, and, saying that his son was very sick, resigned.

So we went to sea without a cook, and thus contributed our share in the conspiracy to murder Lord Nelson.

THE FIRST BREATH OF WINTER

There was a little schooner from Cadiz anchored near us, an ancient craft, built by somebody's grandfather, shaky and patched and sagged out of shape; she carried a farm with her. The pigs squealed dismally while the windlass was clattering, and the hens flew awkwardly up onto the rail and cocked their silly heads at the sea while the crew were making sail. The auspices were favourable, and the schooner got away. We followed her, cleared for Cartagena.

It was beautiful weather – though the sky was pale and the hills were misty in the distance – a 'smoky sou'wester,' such as we have at home. We ran down the Bay and were around Cape de Gata by noon.

The coast beyond the cape was wonderful; high rocky cliffs of gray and brilliant red, with clean little blue coves at their feet, fit for smuggling or elopements or gay adventures. There were a few scattered and lonely ranch houses, with cattle in the fields near them, and two forlorn little villages, huddled down in the steep valleys. For all its beauty, we were thinking, it must be a terrible thing to live in such a place, and more terrible still, having left it, to be forced by inexorable sentiment to look back upon it with affection.

We were nearly abreast the Mesa de Roldan at sunset, about to set a course for Cartagena, when the wind changed, and winter began.

It came offshore suddenly. It was warm at first and smelled of the land, but as it increased in strength it grew cold as the breath of an iceberg and whistled like a winter gale. We took in the big topsail; we went from that to the balloon foresail; we coiled down in a hurry and went for the storm jib on the run; we were out of breath when we got a reef tied in the mainsail, and by the time we had furled the mizzen we were gasping and working in silence. Within an hour's time there was a heavy sea. The sky was black and thick in the east – a sky full of wind. The breeze hauled around till it was south-east, and then flew back to the eastward, and blew like ten men. There was lightning in the south. The glass dropped two tenths of an inch, and the thermometer fell like a shooting star.

We hung on until dark, thinking that it might moderate. Instead, it blew harder. Cartagena was fifty miles away, dead to windward. It seemed best to run back under the lee of Cape de Gata until morning. We wondered how the hens were making out, and the pigs; the last we saw of old man Cadiz, at nightfall, she was fifteen miles off-shore, surrounded by driving rain squalls, taking in sail.

The mainsail was boomed out to port, swelling against the shrouds; the headsails were sheeted flat to ease the steering. In a smooth place we came around, and ran for it. The seas came racing up astern, level with the deck, flinging us forward, head down, at fifteen miles an hour; wind shouting, ropes all alive and humming, white water spouting foam. She settled into the hollows between the waves, her wavering bowsprit pointing up into the black sky, then rose again, fairly leaping up, and lunged ahead. We ran back twenty-eight miles in three hours and rounded in behind the cape at ten o'clock.

It was a comfort to get into the smooth water. But it blew. The squalls came singing down over the hills at the end of the cape, swift as hammer-blows; farther up the bay the land was low, and the wind was fairly singing out across the meadows. It was very cold, and utterly black, except that from time to time we caught the gleam of candlelight in the little village of San Miguel, on the beach half-way up the bay, and off to the north-west we could see the glimmering lights of Almeria. We hove to, under the sail we were carrying, and jogged back and forth between the end of the cape and the beach at the head of the bay. Beach, San Miguel, lighthouse; beach, San Miguel, lighthouse. During my watch on deck we made that circuit seven times.

As soon as there was a sign of daylight, I called the watch below; we took in the mainsail and set the mizzen, and ran back for harbour. They tell me that it blew very hard as we came across the bay, and that the dust from the low point near the city swept out over the sea like clouds of sulphur smoke. When I woke up we were coming in between the mole heads, and we anchored in the same berth we had left twenty hours before.

THE DEMON'S REST

Two days after this we set out again for Cartagena, and arrived. We had favouring breezes all the way, clear skies and smooth water, and we came into Cartagena harbour on the first squall of a savage little storm that was too late to catch us. It was plain to see that the evil Spirits were tired of the game.

We anchored in front of the Yacht Club, and soon afterwards a jovial little man came alongside in a row-boat and asked to be employed as a watchman. He dwelt at length on his honesty and courage, and showed us a thick packet of commendatory letters, two of which were written in Japanese. He seemed to attach great importance to this written record, and left off his boasting, time after time, to bring it out again for our inspection. We hired him, and went ashore.

The main street of Cartagena has no roadway, so that the favourite Spanish amusement of walking up and down can be enjoyed without interruption. Indeed, it is a very attractive city, with a charm and manner all its own. Since Carthage was destroyed, this New Carthage has been prosperous and active, for it has the only natural harbour on the Mediterranean coast of Spain.

We met a soldier who lived in Palma, and he found us eager listeners while he told of the Balearic Isles.

'You have seen the worst of Spain,' he said. 'As you go north now, you will see more and more civilisation: this place is better than Malaga and Almería; Alicante is better than here, Palma is better than Alicante, and Barcelona better than Palma. I am sure that you will like Palma, and I do not say that just because I live there.'

Our watchman was not a cook, he confessed, but there was no other department of human knowledge in which he did not excel, and when he learned that we were going to Alicante he fairly danced with excitement, begging to be taken with us as pilot.

'I know wind,' he said. 'I know all current, all rock, all everything. I go Alicante night time, day time, eyes shut, whatever. Suppose you take me Alicante, we go four, five hours.'

It was difficult to see how he could get the *Caltha* over seventy miles of water within five hours, but we thought that his presence on board might serve as a hostage for the Perverse Divinities, and hired him.

'I go tell good-bye my wife,' he said. 'Three clock to-morrow morning we go Alicante.'

THE SOUTH-EAST CORNER

We came out of Cartagena Bay just as the sun was rising, and shaped a course for Cape Palos, the south-east corner of Spain. The wind was fair.

Our pilot told us a great deal about himself. He had

been in Alicante, and Cartagena, where he was born, and Santa Pola, a small coast town between these two; this was the sum of his knowledge of the round world. He did not understand the compass, and had never used one. He had never seen a chart. He could not read nor write; of this last he was especially proud. 'Suppose I see my name on paper,' he said, chuckling, 'I not know!' Perhaps it was this that led him to attach so much importance to the mysterious Japanese letters of recommendation which he had shown us.

After this, we asked a great many sailors and fishermen if they could write, and though we usually found that they could do so, they were none of them offended at the question. Indeed, in the Rambla de Cataluña in Barcelona there is a row of letter-writers' booths; you go in, and tell the writer what you want to say. . . .

As we approached Cape Palos, still holding our fair wind, we began to feel that at last and at least there was one corner around which we could pass without beating. But there is, in Mediterranean meteorology, a phenomenon known as 'the meeting of the winds.' This now occurred. When we were within half a mile of the cape, the wind suddenly came up ahead. It did not drop and come up again; it did not haul nor veer – simply, it reversed its direction. We sailed from a south-wester into a north-easter without the slightest interruption. It was a trivial misfortune, not worthy of the Demons' previous efforts. But it forced us to beat around the cape. The pilot said that he had been expecting it.

We reached up along the coast, and were in Alicante

Bay by sunrise. The pilot mistook the location of the city, and would have taken us past it, scornful of the chart, had we not driven him away from the tiller.

As soon as we were moored, he began to talk about his brother.

'My brother good pilot, all same me. Speak English, French, Italian, go all over. I no can go Palma now. You take my brother. My wife no let me go. Damn my wife. Never go. Suppose to-morrow come telegram say my wife dead – poof! I go Palma, Barcelona, Glasgow, New York, all over. Damn my wife. You take my brother. No got wife.'

Without waiting for us to reply to this, he went ashore and sent a telegram to Cartagena, and the next day, as we were ready to sail, his brother presented himself on deck and asked to be taken with us as seaman. He seemed a likely man, and we hired him, the more readily since he did not once tell us how good he was, and since it developed that he was no relation whatever to our pilot. We called him Piloto, in memory. He stayed with us for more than a year.

Our pilot said good-by, left us with a final imprecation on his wife – who, in all probability, does not exist – and went back over the old familiar road to Cartagena.

Alicante is one hundred and seventy miles from El Dorado.

THE CLANS GATHER

A short distance to the eastward of Alicante is Cape San Antonio. If bound to the Balearic Isles, you follow the coast as far as the cape, and then set a course offshore, east by north, for Dragonera, which is the nearest point of the Isles. We had this plan.

There was a pleasant sea breeze in the afternoon, and we made good progress alongshore, sighting Cape San Antonio ahead. But clouds had gathered at sunset, and by midnight the sky was thick. When we were within four or five miles of the Cape, from which we were to head east, the wind hauled east. The weather was better organised now, and the clans of evil Spirits better able to interpret our intentions.

We had taken in the light sails some time before, and about four o'clock, there coming a gust with a bite in it, we shortened down to storm canvas, and put a double reef in the mainsail. There was not enough wind to warrant this, but we felt a desire to show the Demons our resources. Moreover, just under our lee there was a cove, called Morayra Bay, where we might run in and anchor if it should be necessary.

There were thunderstorms in the south, and in the black murk astern we could see no less than eleven red lights – the port lights of the fishing fleet, beating up the coast out of Alicante; when the lightning flashed behind them we could see the sharp peaks of the lateen sails, all in line. Then it began to rain, and we could see nothing. We hove to off the entrance to Morayra Bay, and waited to see what the morning would bring us.

At sunrise the wind abated somewhat. We shook out our reefs, turned our backs on the bay, and stood offshore. But this move, of course was noted. Almost we could hear the Demons say, 'There there they go! They're trying to get around the cape!' An outrageous wind came yelling down over the hills from the north-west, raising a steep sea at once, and covering the water with white foam. We turned back and ran into Morayra Bay.

As soon as we had anchored in front of the village, the Coast Guard came off to see who we were and what we were doing there. There were four men in the boat, and all were armed.

It was not until evening that we were fully aware of the trick the Demons had played on us.

We lie close to that wretched village, a huddled group of bare and chill white buildings, crouching there on the shore like a whimpering dog in a storm. The wind yells down through the bare bleak valley behind it, and whips out across the bay in flurries that darken the water. It whistles and moans in the rigging, and screams during the squalls. The water is talking under the bows, and the chain grates on the bobstay as we swing. We roll a little, and shift uneasily back and forth. All the skylights and hatches are shut tight, for it is bitterly cold – a mean, nipping, frosty sort of cold, straight from the Pyrenees, with a taste of snow in it. And it blows like ten men, like ten devils, like Hell . . . .

The sky is clear, as it has been all day, and the moon is shining. There is a steep headland of naked, lifeless rock to the north-east of us, with a forlorn round tower tottering on its summit; away to the south, on the other side of the bay, is Ilfach, a jagged mass of cliff that seems tumbling crazily upward into the sky; the rocks near us are bold and savage – dark caves and gravel talus and patches of beach where the surf is growling – and under our bows there is the dismal ruin of a fort, bearing the date of 1473. The stark grapevines rattle in the wind, and the leaves go scurrying over the bare ground. In the village there is not one glimmer of light. And over all this the wind is howling shrilly like a curse.

Surely this is unqualified misery. This is the Demons' masterpiece. And it is at its worst when one reflects that it should be warm and sunny and pleasant, with green trees and blue water and a happy sky. Iceland would be better, because in Iceland, one would not expect friendliness in the climate. . . . Surely this is the end of the world.

But the Pilot Book, with touching faith, makes a cheerful comment on the situation: 'The town of Tuelada, with a population of about three thousand, is situated three miles to the north of the fort.'

We put on our warmest clothes and set out up the valley in the teeth of the wind.

TUELADA

It was a long three miles, but at last we came to the crest of a hill from which we could see the town. A square church tower rose in the midst of it, with the houses gathered about its foot. The houses were solidly built, as if for eternity, and the streets very clean and finished.

Very soon we gathered some friends about us. The druggist was first; his companions laughingly pushed him out into the street towards us, telling him that this was a chance to try his famous English. He did not speak English, but he took us to the café, where we were joined by the doctor and the veterinary, who also dealt in second-hand horses, and we had absinthe all together, very merrily, though we understood almost nothing of one another's languages. We conversed by signs and gestures and broken phrases, and found our interpretive ability increased thereby, just as blind people find their ability to interpret sounds increased by their inability to see.

Pat waited at the café while the woman made some coffee, and Bill and I hunted out a shop. A very merry and bright-eyed girl waited on us; she sent her small brother out to find eggs and potatoes, and carried on a long and elaborate joke with three of her friends, who had been told that there were foreign curiosities in town, and had come in to look at us.

All at once their levity faded from them, and they bobbed respectful curtseys and murmured 'Buenas dias' to some one behind us. We turned and faced a very droll and jolly priest. I addressed him hopefully, and asked him if he spoke French, but he shook his head and made plaintive and deprecatory gestures with his hands. Noticing how he seemed to consider himself too humble a person for any presumptuous attainments, and yet how at the same time he was feeling his deficiency, I fell to wondering what his life must be like, and if he found satisfaction in his work among these singularly simple and isolated people. I asked him if there was a school in town and he nodded, touching his breast with his finger, but I do not know if he meant that there was a school, and that he conducted it, or that he himself was the school. Probably the latter, for he seemed to be the one person on whom everyone depended. When the boy returned, with the town's last three eggs, the girl asked the priest to make out the bill for her, and he did this, shrugging his shoulders and flourishing his pencil as if to say that he was no dab at bookkeeping. I suppose the girl asked him out of politeness; he added wrongly at first, but the girl discovered the mistake. He laughed, saying, 'I told you so,' and took leave of us in the friendliest manner imaginable.

We went back to Pat, who, I think, was trying not to buy a horse at the moment of our arrival. As we set out down the road for Morayra again our thoughts kept going back. But I thought especially of the priest, left alone in that little untouched world of his. He is there now. . . .

THE FINAL DASH

I

At the end of four mortal days in Morayra Bay, we saw a chance. Rejoicing and jubilant, singing 'Fifteen Men' as we ground the capstan, we clawed the gaskets off the sails and swept out of the bay like a caravel bound for a new world. The wind was still north-west, and blowing hard, and off the end of the cape we ran into a heavy sea, rolling down out of the Gulf of Valencia. We turned back, and anchored in the berth we had left, where we spent the day in varnishing the deck work.

2

On that same evening the wind changed, and came up from the south-west. We did not wait to see what it would do ; we got away at once. The sun had set, and we could see the pale moonlight shining on the walls of the houses in Morayra, until the headland shut them from our sight; nothing, I think, will ever shut them from our minds.

All night the wind kept sobbing and changing, so that at times we could sail our course, and at times no better than north by east. The sea was confused, running in all directions. However, though we did but poorly, we hung on, for unless the wind came due east, and blew hard, we had a chance.

At noon on the following day we saw the hills of Iviza on the horizon. The Isles were there!

At two o'clock the wind came due east, and blew hard.

We talked it over. Some day, the wind would be west. The north-westers were too furious; the south-westers died, or turned to easterlies; some day, the wind would be west. But now, it was thirty miles, dead to windward, to the lee of Iviza. . . . There is no harbour on that side of the island, but we might put into a cove . . . some Godless cove, like Morayra. . . . No.

We set the topsail and the big ballooner and ran for Denia, in the desperate hope of making harbour before dark. This we failed to do, in spite of driving, but there were range lights to mark the difficult channel between the shoals, and we came in without trouble, and anchored between two schooners at the head of the harbour. On each of them a dog awoke and howled as our chain rumbled out.

Denia is worse than Morayra, because it is larger. And one is continually expecting something from it – some evidences of civilisation or comfortable human environment or attempt to make life tolerable – and finding nothing.

The distance to El Dorado is one hundred and eighteen miles.

3

At the end of four mortal days in Denia we saw a chance. The pilot and the Harbour Master told us that we could not hope to make the Isles with a north-wester blowing; a gale from the Atlantic, they said, blows across France, to the northward of the Pyrenees, and falls on the Mediterranean from the Gulf of Lyons; there would be a sea 'as high as the house,' and 'once out,' they said, 'you can't get back.'

Notwithstanding . . .

The church clocks were striking midnight as we made sail.

As soon as we were five miles from the land it was evident that the sea, if not yet as high as the house, would soon become so. Moreover, we were tempted by that opinion that we couldn't get back. We turned about, and though the sea set us to leeward enough to oblige us to take a tack in the narrow channel, the shoals were marked by breakers, gleaming in the moonlight, and we worked in easily enough. We anchored in the berth we had left. Beside us now was a brig – the only brig I ever saw.

4

'This can't go on,' we said. Nevertheless, it did go on. Two dreary days elapsed without producing any change. And then, on the third day, all at once, something happened that altered the whole face of the world. The feel of autumn departed from the air, the sky cleared, the sun warmed the sheltered corners of the deck, and the wind, strong and hearty, blew from the west.

The breeze freshened as we increased our distance from the land, and in half an hour the fight had been taken out of the sea. We set the big topsail, dead before the wind as we were, and reeled off seven steady knots till dawn. The hills of Iviza awere abeam; we were more than half way to El Dorado.

But the Demons had not forgotten us. At sunrise, the wind dropped, and came up from the east.

This was dead ahead again. We tacked over to the southward, towards Iviza, so as to have a weather shore in case we should need it, but by the time we were within ten miles from the land the wind moderated to a normal breeze, and we came about onto the starboard tack again. Lying so, we could just head east-north-east, which was the bearing of Dragonera light. All that day we kept her going, and had seen no land ahead at sunset.

Everything that happened during that night, it seems, happened at the same time. At nightfall the wind began to sob, and there were lightning flashes in the southern sky. It was plain to see that we were to be inflicted with the Burden of Thunderstorms.

The first storm reared up over the horizon in the east, split into two parts, and passed away to the north, leaving a portion of it hanging in the north-east, very black and cavernous, brightly lighted by the white noiseless flames that leaped up from the dark surface of the sea. A storm then appeared in the south. A second came up from the east. Then it rained. Then the storm which had passed around us blew back overhead again, shutting out all heaven, and raining in streams, in sheets – raining solid.

When the rain passed, hissing off to leeward over the water, we saw a light ahead. It bore east-north-east, and flashed every four seconds. A bright glare of deep yellow, just on the rim of the world. That would be Dragonera. We saw it, at intervals, all night. It was the best friend we had. Indeed, except for one another, it was the only friend we had. We claimed it, and called it our light. We cursed about it in cordial enthusiasm. Damned old Dragonera. A good light.

Then two thunderstorms met, just beyond us, one from the east, another from the west. It rained again, soaking, roaring, covering the water with a film of cobwebby white. We sat hunched up in it, like wet birds, and waited. Then it passed, and we steered for our light again. And all this time the wind held in the east, blowing as gently as a summer breeze. This was unnatural, and ominous –we shortened sail in anticipation of some surprising new phenomenon.

There was still a storm in the south, hitherto unutilised. This now came into action, rolling up over us, burying us in thick rain. Some sharp zigzag of lightning fell into the sea near us, with soul-shaking crashes. Then it hailed. We stood by the main halliards, ready to lower away when the wind should come. The hail stones were as big as marbles; I picked one up and put it in my mouth, to feel the size of it. They drummed on our hat brims and on our shoulders, they bounced on the deck like rubber. They were hard as glass, and they cut where they struck.

When the wind came, it came with a rush that made the rigging whistle. We took the mainsail in, the water running up our sleeves in streams as we reached up to drag at the soaking cloth. It blew hard for only a few minutes, and then settled into a tolerable breeze, though it kept changing its direction continually, and would not let us head for our light.

Then it hailed harder. The air was filled with the crash of it. We could see nothing – there was nothing to see except the anchor light in the rigging, and you couldn't raise your head to look at that. The binnacle lamp was out – drowned. The sea, even close to the rail, even during the flashes of lightning, was invisible. The hail stones struck the boat cover and went jumping madly up again, striking our faces under the brims of our hats.

This lasted for perhaps half an hour, though all sense of time had left us. We sighted Dragonera again, and got a light going in the binnacle. If we could get to Dragonera before the east wind came. . . . A storm rolled up from the south-east – a new quarter – but just before it reached us it went back again, and as soon as the edges of the clouds showed us a few faint and very high stars, we shook out our reefs, set the mainsail, and drove her for the corner. We must make the shelter of that corner before the wind came east.

In the cabin, that night, it was warm, and dry, and bright with lamplight. We stepped over the heaps of our wet clothes and went to bed.

We made the corner. I was on watch at dawn, and we had gotten three miles beyond it. Pat called up to know where we were, and could not believe it when I told him; he got up to look, and there was Dragonera, astern. When the east wind came, at sunrise, we were off the entrance to the little harbour of Andraitx, and we decided to run in. We worked in through the narrow passage between the breakwater and the cliffs, and anchored in the centre of the harbour just as the last of the hail storms came tearing in from seaward.

We could hear the sheep-bells on the shore. There were trees on the hillsides. This was El Dorado. We had caught the last tag end of it, we were hooked on in the last port to leeward, but we had caught it; the anchor was down in it, it was ours and we had it, and it couldn't get away.

5

There still remained Palma.

We were subjected to the Trial by Calm. We were

nine hours in making ten miles along the coast, and we towed in the dinghy for three hours of it, to make as much as that. It was dark when we rounded Cape Cala Figuera and headed up Palma Bay. Then a breeze came, and it came ahead.

So, after all, we were forced to beat, even to the last inch. It was a very dark night, and the breeze served us well; we watched the city spreading out and growing more distinct as we drew nearer. Porto Pi light appeared – a miserable affair, but welcome – and soon afterwards the occulting light on the breakwater, very hard to distinguish from the shore lights because of the mirage, which raised them all up and magnified them grotesquely. When we were three miles away we could see lights in houses, and the street lamps, shining on up the buildings near them. We heard trolley cars grinding on the curves, and the occasional hoot of an automobile horn.

We came gliding in, very still, watching the black masts of all the ships against the sky, and the restless reflections of the lights in the glassy water.

We anchored in the centre of the harbour, in front of the Yacht Club, and stowed sail. It was half-past one on the morning of Tuesday, the twenty-second of November.

CHAPTER TWELVE

Palma de Mallorca, In the Balearic Isles

*

ONE expects an island to be remote and provincial. The people who have chosen to live there, shut off by the intervening and estranging sea, are free to arrange life to suit them, and, very naturally, their arrangements are different. They have no one but themselves to consider. If a man doesn't approve their customs, they have a very pertinent answer ready for him. An island people might well be pardoned if they thought their ways better than other men's ways, or the rest of the world no more than hopeless imitators.

We thought to find Palma a complacent little village, out of the world, and sorry for it, rather forlorn in its solitude, and thinking of nothing beyond the wind and the sea and the going and coming of the sun – the boats would be drawn up on the beaches, and the fish nets spread to dry on the stone wall in front of the inn. We fancied that the arrival of the steamer from Barcelona would cause a flurry of excitement, and that the coming of the *Caltha*, a sleek white yacht, flying a foreign flag, would start a topic in the wine-shops that would last throughout the week.

As a matter of fact, we anchored in the harbour without causing so much as a ripple of surprise, and it was not until the third day that the authorities found time to move us out of the way of the traffic. As for the steamer, a fast motor-boat goes out to take off her mails as soon as she passes the end of the breakwater, and she is met at the landing by a swarm of taxicabs and 'buses from the hotels.

Palma is an alert and flourishing city, with a population of seventy thousand. It is much more metropolitan than Barcelona. There is no trace of that sleepy apathy that often attacks people who have, at last, arranged their lives to suit them. The world isn't something remote and separate, away off on the mainland; it is here, and life is now. The charm and serenity of the place take hold on the mind as vividly as the atmosphere of Paris does; life is full of colour and pleasant excitement, and Palma seems an inevitable place to live. Every window seems to have a prospect that would always be delightful, and there is hardly a doorway in the narrow streets that does not cry out to you and ask you to make it home. Certainly there is an air about Palma.

The city has a residential part, and a commercial part, on opposite sides of the principal boulevard; in the one are the houses of the fortunate, and the palaces, in the other the cafés and offices. However, the two are mixed; the biggest club is on the commercial side, and the post office sits among the palaces.

The streets are narrow. 'In these countries, the sun is an enemy.' The trolley cars wriggle through, seeming to draw in their shoulders as they make the turns. At the intersections there are signs fastened to the walls of the houses, with pictures of men driving carts; the direction of the horse's head shows the direction of the one-way traffic. What can be more pleasant – especially if it be quiet starlight, and you are going down aboard a ship –

than to walk through a street where the cornices nearly touch overhead?

As you come up the Rambla from the harbour, you will see on your right, just at the corner of a street that branches off near the fountain of the Tortoises, a sign bearing the word 'Globo.' I do not know if that is the name of a newspaper, or a blood-purifier – at any rate, this is the street to follow. It is about twelve feet wide, on an average, though buildings jut out into it, and irregular corners of ancient houses constrict it. It eludes them. It makes a sudden bend, and runs against a blank wall. It escapes into a wider street. You will know this place by the shawls in the window on your right, and by the fact that it leads to a sort of plaza, twenty-five feet long, before a church. Beyond this, the street narrows to a mere slit, which also ends against a wall. It squirms up a curving flight of steps, receiving contributary alleys at every landing. At the top, four streets meet. One of them is triangular. This seven-sided square is the commercial centre of the city.

Obviously, a stranger can find his way to some particular spot only by the method of trial and error – though it is hard to be convinced of error when every street leads through continual surprises to scenes of fascination. Too often they are seen but once, and lost forever after. But there is always something else.

On the residential side the land is more level, and there are no stairways in the streets. But the little paved lanes pass under archways, often, or under added rooms that have been built out on brackets, and over every wall the orange trees are hanging, and through every iron gate are sudden views of courts and gardens. In these streets, at night, the lights shine up on great closed doors and iron gates and shuttered windows. One may hear approaching footsteps and wait for long minutes before he can tell around which corner the passer-by is to appear. There is a perpetual possibility that something delightful will happen. Nothing happens. Yet the possibility is as undimmed and alluring as ever.

The walls of the Mallorcan palaces rise up like cliffs. Often there are no windows on the lower floors, but only loopholes, and the great arched doorway that leads into the court. But the windows on the second story are twenty feet in height. At the top, a vast cornice hangs over the street, like a roof for all outdoors. Often there is an open gallery along the front, under the cornice ; it indicates a life on the housetop, as the Oriental traditions of Spain, and the climate of these islands, make natural. The starlight, it seems, is a medium most suitable to life in a palace of Mallorca. And down below are those great, cool, sombre rooms; the window shutters are swung out from the top, like awnings; the light from the bright street strikes up against the walls; there are screens of Cordova leather and chests from Granada, and portraits of ancestors who lived ardently a hundred years ago – the architecture is both the cause, and the effect, of the manner of life.

To this consummation the entrance is through the arched doorway and the court. The court is the heart of the house. It occupies nearly the whole of the lower floor; there is a well-curb in the centre – a pleasant suggestion of independence – and at the back the grand stairway leads up; a broad stair, of stone, with heavy balustrades of iron. The whole house rests four-square on marble columns that stand about the court.

The Mallorcan palaces are not so big as the vast fortresses of Rome or Florence, and they have not that air of romantic excitement and unattainable splendour that those of Venice have; they are more domestic, more within the reach of present-day imagination, and seem not too large for one man's use. This is very appealing and reassuring: if worse ever comes to worst, so that one is impelled to make a separate peace with life, Palma and its palaces are always there, on a beautiful island in the sea, 'one of the most delightful countries in the world, and the most unknown.'

The Isles are the very centre of the Western Basin; Spain and Africa and the Tuscan Islands and France surround them at almost equal distances, and Palma was once a port of call on the important trade routes of the world. It was used by Phœnicians and Carthaginians and Romans and Goths and Vandals and Venetians and Moors, and in later times by France and England. It was conquered for Spain in 1225 by Don Jaime of Aragon. For four thousand years, Palma Bay has been an El Dorado. It is impossible to forget, even now, even though one looks out across the harbour through the rigging of a dozen modern steamers, that the fleets of Venice have anchored in that roadstead, and that the long galleys of Carthage have been drawn up on this very beach. And we — we also have known. We had fought for Palma, against the wind and the sea; we were in now, and moored, and could watch the ships coming in – schooners and paregas and feluccas and barques, which had also beat up for the offshore isles, and were tied up, in the quiet water, and called the port their own. As we did.

You will remember the 'old careening riot' of the Caribbees, in the days of the buccaneers, and the 'clamorous crowded shore.' Great days. Men lived rough and free, took part in hopeful fights, drank rum, and worked on ships. On the curving yellow beaches, under the palm trees, they hove down their great butt-ended ships for cleaning. There were fires to melt the pitch. The rum went round, and there was much loud talk and laughter. You remember.

It happens in Palma now. Ships are always careening in Palma, coasting schooners and square-riggers, rolling up huge round bilges as big as hills. And every Saturday while we were there, half a dozen paregas hauled in close beside the *Caltha's* berth to scrub and clean and paint.

Paregas are big, broad, double-ended, lateen-rigged fishing boats, exceedingly picturesque to look at, and built to last a hundred years. They are as shallow as saucers and will go to windward no better than any other basin, but with the wind aft, under their terrifying press of sail they go like witches. The work is desperately hard, as it is with fishermen everywhere, but in spite of this there is never an attempt to make the ships comfortable to live in – the cabins are no more than dog-houses under the deck; like fishermen all over the world, they skip meals and sleep in wet beds, and do not seem greatly bothered by it, because they are so soon to be on shore again.

A parega warps in to one of the lighters that lie beside the quay. She removes all her gear and equipment – ropes, nets, fish-baskets, floorboards, bedding, pots and pans, spare sails, ballast – everything – she is as empty as a tin can. The whole agglomeration is piled in a heap on the lighter. The great yard is lowered and lashed; it is half again as long as the boat. The halliard is made fast to the rail of the lighter. The men heave down – there is a shanty-man to keep the time and take in the slack on the cleat – and the parega, caught by her mast-head, is heeled over until her rail and half her deck is submerged, and her keel rises above the surface of the water. All hands and the cook, with a great deal of talk and throaty discordant singing, turn to with brooms and brushes and scrub the bilge.

But the cook soon deserts. He burrows about in the heaped-up merchandise on the lighter, and having gradually collected his fish basket, his vegetable bag, and the iron bucket that he uses for a stove, he sets about getting dinner. You can see him, through the steam, throwing great double handfuls of rice and tomatoes and onions into the pot, and stirring with a spoon like a spade. He ladles out a sample from time to time, and tastes, lapping his lips, and watching his comrades with an alert, half-amused expression. Another handful of salt goes in, a pint of oil; he takes a few more scooping swirls in the stew, like a man paddling in rapids, and gives the word.

The crew leave their scrubbing brushes in the air, in

the middle of a stroke, and come clambering over the pile of rock ballast like panthers. They snatch up plates and spoons, dip into the pot, and fall to in wild excitement; the loaves of bread go flying from hand to hand, seeming to melt away; some one disentombs the wine-cask. They squat there like refugees among the ruins, with their worldly goods piled up about them; rough and swarthy men, unshaven, yet having a certain air of gallantry; their heads tied up in scarves, sashes of brilliant colours about their waists, some, actually, with earrings in the ears. The ship's boy, who makes a dismal pretence of cleaning some boards, looks towards the group, sniffing the air, and thinking of the days when he shall be captain of a parega, and may have first go at the pot. On the next lighter is another crew; farther along are others still. The clamorous crowded shore.

Here is a savage, reckless way of life, with the true colour of romance about it – impatient men, and costumes out of the play, and ships nearly ready to get to sea again, all under the clear sky, in the bright sunlight, with the blue water reaching away forever and forever. . . . .

We went into winter quarters. Pat and Bill took the steamer to Barcelona, and thence proceeded to visit the Riviera; perhaps, they said, they would take in the winter sports in Switzerland – they didn't know what they might do, or how long they might be gone. As for me, I unbent the sails and sent them to the laundry, arguing for a long time, and in a language unknown on earth, with the extremely prepossessing forewoman of the sail loft about the difficulties of washing a big mainsail, with a wire luff-rope, in a tub. The decks were bare, and the spars gaunt and naked. I put up the old blue pennant that we had carried across the Bay of Biscay, and sat down to work on this book.

Piloto was up forward. He made visits ashore now and again, mostly to the two carabineros, or Coast Guards, who had a little hut, with a bird cage hung beside the door, on the quay astern of us; they were stirring old pirates to look at, in uniform, with faces stained and rubbed down to the colour of old teak and voices like moose-calls; they came aboard once or twice, to listen to the phonograph, which, especially when the record was done on the accordion, they could appreciate, and told me long tales of the contrabandistas, whom it was their duty to apprehend, and asked elaborate questions about New York. Sometimes I found a bit of scraping or varnishing for Piloto to do, to keep him busy for half a day; and of course he washed down decks and cleaned the brass and did the cooking. But for the most part he sat in his fo'c's'le, quiet as a mouse, through the whole length of the day; he looked at the pictures in the *Daily Mail*, and read, a thousand times, backwards and forwards, until they were worn out, the few Spanish books he had on board. And every night at nine o'clock, as the bugles were blowing in the infantry barracks near the cathedral, he came into the saloon and rummaged in the ship's safe – a tin cigarette box – for the money to buy to-morrow's bread.

I sat in the saloon, in front of a rusty typewriter, and wrote. I completed my first draught, up to the words 'and sat down to work on this book,' and then I occupied myself on some other things that I had long wanted leisure to set down. There was a book store in town, and I bought books from time to time, until I had a row that extended the whole length of the saloon on the port side; I brought them down aboard and read them, usually before I went to bed; I read everything on board. Sometimes I made a call, or went to the club, or arranged a tea-party on board, and usually, as I was returning from the post office, I stepped in at the café to read my mail. I invented two new games of solitaire. I worked a great many problems in navigation. Once I did not go off the ship for eight whole days.

And whenever I came on deck at night I said, 'Hi! How are we doing?' to an imaginary helmsman, as if I were coming on watch.

One day, when I was looking over the charts, I discovered that we had nothing of the southern portion of the Ægean. This was a serious omission, because we had tried Spanish charts, and found them ludicrously inadequate, even of home waters, and certainly not to be trusted for anything so distant, and so complicated, as the Greek Archipelago. Accordingly, I wrote to the Chart Office in Gibraltar, and gave my address at the office of the Consul in Palma, after which I thought it best to go ashore to see the Consul, to let him know that I was expecting a package.

I waited in the outer office for a moment, since there was another visitor inside, and then the Consul appeared. He was a slight man, with a small head and stiff white hair, and a manner as alert and quick as a wasp's. A man not ordinary, in any respect. I was ushered in.

'It's quite a trivial matter I've come to see you about,' I said. 'I'm an American, but it happens that I'm here in a British ship, and . . ."

'In a British ship?' he said, drawing out the syllables in long astonishment, as if I had said that I came in a clothes basket.

'Yes,' I said. 'A British yacht. . . .'

'Nobody told me a thing about it,' he said, as if this were the last straw. 'Where are you lying?'

I told him.

'I never heard a word about it,' he continued. 'May I ask what steps you took to have yourselves reported?'

I was a little angry with him. 'I suppose the pilot did whatever was . . .'

'Yes! Yes!' he exclaimed. 'But to me! To *me!* You're required to report to *me*. You must know that.'

'I think not,' I said. 'We're only . . .'

'It doesn't matter. It doesn't make the slightest difference. I have the instructions right here at hand.' He began padding about among the papers on his desk. 'You're not Mr. Spencer?' he asked, suddenly looking up at me.

'No,' I answered, surprised, of course, but thinking that perhaps this question of his would explain his attitude. 'But I'm with Mr. Spencer.'

'Oh, is that it? And has Mr. Spencer done me the honour to give me his address?'

'I don't think so,' I said.

'Who is he? What does he do?'

'Why, we're simply . . .'

'I've no doubt he's rich?'

I laughed.

'I shall get a big fine out of him for this,' said the Consul. 'He comes in here, and . . . . How long have you been in Palma?'

'Six weeks,' I told him.

He rolled his eyes up towards the ceiling at this, but I could see that he was really pleased. 'I certainly shall get a big fine out of him for this,' he went on. 'For failure to report as required. My instructions . . . .'

'See here,' I put in, desperately. 'Mr. Spencer's not here; he's in Switzerland.'

'Ah!' said the Consul. 'That's another story. If he chooses to leave his ship here while he goes off to Switzerland . . . And may I ask you what I'm to do with this?' And he tossed up onto the table a telegram addressed to Pat.

This was a knockout, and he enjoyed it, leaning back, with his finger on the place in his instructions, watching me for the effect it was to produce.

'I'll take it, if you like,' I said.

'Well, then. Very good. Now.' He began reading. 'All vessels, of over twenty tons . . . .'

'We're nineteen,' I put in.

He wilted visibly, but looked up at me as if this were too narrow a margin to gain his confidence, and went on reading. . . . . 'Except yachts . . . .' His breeze left him suddenly, and he lay and rolled in the heavy ocean swell.

'Exactly,' I said.

There was only one thing for the Consul to do, and he did it.

'I see I'm wrong,' he said. 'You see, there was a big yacht in here last week, and she sent up a man to report to me, almost at once. It doesn't happen often, to tell the truth. . . .' He broke off, smiling, and waved his hands.

I was interested in the yacht, which I had seen come in and leave again, and we talked about her for some time, amicably enough, after which I duly reported the *Caltha* to him, and asked him to come down for tea.

'I should be delighted indeed,' he said. 'I hope you'll forgive the lack of cordiality in my first reception?'

I told him that he might dismiss the matter from his mind, and remarked that in all probability he was a very busy man.

'I ought to be in Pollensa this moment,' he said, reaching for his hat.

We parted on the sidewalk in front of his office. 'I do hope you'll come and see me again,' he said, and with that he hailed a cab that happened to be passing, and scrambled out of sight. I realised, looking after him, that I had not spoken of the expected package of charts at all.

I walked slowly back to the harbour. The sun was low, and the slanting yellow light struck the tops of the houses across the narrow streets. I was thinking how small an incident could make a commotion in my quiet life.

For the most part the weather was warm and pleasant, but now and again we had a gale from the north.

The schooner *Roberto*, of Soller, came in, and moored

herself in a very tight corner beyond the lighter that lay next us; this restricted our space somewhat, for there was a lighter on the other side of us, also, and we all lay very close together. Her crew began to unload ballast, in preparation for careening. Her ballast was sand. Loose sand seems a mad thing to carry for ballast. However, she carried it; with block and tackle, in baskets, she discharged about twenty tons of it, piling it on the lighter that lay next us. In the evening, all hands cleaned up and went ashore, leaving the ship in charge of a dog.

After sunset it came on to blow. It came straight out of the north, as cold as Greenland, whistling down through the streets, screaming in the rigging of all the ships, rattling the tin roof of the Health Office like thunder in a melodrama. The *Roberto's* ballast rose up from the heap in swirls, and went hissing gaily out to sea – south, towards the desert, where it came from. It filled the corners of our decks like drifting snow, and though I closed the hatches and skylights, it sifted down in a fine and gritty rain, and fell on the paper as I wrote. The dog was barking with all his heart, meaning to say that things had gotten beyond his power to control them.

The *Roberto*, with all the ships in line behind her, shifted down to leeward and squeezed us between the lighters. There was a short choppy sea, and we lurched and staggered and bumped; it was a horrible sensation, like being ashore on a bar. Piloto and I, with coats buttoned tight and eyes shut, made our way about decks, like men in a sand-storm, putting over fenders. One by one they popped like rotten apples, and the cork filling went drifting away with the sand. We patched up what we could, using old rope and scraps of canvas.

The schooner's skipper came running down the quay and scrambled aboard. He stood for a moment clutching his hat, watching the disappearance of his ballast. Something must be done. He caught up a bucket, and threw water at the pile. No use in that. It never reached the sand. The wind turned it to fine mist, almost before it was out of the bucket, and it went singing over the breakwater, a quarter of a mile away. The dog howled.

About midnight, the paregas began to come in. They must have had to fight for it, for the wind was blowing right out of the bay. In the black night I could just see them over our bows, double-reefed, setting storm jibs no bigger than handkerchiefs, racing in close under the bowsprits of the line of anchored ships. One after another, rushing blindly in. I could hear the men shouting excitedly as they got their anchors ready. All the Palma boats made port that night.

On the twenty-fourth of January I got a telegram from Bill in Paris – 'Ah, yes; the winter sports,' I said, as I read it – telling me that they were coming back, and that they would stop in Barcelona to look for a motor. We had taken out the Old Unfaithful, and during all the time we were in Palma it lay on the forward deck, in pieces, in the wind and the rain; this was inadequate punishment, perhaps, but the machine's sensibilities were blunted by sin. There was every prospect of long periods of calm during the summer that followed, and we had done a great deal of worrying about a motor. As it turned out, however, Bill and Pat found nothing in Barcelona, except at the prohibitive prices that the import taxes made necessary, and we sold the old motor for junk, and sailed without one.

On the morning itself, I went over to meet the steamer, but they did not appear, and the man whom I sent aboard to look for them came back shaking his head. So I rowed back across the harbour and had breakfast; just as I was through I heard Pat hailing me from the deck. Bill was up at the Yacht Club, guarding the trunk which he had lost in Penzance, and had found again. There they were.

Their first question was in respect to the weather – to which I replied that if we were careful to choose a time between two northers, we could get away at any time – and their second in respect to the exploring which they expected me to have made over the rest of the island. But I had postponed all exploring until my work was out of the way, and knew nothing of the island beyond the limits of the city itself. It was all one to us where we went, since everything would be new, and we selected Soller, because of the suggestion of the schooner *Roberto*.

We left in a diminutive 'Pullman,' a dainty car, as neat and precise as a toy, in which the brass was brightly polished, even the hinges of the doors, and there were linen slip-covers on the seats.

The line runs up through the level country of the central plain, where the almond trees were in full blossom – though it was only the last day of January – and the dark olive trees made spots of deep shade around the farms. Ahead of us we could see the mountains that range along the north-west coast of the island, and as soon as the train entered them we began to climb. By the time we had reached Buñol, the high bare rocks had shut in on all sides of us, except that through the steep pass by which the train had come up we could look back over the plains and see Palma, spread out along the shore of the bay. Buñol is a meagre and forlorn little village, sticking to the side of the hill as if it had been thrown there, and seeming to hold itself in a tight grip of restraint, as if it feared to go mad from loneliness. Just beyond it we went into a series of tunnels which lead through under the saddle of the pass.

We came out on the other side and looked down on the roofs of Soller. I am sure that the inhabitants lie on their hearths and look up the chimneys at the train. There was a church in the centre, and all around it the gray roofs. The orange trees begin at the limits of the town and spread up the steep slopes; above their limit of culture the bare cliffs rise up like the rim of a cup.

The station was far below us, and we scuttled and roared down the side of the valley, in a long zigzag, to reach it.

There is a gray light in the streets. Because of the surrounding hills, the sunshine is direct only in the very middle of the day, and the light of the sky sheds a cool clean radiance over everything, and touches the houses and the people and the whole aspect of life with an exquisite and friendly sort of loneliness. The town is hidden away, it has vanished around the last corner of life, and has no thought nor sentiment that is out of keeping with its serenity and its simplicity. A noisy little stream flows through it, and over the garden walls the oranges and lemons hang and look down at the hurrying water, and see nothing else, in all their lives, that suffers any change.

The hotel is quite, quite new – in fact, portions of it were still unfinished, and the numbers had not yet been painted on the doors of all the rooms. The manager was most cordial, and showed us over the place with a schoolboy's enthusiasm, as if it had never entered his head that we could have seen finer rooms than these.

We rambled off down the trolley track and took the road that leads out through a very deep and narrow valley to the Port. Here, surely, is a place that is around the corner from everywhere. It is remote even from Soller. It has everything it needs. The shape of the land that forms the harbour leaves nothing to be desired; it is just right for shelter and for easy entrance. The village is built along the curve of the shore, with all the houses facing the water across the single street – the sort of village I like best in all the world.

It was evening then, and we went through on the street to the rocky point where the lighthouse is, and sat for a time looking out over the dark sea towards the west. The white-caps were rolling endlessly along, but they died at the harbour mouth, and the little yellow lights that were beginning to come out one by one in the village behind us were reflected in water perfectly still. Behind the mole lay a schooner and a big parega, and the beach was crowded with fishing boats.

We had half an hour to wait for the trolley back to Soller, and we went to a café and ordered coffee. The floor of the room was of stone, and the high ceiling was supported by gray stone piers set in the thickness of the white plaster wall. Off at one side was a mechanical piano, and the fishermen danced together while one of their number ground out the music. It was a strange, unreal sight, but full of charm, none the less – fishermen, with patched clothes and heavy scraping boots, clamping their cigars in their teeth, dancing together in a café in Puerto Soller. . . . The Signora of the house came and went, and the patron talked earnestly with two friends, also fat, at a table in a corner.

Then the car came, and we went back to the hotel. It was the first time I had slept ashore since Granada, nearly four months before.

It had been our intention to walk back to Palma on the following day, but we spent the morning in climbing mountains and eating oranges, and were in no mood for anything but an afternoon's enjoyment of the quiet atmosphere of Soller. We returned by the evening train.

Naturally, if the whole island of Mallorca was as pleasant as this, we should have no right to leave it within the year. But we thought of Italy, which lay ahead of us, and the Isles of the Ægean, and tried to call up resolution enough to proceed. Some places are like this – so lovely and so congenial that one calls them 'demoralising,' and sees nothing but emptiness in life without them. It happens with people, too; you can't, by any effort of will, see life as more than half complete without them. As a matter of fact, if it hadn't been for the football game, we might perhaps have been in Palma still.

For all I thought my days in Palma had been so quiet,

I found, when I came to talk of them, that I had much to tell – but this, possibly, was because I had had no one to tell of them before. The others had had fewer incidents, and more events. They hadn't, of course, been near Switzerland; they had avoided winter so far as they could. The Riviera had been enough for them. 'Enough,' forsooth! They had gone straight to Paris, as the most suitable expression of their state of mind.

One day, when we were taking a walk through the outskirts of the city, we came upon a football field, and went in to watch. It wasn't long, of course, before Pat had taken off his coat and joined the players. Bill and I, who knew his reputation and his skill, were prepared for the next step, which, indeed, followed very soon; Palma was to play Barcelona on the following day, and the captain, coming out of the track house when the news was brought to him, approached Pat, after watching him for a few moments, and asked him to play. Pat was reluctant to accept, at first, but the captain convinced him, and he signed on, and had his picture taken with the Palma team.

We went back to the ship. The sails had come from the laundry, and we set to work to bend them. It seemed incredible that we were to go to sea again. Our whole thought had been turned inland – we had taken notice of trees and roads and houses and the interiors of theatres – and here we were, bending sail, bound for Italy! It is sufficiently exciting, and sufficiently wraps one around in a complex of enthusiasms, to step aboard of a ship, even as a passenger, and go to a foreign country; but we were going under canvas, and it was we ourselves that made the ship go. The *Caltha's* mainsail seemed twice as big as it had seemed before, and all the gear seemed hard and heavy and stubborn; the thought of a ship before the wind, roaring through the water, seemed absolutely terrifying. This feeling is usual enough, I imagine, to one who looks up at a ship's bow as she lies at anchor, especially if she be a square-rigger, and big; the sea is so mighty and relentless and indifferent, and the big bow will meet it, be smashed in the face by it, and yet go. It gives one a stunned feeling, deep down in the soul.

This was only the first week of February, and though the almonds were in blossom ashore, spring had not yet come to the sea. There was still a possibility of a winter norther; we took note that we had Port Mahon, at a hundred miles' distance, and Bonifacio at two hundred and eighty, for shelter in case we should need it. However, we held a fixed conviction that spring was waiting for us in Italy – rendezvous, surely, to keep a man's heart in a flutter. We overhauled rigging, and stowed things away below, as jubilantly as though it were already May.

Bill and I sat on the side lines at the football game, cheering at appropriate points, and continuously interviewed by reporters, and others, who wanted explanations of Pat's ability. 'The trouble with football, for Spaniards,' one of these men told us, 'is that the game really isn't suited to our temperament. Each man gets excited and plays for himself and forgets all about the team. Boxing is more our sort of . . . Ai! Ai! Palma! Palma!' Indeed, it was a wonder that the spectators could be kept off the field. The whole game was a tumult of yells and thrills. And Palma won.

Pat came out of the dressing-rooms, after the game, through a cheering and applauding crowd. Bill and I achieved something of reflected glory. We were taken to the Palma Club, where they gave us beer and cakes, and because our ignorance of one another's languages made conversation impossible, we took it out in cheering and in drinking healths. Most of the cheers were for England, though there were no Englishmen present.

Of course Pat was so lame that he could hardly walk. When a delegation came down aboard to ask him to play again on the following day, he rubbed his legs, and said that we were unfortunately going away at noon. Having thus committed ourselves to action, we got our Bill of Health, took the covers off the sails, and made all snug for sea. The sky was gray and cloudy, but the glass showed a tendency to rise, and the wind was west.

It was just after two o'clock on the afternoon of the twelfth of February when we pulled out of the old berth and made sail. The two carabineros were out in their boat to wave their caps, and on the quay astern were three members of the Palma Football Club, hopeful to the last.

The breeze was very light. We slipped along past the end of the mole as silently as we had entered, that black November night which seemed so long ago. A soldier and his girl were leaning on the parapet at the end of the mole, watching us. When we came up on deck after supper we were off Cape Blanco, headed east. Nothing was left of Palma but a few winking lights, close down to the water, and the whole island of Mallorca was no more than a dim gray outline of hills against the dim gray sky.

'The Golden Isle,' they call it, and 'the Enchantress of the Mediterranean,' though so small 'that a swallow can fly across it in an hour.' There it is. Hail and Farewell.

You would think, perhaps that we would be despondent now that we had left our El Dorado behind us.

But Italy was ahead.

CHAPTER THIRTEEN

The Hounds of Spring

*

After dark the wind dropped to a barely perceptible breath, and it was not until three o'clock in the morning that we rounded Cape Salinas. The dark land, with a ragged fringe of trees on the crest, slipped along slowly under the stars; the surf along the shore gleamed white in the faint starlight. We said good-bye to Mallorca, and found a sort of satisfaction in the quiet tranquillity of it, as if this made it all the more certain that we should find it waiting for us when we came back again. I don't suppose it is possible to leave Mallorca without planning to come back. But when the sun rose, very hot and yellow, the wind failed altogether, and we met a big long sea rolling in from the south-west; we were all day wallowing along the coast, never more than five miles off the shore, and making less than a mile an hour. Certainly, it is very hard to leave Mallorca.

About four o'clock we saw two paregas come right out of the cliffs. They crept slowly offshore over the shining gray water. If they could come out, we, perhaps, could go in, and it would be better to wait at anchor than roll and tear at our gear as we were doing. There was a little cove shown on the chart; we came about and headed towards it.

This is an ideal coast for smugglers. We knew more of the traffic now, and we knew that the sight of a strange vessel, under a foreign flag, heading in for a deserted coast at sundown, would be sure to excite suspicions and raise hopes. There was only a lonely ruined tower in sight on the whole stretch of shore, but we knew that someone would be watching us, with a telescope, from some invisible window, or from a corner in the rocks. We quite obviously weren't one of the regulars, but we might have come from almost anywhere, and we might have met almost anybody on the way; there must always be a first time for a new vessel in the trade; we had a likely look about us. Sure enough, within half an hour after we had come about, a long gray motor boat came out of the cove and headed towards us. If we were what she thought us, and she were what we took her for, the Law would be the enemy of both of us; it was pretty to see the confusion of hope and nervousness with which she watched us. We knew that she wasn't what she was supposed to be, and she knew we knew it. And she couldn't make us out.

There were nine men aboard of her, all staring at us. As she crossed our stern her skipper climbed up on the rail and drew in his breath to hail us, but we stole his intention from him by hailing first, and offered fifty pesetas if he would tow us into the cove. We could see the thought pass through his mind that this last-minute caution of ours was unnecessarily elaborate, but he decided to humour us – we might, of course, be very valuable – and passed us a line.

We took in sail as we went, and rolled wildly as soon as the steadying canvas was down; the motor boat, rolling as wildly, went purring on ahead of us, heaving in and out of sight over the smooth backs of the rollers, switching her mast back and forth as if she were struggling to get away from the hawser. The cove opened up ahead; we could see the quiet silvery water stretching back into the land, and the little silent village on the shore; we came surging in through the narrow entrance with the breakers roaring and spouting on either hand. Just as we got inside the sun went down, and it was dark at once. We anchored where we were told, and lay and rolled all night, deep and slow and easy. The motor boat anchored near us, like a watchdog, but no one came aboard of us, and we might have been loaded to the roof with tobacco.

The village of Port Petra is desperately small and lonely, and has a look of being completely out of the world. When we noticed that it had no street, but only a rough, rocky passage between the houses, it struck us that we had seen something very like it before. Morayra anchorage, of course. But it did not have the dismal, accursed look that Morayra had; we saw it in decent spring weather, moreover, and not in howling winter. And it seemed quite contented to be no bigger or finer, for all there were but ten houses in it, and these so closely huddled together that one roof might have covered them all. Two or three children who were playing on the beach stopped to look up at us as we rowed ashore; the fisherman seated happily at the foot of a sunny wall nodded to us in a friendly way, but showed no interest or curiosity.

We walked up the road, since there was nowhere else to walk.

The fields were brown, and had a melancholy autumnal look, but the almond trees that hung over the walls beside the road were thick with spring blossoms, and we had not gone far before we heard a bird singing in the woods. This was the only songbird that we had heard in all Spain, except those two in the cage at the carabineros' hut in Palma. One songbird does not make a spring. But it was a sign. Spring was somewhere. There we were, waiting; and the ship, rolling gently on the raking swell in the cove, lay idle, but expectant, under a cloudless and breathless sky. Somehow it seemed very hard to bear.

We went back into the village, since there was nowhere else to go. One of the houses had '56' painted above its door; it was the only numbered house in the village. This gave it a certain distinction, and a public aspect, but we dared not assume that it was a café, even though the door was hospitably open, and we could see a primitive sort of bar within, with bottles on the shelves against the wall behind it. We ventured timidly to the doorway. Why, yes; this was a café. As if – did we expect to find a Spanish village so remote and uncivilised as to be without one?

While our coffee was being made the proprietor brought out a large brass tray of glowing embers and set it on a rack provided for it underneath the table where we sat – the only means of heating, apparently, in the whole house, except the fire of twigs in the kitchen stove. This done, he went back to his chair, took up the net he had been mending and talked to us, steadily, and in perfect confidence that we were understanding every word of what he said. He talked of what was uppermost in his mind: ships and passages, the state of the wind and the sea, the harbours along his coast, and, out of respect for the fact that we had come from far away, of Barcelona, which was, for him, the end of the world.

He had not known that the English language was so different from the Spanish as to preclude understanding the one from a knowledge of the other, and when he was told that the two were of separate families, and were quite unlike, he stretched his fists luxuriously over his head, yawned, and said 'Bueno!' meaning that he was glad to know the facts of the matter, but that it would make little difference to him.

We went several times to the café – there being nowhere else to go – and became acquainted with all the inhabitants of the place, besides the carabineros, who hover between the status of actual human inhabitants and lifeless symbols of Law and Order. The proprietor's wife was a sad-faced woman, dressed in black, as if it seemed appropriate, who gave the impression of having long ago closed her mind to every stimulating thought or joyous recollection. Some very bright-eyed and noisy children came in to play with marbles and whip-tops, and she watched them without the faintest expression to indicate that she understood what was going on. It was impossible to be sorry for her, because she didn't know that she was unhappy. From time to time a rather pretty young girl came and went through the room, carrying a water jar, and the soldiers who were lounging in the doorway looked after her as she passed. Her we thought pathetic, since there was no real chance for her to have anything in life that was not dull and stupid and useless. She seemed to know this; there was about her a hopeless, abandoned air, as if she felt herself gone, and negligible. Even if the attentions of one of the soldiers had been acceptable to her, she could get no further than a stifled sort of aspiration. In the course of time, she would become sad-faced, and wear black, as seeming appropriate, and watch the children at play on the floor with a slow stare of incomprehension.

That night there was a breeze from the west. We asked the proprietor what he thought of it, and he said that he thought it good for something. We left at once, gliding out through the entrance in the starlight, leaving the village very still and dark behind us. The wind was very light all during the night, but at dawn it came up fresh and sparkling, and we crossed the North Channel and ran the whole length of Minorca during the day. At eight o'clock in the evening, with the lights of Port Mahon glaring at us very clear and bright from under the dark mass of the land, we set the big topsail and the ballooner, streamed the log, and put her on the course for Asinara, off the north-west corner of Sardinia, two hundred miles away. The wind held strong and steady all night, and when the early clouds lifted at sunrise the last tall peak of the Balearic Isles had gone down into the sea astern.

It seemed a long time since we had been at sea. We felt free and unattached, related to nothing in the world. But we quickly fell into the old ways again; the round of watches and meals came back, and the feel of the moving ship under us, so different from the easy, sluggish motions while riding to an anchor, became again as natural as daylight.

At dawn four lonely seagulls appeared out of nowhere,

played about astern of us for a time, and then went back again to nowhere. That strange cry of seagulls sounding like ironic laughter . . . they made the sea seem more lonely than before. We had expected to sight nothing on this passage, and had made up our minds to go rolling over an empty sea like the last living thing in all the world; the Spanish coastwise trade would go down to the westward of the Balearic Isles, and ships bound for Italian ports would pass to the eastward of Sardinia.

But that afternoon we saw a ship. She came up from the south, a square notch in the sky, and passed close astern of us, so that we could take her picture. 'A macaroni boat,' we said, 'bound to the Gulf of Genoa.' As she passed no more than a hundred yards away, her skipper came on deck and waved the Italian flag at us, flapping it over the rail as if he were shaking the crumbs out of a tablecloth. He was evidently lonely, too; we could almost see his jovial grin of greeting as he bundled the flag up in his arms and went below again. He was well to windward of Genoa – prudently, for he was in ballast, and if it should come on to blow hard out of the Gulf of Lyons, he would need every possible mile of westing. I wonder what happened to him, later. . . .

After all, it was early in the year, and not too late for a gale of wind; the sky was low and heavy, and the sea had a hard, gray look. It was cold; we sat at the tiller in sweaters and oilcoats, with our old September canvas wrapped about our knees, and the watch below crowded into the galley at meal times, to be near the stove, like vagrants around the gratings of a bakery. This wasn't right. Where was spring? To believe in spring, with that wind moaning in the rigging and the feel of snow in the air, was an act of Faith. To believe that Italy lies just ahead seems always an act of Faith.

The breeze freshened during the night. When I came on deck in the cloudy darkness just before dawn we were making six knots, rolling deeply, and spreading the phosphorus from our bows in a broad spearhead of cold white fire. There was a nip in the wind at dawn, and the glass was falling.

At seven o'clock I made land on the starboard bow – Asinara, east a half south, twenty-one miles away by the log. This was just right. But the aspect of it killed all hope of spring: two peaks, down in the sea, gray and misty and dim, like a headland in Tierra del Fuego. Bill came on deck at eight, struggling into a stiff oilcoat, and saw the land; at first he was enthusiastic at the landfall, and later not so enthusiastic. Pat, hearing us talking of hills, climbed up on the side of his berth to look at them – and, after a look, went down again. In the north, black clouds were rolling up, shutting out half the sky, which had become opaque and uniform, and rain-squalls were chasing darkly over the face of the sea. As the hills loomed more and more their tops were cut off in the mist; the clouds spread until the whole northern sector was as thick as lead, and ragged streamers, of a greenish hue, sprouted up from their upper edges. Something was coming.

The wind grew, all during the morning, and a heavy sea rolled up. The glass was fairly tumbling. At noon, with Asinara abeam – the lighthouse was a mere tottering smudge of white, like a ghost – I worked out a course to Bonifacio: north fifty east, forty-two miles. We should have need of a harbour.

Bonifacio lies within the Straits, on the Corsican side. To reach it before dark we should have to carry sail. The Pilot Book confirmed our resolution; ledges and lighthouses and cliffs with caves in them, and a harbour 'difficult to recognise.' Yes; before dark, certainly.

We made no more concession to the first squall than to take in the spinnaker; at the second we doused the foresail; the third was actually on us, black and ugly, filled with pelting rain, darkening the water in streaks, before we lowered the big club topsail. We got it down an inch at a time, successfully, which was no mean achievement, seeing how badly it wanted to blow out over the peak halliards. It came down on the windward side of the main, plastered flat against the canvas, and we laid it along the boom to furl it, and got it in on deck. Then we went for the mizzen. It was broad off, of course, out of reach, and stiff with salt and rain; we quieted its mad struggling finally, and furled it snug. She was under mainsail and jib, then. And sail enough, too.

We didn't expect the wind to hold. It would go down at two o'clock, we thought. But two o'clock passed, and it blew harder. The clouds were swept away, and the sun shone brilliantly; tremendous waves were rolling up, their tops whipped off in whistling spindrift, filled with rainbows; the whole surface of the sea was deep blue and foaming white. There was too much of it; too much sea, too much wind, too much speed. We wanted things to stop for a moment, to give us a quiet interval in which to collect our thoughts. There was no longer any question of reaching Bonifacio before dark; we were wondering only how we should find the harbour entrance when the coast was sighted, and how we should manage to run in in safety with that bellowing wind behind us. In all probability there would be a compact and tangled mass of fishing boats lying beside the quay, manned by pirates and bandits who would wave their arms and scream blighting Corsican curses at us as we came splintering into the midst of it. . . .

However. The seas were breaking all around us, and over us, flinging us forward, head down, roaring and wallowing. We did nine knots at the worst, and as each wave jumped up under our stern and caught us we leaped ahead dizzily, and the log on the taffrail spun like a top. It was time to do something. . . . That whole mainsail was too much to carry. But it was too much to take in. As for heaving to, the time had passed for that; the seas were like breakers on a shallow shore. But it was a simple matter to lower the peak, and we got the throat down five or six feet by a purchase hooked in the second reef cringle. This was the best we could do. The sail set like a great bag, the gaff sweeping out almost to the crosstrees. She went easier so.

Then we saw land on the port bow – very high land, covered with snow. It might be Cape Blanco, on the southern end of Corsica . . . but if this were so, we had missed our harbour, which lay to the northward of the cape, and there would be nothing for it but to run on through the Straits in the dark and spend the night hove to close up under that unknown shore on the other side. There were shoals in the Straits, too, and islands that we should have to pass. In half an hour more land appeared, but did not help us. It would be best to keep up to the northward to make sure – best, that is, from a point of view of piloting, since only so could we keep our harbour certainly to leeward, but quite mad from a point of view of seamanship, since we should have to take the sea abeam. It was no sea to take on the beam. However, we eased up, and tried it.

The ship was thrown about like a stick of wood in rapids. One of those howling combers would catch us, dump a few tons of white water on our decks, and send us whirling. It boiled in over the stern like suds, and broke over the rail on both sides, as far forward as the main rigging; half the time, it seemed, the bowsprit was ploughing under solid water, and the decks were no sooner free of one wave than another came aboard. And we were going like a locomotive. We were charging down on that half-seen coast, over the backs of the hills of water, dropping into the valleys between them until everything was hidden from us, and we from everything, surrounded by a steady halo of rainbows in the smoke of the spindrift. But we got up to the northward.

I went below to consult the chart. It was an extraordinary change of surroundings to come down through the hatch; the whole 'house' of the ship was leaping and capering and flinging through space in an unbelievable way, but the growl of the waves outside was muffled and the wind was gone. It was warm and quiet and secluded. The books in the shelves shifted contentedly back and forth; a sailor's 'housewife' was swinging gaily in circles on its hook. The storm was outside. I stood there for a moment to enjoy it. Then I braced my feet in the angle between floor and wall, took out of the rack the big general chart of the Mediterranean, which had a detail of Bonifacio Harbour in the margin, and unrolled it to see where we were.

The whole south-western coast of Corsica is backed by a range of mountains; there are a dozen snow-covered peaks, and the one we had first seen might be any one of them. The coast at their feet was a succession of capes. I dumped the chart back into the rack again and dragged out the Pilot Book. The capes were all described as 'high and rocky.' We could see them only when a wave lifted us, and when the haze of spray blew clear for a moment. One cape after another, and all alike. There were no lighthouses, no buildings, no islands . . . if only we could pick up some definite identifying feature. . . . Just then a paragraph in the Pilot Book seemed to leap up at me from the page:

'A new beacon on Monachi Rocks has been completed; it is in the form of a white tower, consisting of two truncated conical sections, one above the other; the whole structure is sixty-one feet high; it is named Moines Tower.'

I looked at the chart again, and found Monachi Rocks, a tiny speck, close to the shore. There was no beacon there when the chart was made. But in the Pilot Book there was a beacon. If there was any honour among those patient clerks in Washington, we should sight that beacon. And we would be to windward of our harbour, safe enough.

A hail came down to me from the deck; two voices, shouting together. 'Hi, below!' they yelled. 'A white tower, close to the shore, dead ahead!'

Good old Pilot Book. I stuffed it back into the rack again and went up into the wind.

Between waves we could see it, white, rising up against the dark, misty background of the shore, with white surf at the foot of it. Five miles down to leeward was Bonifacio Harbour. We squared away again, and ran for it.

As we drew near the details grew visible: Cape Feno light, with the cross on the crag behind it, the citadel on the cliffs, the windmills and the wireless station. It was all as it should be. Even the entrance lights, two little white lumps on the gray rock . . . only, there was no entrance. The line of cliffs was continuous, and the surf was breaking all along the shore. We passed Cape Feno – still no entrance. Even at three hundred yards, when we could hear the rote above the noise of the wind in the ropes, there was no opening; it was like rushing at a blank wall. We went forward and got the anchor ready, as a matter of form. At two hundred yards we were still anxiously looking. The big seas rebounded from the cliffs and danced – sharp steep points of water that rose and fell soundlessly, incredibly nimble, like crazy things. The deck was prancing under our feet. Through this boiling nonsense we came shearing down on the light, straight for the solid rock, so close that we could see the panes in the windows of the light-keeper's house, and the tiles on the roof. Then the harbour opened up.

Deep emerald water between high cliffs; a sudden turn to the east; and we looked down the whole length of the harbour, barely ruffled by the little cat's-paws of wind that went chasing over the surface, and saw the quays and the idle fishing boats and the tall French houses standing demurely under the hill. The rollers vanished, the wind went shouting through the sky high overhead, we came gliding in, very stately, very deliberate, spreading ripples from our bows, and let go the anchor at the harbour head.

We had run forty-two miles in four hours and twenty minutes.

We bundled up the stiff mainsail in a great wet mass along the boom, peeled off our oilskins, and stood on deck and looked about us. Bonifacio, at the southern tip-end of Corsica, a port as snug as a wayside inn.

CHAPTER FOURTEEN

Vogue La Galère

*

WE were in harbour all the following day, for the wind went down with the sun, and left a big glassy sea rolling through the Straits; the worst sort of weather, always.

Bonifacio was once a nest of pirates – it makes one faintly envious that the pirates should get all the best things. But previous to that, of course, it was a Roman port, and it is pleasant to think of the long galleys coming in, with the rowers' heads all bobbing up and down in time to the stroke, and the long oars, like the legs of an insect crawling on the sea, churning up the quiet water, creaking and splashing, echoing back from the cliffs. It is easy to picture the place all a-swarm with Romans; the galley with her nose on the beach, the men clambering in and out, the air humming with conversational Latin, and P. Cautious Furious, half pilot and half centurion, standing moodily on the rocks, out of the smoke of the fires, impatiently waiting for supper. And then the pirates came, and the picture grows confused; for who knows what Corsica was like a thousand years ago?

True, the medieval aspect of life is uppermost in Bonifacio. The high citadel looks down upon the town with a stern air of patronising benevolence; the narrow and dirty streets are made more gloomy still by the crumbling flying-arches that cross them from wall to wall and keep the crumbling houses from collapsing against one another's faces; there are beggars and deformed idiots and thousands of subdued and joyless children; the blank doorways open on steep, worn stairs that lead up to poor and dismal habitations; the priests in the streets seem haughtily superior; the soldiers who lounge at the barrack gates have an arrogant and half-contemptuous air. The huddled little town has come down from the Dark Ages, unchanged. But the central idea of the Middle Ages, the dominating and vitalising spirit, the medieval mind, is gone. The electric lights in the houses seem to bring no light to the rooms, and the motor-diligence that connects with the railway is no more than a scornful taunt. Instead of having 'old-world charm,' the place seems merely 'backward.'

Moreover, the absence of hot summer sunlight made it seem not even Corsican.

We got away on the second day, but a cold and drizzling rain killed the wind, and we came back. We beat into the harbour, and worked up the whole length of it in short tacks – a feat which, to judge by the staring amazement of the inhabitants, had never before been accomplished. They gathered in groups on the quays, our bowsprit poking into the very midst of them sometimes as we came about, and we could see them high up on the citadel, leaning on the parapet to look down. Their own method of entry is to strike sail, lower masts, and unrig off the harbour mouth; then they can row in with dignity. Mediterranean small-boat sailors are not 'progressive'; in a pinch, they depend on the good old method of oars, and the business of handling a sailing vessel under sail leaves them astonished, and somewhat sceptical, as at a new form of impious self-assertiveness.

Late in the afternoon of the third day we thought we saw another chance. In that shut-in harbour, which misses complete seclusion only by not having a roof, it was impossible to tell what the weather was doing, but the sunset was good, and the clouds overhead were undeniably moving from the west. We made sail and stood out. Off the entrance we passed a fisherman, who took back some letters to post for us; he seemed delighted at our confidence in him, like a small boy entrusted with an unusually important errand; he heartily wished us 'bon voyage,' and stood idly at his oars for a long time, looking after us.

But the breeze died at nightfall, and we were all night in getting through the Straits. It was not until dawn that the islands of Lavezzi and Razzoli were astern of us, and we looked ahead into a new sea.

A new sea – we had been counting on it. Surely, the high mountains of Corsica would stop those winter westerlies that come from the Gulf of Lyons. Surely, on this side we should find spring. 'Beyond the Straits lies Italy.' If ever the sea smiled, if grass ever grew green, or buds burst in warm sunshine, this was the place. But our sea was gray and hopeless, covered with tumbling white-caps. It rained. The barometer went down to twenty-nine, point four, and stayed there. The wind hauled into the east north-east – right in our teeth – and blew hard for a week. For eight hours we sliced into it, making a scant three knots, five points off our course, with our jib wet half way to the masthead, and every rope taut and humming. The remaining six days of our penance we spent at anchor in Porto Vecchio Bay, on the eastern coast of Corsica.

This is the loneliest place in the world. We came in just at the end of the day, and the sunset through the clouds gave a colour of deep and solid purple to the surrounding hills, and cast a sad and hopeless blue light across the water, as if the sun were never to rise again. A barquentine from Viareggio was anchored in the centre of the bay; she lay all dark and silent as we swept past her, her spars black and sprawling across the sky. There were no lights in the village. There were no boats, no men, no birds, no sound except the faint roar of the surf on the rocks outside, and the sighing wind in the pines at the head of the bay. The light faded from the sky as we were stowing sail, and there were no stars.

The barquentine was bound to Barcelona, and this was just the wind for him – except that, with it, he couldn't get out of the bay. He had come in during the westerly that brought us to Bonifacio, which was the worst possible wind for a ship bound west, of course; now he had his precious easterly, and couldn't use it. The same wind would serve us both for leaving the anchorage, but, once outside, he would be praying for a shift, while our wish would be for continuance. And in consequence we both kept silent, from a feeling of sportsmanship. Besides, it's an ill wind that lasts forever.

Each night at sunset it faltered, dropped, blew from the westward for an hour, and then hauled back to the east north-east. We waited. A time would come when it would go into the west and be unable to get back. . . .

On the shore at the head of the harbour was a warehouse marked 'Société Marseillaise de Bateaux à Vapeur,' and there was a large stock of cork slabs piled on the quay before it, waiting for the next steamer. There were a few lighters for loading and unloading, and one or two disconsolate rowboats, chained, padlocked, and forgotten. Grass was growing in the yard. The shutters of the warehouse were closed tight. The possibility of a steamer's calling seems very remote. The whole place seems remote.

The road winds up a hill to the town. We came upon rickety hen-houses and pigsties first, and then a waggon-builder's shop, with two men listlessly at work in it, and then the town. It is built entirely of gray granite. There is a raw, unkempt look about it, as if the inhabitants were beyond caring what became of things. Indeed, people seem to live there out of sheer indifference. The place is dangerously malarial in summer and is then nearly deserted. 'Nearly' . . . a very nice problem of weighing chances, I thought, on the part of those who stay behind.

We sauntered through to the other end of the town, and then, returning, dropped in at the café opposite the church. A lounging youth with a whip hung about his neck moved aside in the doorway to let us pass. Within: an uneven and much-worn floor of boards, dusty, with holes broken through into the cellar; high windows, over which the shutters were closed and propped – the only light comes through the doorway; a dingy billiard-table with the legs wedged up on shingles, and many tears in the cloth; a marble-topped layout for drinking, with three chairs which had frazzled seats and broken backs. The walls were dark with smoke, and bare, except for a notice which indicated a recent reduction in the price of all drinks. The lounging youth brought us very bad coffee, and we sat and talked of the place we were in, and of places. A flat and meagre environment, as rare, and hard to find, as a perfection of sumptuousness.

A motor-car came across the Square, and we went to the door to see it pass. All the other doorways were filled, too. Having gotten out of our seats, we could think of no real reason for going back to them, and we went on down the street to look for eggs.

We appeared suddenly – and startlingly, too, evidently, for the woman jumped – at the door of a likely-looking shop. The place was sombre and barren, with a stone floor. The woman was seated on a low stool before a fire of brush, making waffles. She thought that she could get us some eggs, and drove the chickens out of the chairs while she went somewhere to look for them. There was twenty centimes in change after paying for the eggs, and we bought a waffle with it. It was very cold and dead, soggy with the steam it had generated in the pile, and doughy inside. Moreover, it was made of black flour. We took one bite each, on the road outside, and threw what was left into the bushes. Three dogs rose wearily from the dust and went in search of it.

We did not go ashore again. We sat in the cabin, reading or playing Russian Bank, watching the barometer and listening to the wind. And, one night, it shifted and died. Died, with its back to the west. We could not trust it, at first; yet in the morning it was still there, faint, but confident, and undeniably from the west. The barquentine was gone.

We got away at once and dropped slowly down the bay. The high, bare mountains with the snow on them, the swamps and the empty pine groves – as for the village, it was easy to ignore it – gave the place a primeval, virginal quality; it might have been a newly-discovered land at the remotest end of an unknown continent, and we, as discoverers, following the traditions of our calling, might have called it 'Better-luck Harbour,' or 'Welcome Bay,' to show that nothing could make us downhearted.

Indeed, nothing could. Italy – and spring – was ahead of us, one hundred and seventeen miles, and the wind was fair.

Our barquentine was away to the south, beating up for the Straits. The wind was light, and shifted several times, but it kept to the westerly sector, and we dropped the coast behind. But the mountains were still plainly visible; indeed, we kept that line of snow in the sky astern of us for more than eighty miles. In the afternoon we were far enough away from the land for the wind to get at us through the Straits; it hauled towards the south, and blew harder, so that the sails filled again, and the log, which had been hanging idly, straight down under the stern, straightened out and marked the miles again. It fell calm at sunset – a clear yellow sunset, behind the mountains – and we made no more than fifteen miles all night.

The day came in clear and brilliant; a big clean sunrise, in a sky without a cloud. The wind blew gently and steadily from the west. Monte Cristo was abeam at dawn, and later Giglio and Giannutri and Elba; far down over the rim of the horizon to the east we could see the faint and misty outline of a mountain – Mount Argentario, in Italy. In Italy. And spring had come. A miracle, of course: that spring should come on the very day that the first peak of Italy lifted out of the sea. We skipped about decks, taking cross-bearings of the islands, marking our position on the chart a dozen times, measuring off the distance that remained to go, in all possible eagerness and excitement. Was it spring you wanted? Why, you had only to . . . .

There were clouds in the south-west. They rose up quickly, and at sunset the sky was covered. The wind backed to the south-west. A veil of hissing rain came trailing over the water, shutting out the sky and the islands, and stealing the colour from the sea. Spring? Spring was a word the poets used. Let it go. We had sailed gray seas before. . . .

My watch began at midnight. When I came on deck the wind had gone into the south, and was blowing fresh; the lights of Civitavecchia were spread out before us in a long line, and the scurrying seas, slipping along, shut them out, and showed them again, in travelling waves of darkness. The big breakwater light was flashing with a sort of sullen fierceness, whirling long arms of light that flashed in turn on the tall spars of the ships in the port and the towers in the town and the black water. Over the shallow sand-banks the waves were breaking noisily, and the big seas rolled thundering in against the moles. And this was our Italy. . . . It was like the dock lights of Liverpool, as you look back at them, through the rain, from down off the Bar light-vessel; a cold northern country, cheerless and wet and bleak. As if there were never to be any spring again . . . ever . . . anywhere.

At half-past one we were close in, reaching up along the mole, looking for the entrance lights; the watch below turned out to shorten sail and get the anchor ready. The wind was blowing directly out of the harbour, and we took a great many short tacks to get in; once past the thumping rumpus at the end of the mole, we were in smooth water, and we were closely followed by a rowboat in which two men were fishing; she carried a bright acetylene torch over her bow and shone it in our eyes as she nosed about us like an affectionate puppy. But we forgave the men because they were speaking Italian.

We worked into the inner harbour and dropped anchor in the very centre of it, under the walls of Michael Angelo's fort. Civitavecchia, 'the principal seaport of the late Papal States.'

At six o'clock a steamer came in from Sardinia, whistling excitedly, in a panic of sobbing haste, to get us out of her way; a towboat came surging up alongside, wild with the importance of her function; we turned out in our pyjamas and hove anchor, and the towboat yanked us out, stern first, as if we had been a naughty child that insisted on sitting down in front of a procession. The steamer dropped her anchor just where we had been, and seemed satisfied.

From Civitavecchia one may take a train to Rome. We left the ship in charge of Piloto, and frequented the trail of the tourists for a month.

CHAPTER FIFTEEN

The Tourist Trail

*

THE Tourist Trail is an excellent institution. It leads to all the orthodox 'best places.' missing nothing; it avoids all worrying difficulty and excitement; it is crowded with People from Home.

Now orthodoxy, of course, is the first essential of foreign travel; excitements – such as buying a railway ticket – spoil endless days of complacency; one is never so happy, really, as when closely surrounded by People from Home. It is so pleasant to be met in the portico by a happy band of intelligent guides who know exactly what one wants to see; it is so satisfying to escape dexterously from the clutches of the rogue who earns his salary by selling tickets; it gives so great an elation of conscious pride to know that the loud-talking and conspicuous people who are now admiring the Queen's bath are actually natives of the Home Town. These things produce such confidence in life.

Why, a tourist had written in the 'remarks' column of a Visitors' Register in Rome, 'Travelling since October 15, 1921, all over Europe.' A very appealing thing, I thought it, and rarely met with in these days of propaganda. If he had travelled off the Trail, we should never know of him at all. And yet, to look at him, you would take him for no more than a commonplace, unimaginative dealer in small potatoes, who never in his life had lived dangerously. But what things he has done! And so cleverly, too. For he has conquered a world, without the necessity of giving anything in return.

I think that it is a habit with him, now. No doubt that in the beginning his wife had reminded him that he always was careless about things, and, fortified by this, he himself had remembered that he had never been able, deep down in his heart, to trust foreigners. It was his great idea to avoid being a foreigner himself. He pretended to compromise with caution in the beginning; until he learned the ropes and got the hang of the languages a bit he would let the guides help with the details. And then it turned out to be so simple to let them do everything. It gave you time to enjoy things, and you got so much more – well, he never would have known, just by looking at it, that that lamp had been burning for four hundred years. Interesting little details like that – did you get that, Harriet? – he would be sure to miss, by himself. No, no; let them run that part of it. And besides, the People at Home need never know. And it's a habit with him now.

Of those who follow the Trail not by habit, but by a natural mental inclination, the best example I ever saw – and the most extreme – was Michigan Charlie.

We met him in a pension at Venice. That chilly little dining-room on the third floor, at the corner of the house, so dusty and tattered and familiar – it was there. The missionaries from Ceylon had left the room; the two Frenchmen in the corner were deep in a discussion of the commercial possibilities of the Adriatic; Belinda was clearing away the cups and plates; we were four at table together. And Michigan Charlie, pushing back his brass bowl of peanuts and oranges, with the air of a man who comes at last to business, opened the conversation by asking me how many hours my Guide allotted to Padova. For the life of me, I couldn't say.

Charlie pointed out that all his Guides were lamentably deficient in this respect, and that he had been unable to discover if the fine sights of Padova were sufficiently meagre to allow of his return to Venice by the evening train. I thought this an explanation, but no excuse, and since he was obviously expecting me to say something, I remarked that my own Baedaker was dated, as I remembered it, 1897, and that I thought it probable that ten hours in 1897 would count as five to-day. Charlie looked sidewise at me, and ate a peanut.

Bill covered the awkward silence by saying that it would perhaps be pleasant to spend the night in Padova after all, even if it was not a matter of necessity. Charlie seized eagerly on this, as a topic. That was just the point. Pfefferkegel gave fifty-seven hours to Venice, and allotted sixteen pages; Holtzknopf gave Padova four pages and a-half. It took but a moment to figure the proportion, but the authors were different. Was the result dependable? Should he risk it? Because, you see, the morning trains accommodated themselves so ill to the hours of the opening of the Galleries that a night in Padova would seriously throw out the schedule; he had one whole gallery, besides one side of a room in another, left to do in Venice; he really must be getting on; there was a Virgin and Child by Somebody-or-other who had already waited for him as long as he could reasonably expect. Charlie smiled ruefully and remarked that he was getting nowhere. Bill and I exchanged glances of sympathetic understanding at this, and asked Belinda for another carafe of wine.

The fourth man, filling another awkward pause, came into the conversation then, and declared himself to be an architect from Denver. It was pleasant to see with what relief Charlie received this information, for he had come upon our friend, that very morning, in the act of making a sketch of the Rialto Bridge, and had, of course, passed by on the other side; now that the man was known as an architect, his eccentricity was excusable, and Charlie felt all right about it. The architect looked across at us, silently requesting credit for having turned the subject of the discussion, which we accorded him by filling his glass. Charlie said that he had at one time spent many years in Denver, and the two set about discovering mutual friends in that city.

'Did you ever know a man named John Purcell?' asked the architect.

'Oh, yes, indeed,' Charlie said. 'Jack was one of my best friends.'

'Then you'd know if he married that girl he was once so fond of, years ago. I can't think of her name.'

'Her name. . . . Ah, I'm afraid I don't remember, either,' said Charlie, and added cautiously, after a moment, 'He is married, I know.'

'But you don't know if it was to that girl he was engaged to for so long?'

'I couldn't say, offhand,' Charlie answered. 'I have it all down in a card file at home.'

Surely, here is a natural mental inclination.

I told this to a girl we met in front of the Vittoria Emmanuele Monument in Rome.

'Ah, yes, of course,' she said, 'you have to be different, don't you?'

She was one of them.

I submit that she missed the point. You can't do everything, anyway; why not select for yourself the things you'll do instead of asking someone else to make the choice? It's yourself you're trying to develop, and not some abstract idea of culture. You'll learn more if you go your own way. And there's such a wealth of innocent fun in all the little toy difficulties, besides.

The ghost of that girl comes floating between me and my page.

'And if we want to do it the other way, why can't you let us?'

I'll not argue with a ghost, madam.

Charlie, my friend, my sincere good wishes go with you; may all your paths be pleasantness, and all your ways be peace.

Why, if it had not been for Charlie's urgent advice, I should never have seen Santa Maria dei Miracoli.

CHAPTER SIXTEEN

The Slogan of the Vikings

★

Now in all this time there had been no spring. There were a few warm and sunny days in Rome; the trees that hung over the brown water where the Arno flows through Florence were of a fresh and tender green; there was one night of misty moonlight in Venice. But these things do not make a spring. The world seemed nearly perfect, but there was an empty space where spring should be.

And when we came back to Civitavecchia again, watching, from the car window, the big breakwater light flashing on the spars of the ships in the port and out across the dark sea, the wind was blowing maliciously from the rainy south-west, and the white spray of the heavy surf was flying across the top of the forty-foot mole like scudding smoke. Day and night we heard the rush and thunder of the breakers, and though we lay at the very head of the harbour, our rigging was white with crusted salt. Cold winds and white rain and a dim gray sea of driving spume – that was Civitavecchia at the end of March. It was a 'late season,' everyone said.

But in Naples it is always summer. The winter gales rarely penetrate so far, the Pilot Book assured us – as if no gale would dare thus to attack the very heart of Italy. A gale, in Naples Bay? We couldn't believe it. The phrase '*O dolce Napoli*' came to our minds, and we could not dismiss it as meaningless. We remembered the slogan of the Vikings: 'Let's go and see.' If the weather wouldn't change, under the circumstances, then we could change the circumstances.

We left on the fourth of April. The wind was right on shore, and there was a heavy sea rolling in from the southwest – a sea out of all proportion to the wind then blowing, or that blew the day before. For two hours we stood out close-hauled, right into the seas, to gain an offing from the bad lee shore behind us. But there was no power in the wind, and it was too rough to do more than dance and wallow, and we turned back.

Almost at once the wind dropped dead. The canvas slammed and cracked above our heads, and the booms wrenched at the sheets. It didn't matter which way we headed. But after the sun went down we found a few puffs to help us, and by half-past nine we were close up to the entrance again, where we were met by our old antagonist, the Sardinian steamer, coming out. We showed a brighter light, up forward, and she whistled to tell us that she saw it, and would pass to starboard, that is, ahead. But she left us very little room. The big gleaming seas were rushing in on the end of the mole, just at our rail, and the steamer, plunging and muttering, with rows of lights in her high black side, was right across our bows. We could see the people on her decks, looking out into the darkness at us; they were thinking themselves very secure and snug, no doubt, and us very forlorn and lost. They were in for a bad night, but they hadn't yet discovered it.

We tied up in the berth we had left. In the morning, the wind was in the north; the seas would be as bad, of course; indeed, they would be worse, because there would now be three sets of waves, one running over the other. But we could not consent to throw away a fair wind and we got under way at once after breakfast, the same crowd of loafers casting off our stern lines from the quay that had been there the day before. A ship leaving harbour will always bring a crowd to watch her go – a pathetic fact, when you stop to think of it.

The rough water checked our progress, of course, but before noon the wind backed to the westward again, and freshened, and we began to go merrily, with the breeze abeam, fifteen miles offshore, well clear of Cape Linaro, and away from the shallow water. The whole coast is flat and uninteresting, and was nearly out of sight when the sun went down. At midnight we picked up the light at the mouth of the Tiber – a black night, if ever was, starless and clear and heavy; a night in a thousand for seeing distant lights – and Cape Anzio, which was the next in order, was abeam when it was extinguished just before dawn. Though, properly speaking, there was no dawn; the sky took on a uniformly lighter tone in all directions, and the day came in from all sides at once.

It blew hard all night, and increased during the day; we carried everything, alow and aloft, and we fairly flew. The waves clutched at the hurrying stern, heaved under the lifted bilge, slammed against the bows and went rolling back in tumbling foam. She lay over to her rail, plunging and skipping, trampling it under her feet, poking her bowsprit into it, rearing up to look ahead for more. She felt that breeze. It did her good. And bound south too.

The Mount of Circe was abeam; offshore we had Zannone, and other islands of that group, 'used as places of exile by the Romans.' This was grand going. We were beginning to look ahead for the land that lay across our course and marked the final turn of the road.

There is hardly anything in life more pleasant than this: to sight land far ahead and watch it grow from a vague shape into something solid and real; to see hills and forests and fields appear, towns and harbours and houses, surf on the rocks, boats pottering along the shore, and people, planted there on firm land, going about their own affairs without once looking out to sea. And you come down upon it and join with it. That it should be there, and real, always seems wonderful. It's as if you dreamed a whole colourful world, with people in it, and saw it take on actuality before your eyes.

Long before noon the land appeared, very indistinct and uncertain, too high, really, to be land, yet too solid and fixed to be a cloud. This was Ischia, on the north-west side of Naples Bay. It was thirty miles away, and time after time we lost it again in the clouds that swept in front of it. But Ischia it was, and in Naples Bay.

Later, the clouds thinned, and we had glimmerings of pale sunlight. Ischia was in sight all the time now; high land, and sharp hills with patches of trees on their sides. Away offshore the sun broke through and shone down on a few acres of tumbling gray water, and in the centre of it there showed a sail. It was a big yawl, running dead before the wind for Ischia passage. She would come thrusting up on a wave until the whole of her black hull was visible, and we could even see the white water under her bows; then she would sink again into a hollow and leave the gray sail to mark the spot where she had been.

Then we saw another sail ahead – a tiny rag of brown canvas, dipping in and out of sight between the waves. We bore down very fast and passed her; she was a little open fishing boat, and the four men in her, who were reefing, looked up and raised their hands in greeting to us. A moment after we had passed them they hove up and sheeted home and came staggering along through the passage behind us.

The land flashed up on all sides; we could see the windows of the houses on Ischia, and the dark tower of the castle, built on a steep rock that jutted out from the shore. Through the gap ahead the outline of Capri, as flat as cardboard, seemed like a tipped-up portion of the gray sea. We rounded the gas buoy on Vivara Shoal, and squared away for Naples.

The wind was whistling through the passage, and for all we were romping along at such speed it was some time before the shores ahead of us grew definite; the city looked like a long line of gray rocks, and all but the lower slopes of Vesuvius were hidden in cloud. It was not hard and forbidding – the associations will not permit it to seem so, but certainly it was not the Napoli of the song.

The town of Pozzuoli began to form in the mists to port, and soon afterwards we made out an enormous range of high blank buildings in the confusion ahead. This was the barracks, mentioned in the Pilot Book as the first conspicuous feature to be picked up by a vessel bound in through Ischia Passage, and making a range for the harbour entrance. We steered for it.

We set the mizzen, which we had taken in four hours before, and then hove the ship to, took in the mainsail, straightened out the gear, and cleared the anchor. Two schooners were beating out from behind the mole, serving to show us the entrance; they were ungainly, high-bowed boats with big foresails, and they came careening out over the seas like rocking-horses, pushing great long bowsprits that poked the sky and rooted in the sea. When we looked up from watching them we found the lighthouse close aboard.

While we were reaching up the harbour Piloto went below and set the table and cooked the last of our Civitavecchia beef, so that dinner was ready as soon as the anchor was down. There was a roar of traffic on the shore, and a million lights appeared in the twilight – we had not been in a harbour so big and busy since we left Liverpool. It seemed exciting, and filled with adventurous possibilities. We couldn't wait to see it.

Pat and I went ashore, but, of course, we saw nothing – you cannot pick up gold in the streets. It was late, and everything seemed finished and put away for the night. We could not manage to find the centre of things, and every street we tried seemed to be leading us away into stagnation. In an hour we came back to the place where Piloto was waiting, climbed through a gap in the high iron fence near the port office, and rowed out through a black alley between the dark still ships. The clouds had cleared, and we could see the red glare of fire in the crater of Vesuvius, shining up on the smoke.

In the morning Pat went to ask the Captain of the Port where we should moor, and he told him to select any berth that pleased him along the San Vincenzo Mole. 'Anywhere except in the harbour,' that meant, for the San Vincenzo Mole is a mile in length, with deep water all along it, and no real shelter anywhere except for a big ship. We went to the end of the line, in the last berth to seaward, before we could find a place to get in, and there for two days we lay and rolled like a drifting jug.

Guido Fiorentino called on us, to make us welcome in the name of the Naples Yacht Club. He told us that the berth where we were lying was not considered a part of Naples at all; why didn't we, he asked, get under way and come over to Santa Lucia? We stared at him, and made him tell us again. He had said it. There was a place called Santa Lucia. Santa Lucia, in Naples Bay. As if a man should come to you and say: 'This is Aladdin's lamp.'

Santa Lucia is off to the westward of the city, away from the port. There is a range of big hotels on one side of it, and on the other the high crumbling walls of the Castello dell' Ovo. On the north a boat-passage leads through under what was once the drawbridge of the castle, into Posilipo Bay, where there is a long curving sea-wall and a line of trees in a park. To the south, across the Bay across six miles of blue water – is Capri and Sorrento, with the purple hills behind it, Pompeii, the Valley of la Cava – and Vesuvius.

The harbour is used only by small fishing boats and yachts.

We came in at the very end of the day; the sky was all bright behind Posilipo, and the water blazed like fire. We rounded in through a great cluttering swarm of row-boats, and Pasquale came out from the club and took our lines ashore. There was a hum of happiness all about us, in the very air, and the sound of many voices. Just astern, on the terrace of a restaurant on the quay, a man was singing *Sole mio*.

And the weather changed; completely and definitely for ever.

CHAPTER SEVENTEEN

Sempre Felice

★

We of the *Caltha* belong to the Rag and Stick School of Seamanship. We don't like motors; we prefer sail. We would rather be becalmed for a day, and sail when the wind did come, than operate a motor and arrive the day before. Moreover, we never saw a marine motor that was easy to start, or that would run properly when it was started. Motors encumber the ship, and impair sailing qualities; they demand constant and loving care, and when they are called upon in some emergency, they do not answer. We don't like them.

But it was plain to see that there was to be but little wind during the summer that was before us; there were many miles and many places left untouched in our programme and, if we wanted to achieve even the half of it, we must have a motor in the ship. And Naples was our last chance to get it.

We poked about the town, looking in the windows and turning the pages of the manufacturers' catalogues, but no one seemed to make anything exactly appropriate to our purpose. We went to one of the English shipbuilding firms, though we knew that they cared for nothing of less than a thousand horse-power, and were told, as we expected, that though it was not precisely in their line of work, still they might look about and see if something could be done. At the end of three days they reported finding a second-hand motor that could be made to answer if it had a new propeller of a lower pitch than the old one; it would take two two weeks to make the wheel, they said, and in the meantime the motor could be set up in the shop for our inspection. This sounded satisfactory; we should see it actually running, once at least. As for the two weeks of waiting – well, we were in Naples.

We made sail and went across the bay.

Early in the afternoon we came into Sorrento. The harbour is a very small one, made by a single breakwater that curves out from the shore. There is space at the foot of the cliffs for a single row of houses, and for the fishing boats that are pulled up on the beach; up above, the hotels and the villas are built on the very edge of the wall that rises from the chimney-pots.

We had tea on the terrace, and sat for a long time looking down at the *Caltha* lying on the still surface of the clear water; the bottom of the harbour, with the anchor chain trailing across it among the rocks and weeds, was plainly visible under her keel. In the distance, Naples was a low cloud of purple; the sea was blue – that Mediterranean blue, which you can almost never see without a catch in your breath, a gasp of incredulity that anything on earth can be so lovely; Vesuvius, posing theatrically, stood at the head of the bay with the level sunlight shining golden on its plume of smoke.

Behind the hotel there is a garden; lichen-spotted statues and banks of blazing flowers and wistaria dropping from the pergola overhead; at the end of the long path an iron gate leads out into the street. Here, in the Square, the protecting saint of the town stands on his pedestal with one foot resting on the head of a dolphin; he looks down the length of the street with a calmness that can come only from having watched the same scene for a hundred years. At the end of the street there is a place where the road crosses a ravine on a high bridge, and from there we could see the sun going down behind Ischia, radiating in flaming bands from the very top of the purple hills. Behind us the tower of the church stuck up into the light.

As we were returning, we saw a shop filled with toy boats. There was a pleasant old man who had long ago left the actual sea, but now expressed his continued friendship for it by making these little ships; we bought one each and sailed them in the harbour when we came back, though it was nearly dark.

After dinner we brought the phonograph up on deck. Naples was a glittering band of light that just showed over the curve of the dark water, but the power-house had failed Sorrento, and the whole town, save for a candle in an occasional window, was in darkness. Some men were fishing along the breakwater, and their light shone down on the clean, sandy bottom and the shadowy, darting fishes. There was not the faintest lap or ripple of water anywhere; the sky was breathless. We lighted matches and held them up, and the flames stood steady and unwavering, like a candle before a shrine. We played the records of all our Neapolitan songs, and people up above us in the darkness applauded after each one, and shouted 'Bravo!'

We were away before the sun was up, because we had been told that there would be a few hours of early morning breeze. But the wind didn't come, and we drifted slowly along the shore on glassy water, like a fascinated ship, silent, except for the faint, rustling noise of the drooping sails. It was noon before we got a breeze to take us across the Bocca Piccola. We beat up under the high walls of Capri and anchored in the harbour.

We sailed our boats again. We thought that the children for whom we had bought these little ships would be pleased to know that they had sailed at Capri, but as we considered it further we saw that the fact would add nothing to the child's imagination, because a ship is a ship, for anybody, and may quite naturally be assumed able to sail anywhere.

It blew hard during the night, and I was out on deck to let out more chain. The night was black and starless, and the seas were thumping on the breakwater. It was a strange contrast to the environment of a few hours before. The wind continued through the sunrise, and we had a fine brave breeze to take us back across the bay again, so that we were sorry we had bought a motor, and resented the necessity for it.

As soon as we were moored we went uptown, and looked about us in a new mood, almost surprised that Naples should not be altered in accordance with our enthusiastic attitude. It did not seem excited to the degree that circumstances ought to warrant. Sorrento and Capri had been there, all the time. And Naples took the fact for granted. This would never do.

We wanted Naples to show its heart to us, to confess that it felt towards life as we felt, and had seen what we had seen. We went up the hill for dinner at Bertolini's.

The view from the terrace was lovely, of course; the moon came up behind the peaks of the Apennines, and we could look down on the whole smooth bay and watch the fishing boats and slow coasters and big steamers moving about across its surface, as if the whole world were some beautiful dream-made toy that we could take up in our hands. But we could find no excuse for the man who, having such a location at his disposal, had not made the best hotel in the world there, and the gentleman from East Orange, whom we met in the bar, would not introduce us to the two lovely girls whom he actually admitted to be his daughters. We came down the hill in a mood of dangerous disappointment.

The next night we tried again, with expectations just as arrogant, and went to the Excelsior, where we should have gone in the first place. As we came up the steps we were discussing whom we should like most to meet, for, though we could think of no one whose presence there was really possible, we were insistent that something should happen. As soon as we had taken our seats in the dining-room I looked up and saw Russel Armstrong.

He had prevailed upon Mr. and Mrs. Richard Higgins to come with him to Italy – or possibly it was the other way about, for each side in the controversy seemed to want the credit of having brought the other. They had come through from the other side of the continent, and had arrived very tired and out of patience with the railways, which was exactly as Russel wanted them to feel, because he wanted them to enjoy Naples. 'Life is an adventure here,' he said. 'You never can tell what's going to happen.'

It turned out that they were planning to drive over to Pompeii and Ravello and Amalfi on the next day but one, and they invited us to come with them. We protested feebly at this hospitality, but Russel said it was very important to him that Mr. and Mrs. Higgins should like these favourite places of his, and that he knew how greatly it would add to their pleasure to have us with them. Before such cordiality as this there was nothing for us to do but get ready to go, which we did. We packed our things in Russel's old 'container,' which still bore on its end the faded 'R.A.' that he had asked me to paint for him when he left Paris to go out to Compiègne in the spring of 1918.

In the morning a car was waiting for us in front of the hotel, and we drove out through the lava-paved streets – a romantic idea, this lava, but unsuitable for paving – and followed all around the shore of the bay through Torre del Greco to Pompeii. We had seen it before, but it deserves many visits, and we wandered very happily through the terrible streets. It occurred to me that if you wanted to learn to appreciate Pompeii you should be a custodian there, and live in that dismal little house near the Forum, in full view of the mountain, and frighten yourself out of your wits by thinking of ghosts.

We went up the Valle di Pompeii to la Cava, through a country of small villages and macaroni factories, and came through a gap in the hills on to the coast road that runs from Salerno to Amalfi.

It is very much like the other coast roads that are like it – it winds along the faces of the cliffs, around the shoulders of the hills, sometimes high up, looking ahead and back along the whole range of the coast, sometimes down beside the water, jumping across chilly ravines where there are ruined 'pirates'' villages, or through the streets of little fishing towns. These sights gave me a feeling that many of the things I had imagined in moods of airy fantasy – houses in caves and villages under the arches of bridges, beautiful girls who lived Romance, bold men who walked through all their days hand in hand with Crime and Danger – were real and actual, and that this was the place. But it would never do to believe it true. Because, you see, if you were sure. . . . And yet it would never do to be sure, either.

The driver pointed out Ravello on a hill before us, an irregular group of houses on a steep ridge. I noticed a row of white posts on the very edge of the cliff – a pergola in a garden, looking out over the world – and began to hope that it was there that we should spend the night.

We turned off from the main road and climbed to the town by looping up the sides of the valley that lay behind it. The little square has a church on one side, and houses on two, but on the fourth there is a stone seat and a parapet, level with the tops of the trees that grow on the side of the valley. In this church, though I had forgotten the fact until I saw it, is the famous and marvellous Romanesque pulpit, a wonder of inlaid marble, resting on twisted columns on the backs of six lions. I saw the sagging hinges of the gate, and the worn steps that lead up to it; I stood close beside it, and put my hand on the head of one of the lions – and up to that moment I had thought it no more than a picture in a book. So long as I had seen it merely drawn or photgraphed, I had thought its existence natural enough, but now – now that I saw it actually to be true, I could not accept it.

We went up the Square through steep streets of irregular steps; cypress trees shot up into the sky behind the walls on either hand, and we could look into forgotten gardens with mossy paths and purple flowers and great red wine jars standing in the spattered shadow of the ferns. When we arrived at the Hotel Belvedere we were unreal and excited, and in a mood to float off into space. It was the place I had seen, with the pergola on the edge of the cliff.

We sat on the terrace in the twilight. The church bells were ringing in the village down in the valley, and we could see the little figures of men and mules winding down the hillside paths into the streets. The lights came out one by one, gleaming deep yellow against the blue-black background of the sea. There was no sign of life down there then; we might have been alone in the world. We kept thinking of coming here for ever, and kept speaking of it. It seemed as if we should do some irreparable harm to the scene by leaving it; as if it existed only while we watched it, and would vanish while we turned our backs. But it has not vanished. It is there – to-night. It is always there.

When the sun came up, I was sitting on the window-sill of my room, looking at that same village down in the valley. The sky was all one blaze, and the sea was bright. The whole atmosphere was too delightful, too serenely lovely, to put into words; the phrases for the description of such things are well worn, and slip from the mind without leaving an impression. Almost it is too beautiful to think of coherently. Not that coherency matters. But I should like to think that I had done what I could to share it.

The Capuccini Hotel at Amalfi is the place where the old monk sits on the pergola wall in the pictures, with the sea and the distant headland behind him. All my life I had told myself that some day I should sit there too, and have lunch under the same pergola.

And as soon as lunch was over we went to Sorrento, where, at the beginning of that very week, I had promised myself to return. This is the place where such things happen.

At Capri, the steamer took us alongshore past the harbour to the Blue Grotto, and we went in. The chief charm of it, I thought, is in the method of entrance. The opening is very small, and an ordinary rowboat could not pass; the boats used are specially built for the purpose, holding only two people besides the boatman, and their gunwales are battered into splinters where they are flung against the rocky walls on rough days. Our day was a rough one. The entrance was choked by every wave. The boats, each with their boatman and two cowering passengers waited their chance to duck in through the arch between waves; the pressure of the rising water within blew off the wave-tops in spouts of roaring spray.

There was a girl in a blue hat whom I had noticed on the steamer. When her turn came the boatman motioned to her to lie down on the floor of the boat. She drew herself into her husband's arms, laughing up into his eyes as if to remind him that she had done as much before; and then the chance came; the water roared out over them like the Horn of Doom, and they vanished into the centre of the earth. It was a startling statement.

That night, when the steamer came back from Capri, we saw Santa Lúcia from the other side of the picture: we were among the tourists who were rowed through the excitement, instead of being a part of the background, as usual, seeing the excitement from within.

But, indeed, the excitement had spread all over Naples. The streets seemed more gay, and our favourite café more friendly; the shrines on the walls of the houses seemed to have a new sincerity about them, to replace their former tawdriness; the people who sang in the restaurants seemed more human artists than they did, and the ships in the port, and the taverns along the waterfront, seemed to hold possibilities of endless escapades. Life in Naples, Russel had said, was an adventure; you never could tell what might happen. We saw it no longer from the outside, a stage set, a piece performed; we saw it from within. It was our adventure.

Two days after our return, when Russel and Mr. and Mrs. Higgins had gone to Paris, the shipbuilding company sent a towboat for us. We were dragged away from Santa Lucia and anchored off the Works in the main harbour. The towboat's crew used chain heavy enough to hold the *Majestic;* they seemed to be making plans to keep us there for a long time.

The motor was set up in the shop on a timber foundation, looking very efficient. The starting handle had not yet been rigged, but two men wound a rope on the fly-wheel and spun it like a top, by walking across the room with the end of the string. It started off merrily enough, and ran with great confidence and spirit.

The first day's work began at two o'clock in the afternoon with the arrival of five workmen. It ended at four. There were days when three bolts were tightened, and nothing else done at all. There was one day when a steel plate was brought aboard, measured and marked, and taken back again. It required some part of each of the first nine days to set the reverse gear in place and bolt it down, and we had a constant feeling that it might at any time be taken entirely out again for the solution of some new trouble. The floor boards were taken up, so that the saloon looked like the inside of a wreck, and we had our meals with the table set down on the ballast, on the level of our knees. The cabin was piled high with all the movable furniture in the ship. The linoleum hung over the boom. The deck was cluttered with planks and scraps of greasy canvas.

The base of the motor was brought aboard and set in place, but the bolts did not fit, and a day was spent in discussion as to whether it was better practice to decrease the size of the bolts, or enlarge the holes. And even when this had been decided, no step had been taken to align the motor. The propeller, after a week of argument and diving, was sent back to the shop to be turned larger so as to fit the shaft; it was perfectly evident that the hub was too small, from the very first, but reluctance to admit anything kept alive a long series of experiments. The diver came up, time after time, and said that it needed a fiftieth of an inch, all around, but the chief mechanic said that he didn't see how this could be true, and sent the diver down again.

On the eleventh day Lorenzo began to see himself, in the mirror of our comments, as something ridiculous, and took steps. On the twelfth day the starting gear and the exhaust pipe dawned over the horizon of difficulties. On the fourteenth day the carburettor and the water connections forced themselves into the calculations.

This was the Directory of Personnel:

Theory Guiseppi, the chief mechanic. He has a steel rule and a thickness gauge; he allows nothing to be done in his absence, and he is present for an hour a day.

Luigi the Lifter. He sits all day long on the fore deck beside the hatch, holding a rope in his paws; when there is something to be lifted down below, the rope is attached to it by those in the galley, and Luigi lifts, without rising from the box on which he sits.

Roberto the Revolt. He has a wife and child to support; were it not for them, he says – he breaks off, and places the first finger of his right hand crosswise in his teeth, bites it savagely, glaring, and shakes his head like a growling terrier with a rat.

Bold Lorenzo, who believes in courage. He aligned the motor one afternoon while Guiseppe was ashore. For this he nearly made the Supreme Sacrifice, but the Chief Engineer of the firm pronounced the work well done, and so saved him. It took him two hours.

Pietro la Piccirella, the wrench-passer. He passes

wrenches, and fishes up washers and nuts that have fallen into the bilge.

Deep Tony, the diver. He sinks in the sea, and rises to say that the hole in the propeller hub is too small for the shaft.

Giovanni the Scream, diver's helper. He asked me to take his picture wearing the diver's helmet, as a gift for 'mia amorosa.' He has told her that he is the diver.

Black Angelo the Silent, diver's helper. He helps the diver to dress, holds the air line, and turns the pump.

On the fifteenth day we went for a trial trip. The motor ran – though it stopped twice, for no assignable reason, within a mile – and the ship did move – though it was evident that we could hope to make little progress against a head wind, and against a head sea, no progress at all. It would not be fair to say that we were delighted with it. But we were greatly pleased to have it finished. We put the floor boards down again, cleaned up the ship, and restored things to their former state, so that it was quite as if the motor were not there.

On the sixteenth day the exhaust pipe was wrapped with asbestos. When it was done, and the mechanics had gone ashore for the last time, taking their tools with them, and asking for presents as rewards for their skill and speed, which they did not deserve, and did not get, we could think of no good reason why we should not go back to Santa Lucia.

We dropped the ponderous mooring and started the motor. Halfway across the harbour it stopped, because of a bad plug. The plug was changed, and we went on,

Just after we had rounded the end of the San Vincenzo Mole it stopped again, and no diagnosis would reveal the difficulty, nor any changing of plugs effect a cure. We spent half an hour at it, and then covered its face. We went into Santa Lucia under sail.

There is a glamour about Santa Lucia, and an excitement, that nothing can escape. We came in with the last of the evening breeze. Just behind us was the steamer, coming back from Capri, rolling in the beam sea, spouting black smoke. The boats were coming out from the shore in a swarm to meet her, their gunwales bumping, their oars tangled in intricate confusion, their rowers shouting and arguing and bursting out into snatches of the old inevitable songs. The tourists, with their wraps and baskets and parasols, moved through the tumult stiffly, like smiling images pushed from behind, sitting very straight, with a great assumption of calm, yet shivering with a communicated excitement, as if they could hardly wait to tell of their experience. They had been to Capri, and had now returned to Santa Lucia – and they were touched with inspiration. And through the throng of boats the *Caltha* came sweeping in, scattering them before her like floating chips, letting them close in behind her like the sea itself; her bowsprit was soaring above people's heads, her big club topsail thrusting up into the yellow sunlight.

Just outside the breakwater, their sails gleaming like old silver, were three of the club knockabouts, dipping and skimming like swallows. In the narrow lanes of open water inside the harbour an eight-oared shell was shooting dangerously up and down, stopping short, with all oars reversed and holding water, when some crazy warped little boat of naked boys blundered out into its path. It seemed as if everybody would be run down and sunk. Over near the drawbridge, in a veritable village of boats, fishermen are piling nets, their trousers rolled to the thighs over their brown legs. The boys dive for pebbles and scream. On the streets above, hundreds of people are leaning on the balustrades to watch – young men who sing songs, very attentive to dark-eyed girls in white dresses and floppy hats who laugh and twirl flowers in their hands and tap on the pavement in time to some imaginary dance. In the restaurants the orchestras are playing, and some one takes up the chorus of a song, singing as if he were alone on a hilltop, singing 'as if his heart would break.' And the twilight deepens and the colour of the sky becomes too lovely to endure, and the lights come out along the Posilipo shore – and you would sing, too. For you cannot escape the glamour and the excitement of Santa Lucia.

A man was waiting with our supplies, and Pasquale brought a great sack of bread, which he dumped down on deck like so much cord-wood. We went up to say good-bye to Signor Fiorentino, and he took us into his bar and bought champagne for us, and toasted the *Caltha*, and we drank to him, and to Naples, and to the Island of Cephalonia, off the west coast of Greece, which was where we were going.

We went down aboard, carrying the laundry bag. Piloto put up the lights. Bill started the motor. We hauled ahead to the small anchor, which had been out over the stern, close to the breakwater. As soon as it was apeak Bill put her into reverse; we backed away, swung clear, and went ahead. The bay was very dark. As we passed through the little entrance, Signor Fiorentino and four or five members of the Yacht Club came out on the terrace and cheered us. 'Good-by, *Caltha!*' We cheered in answer. They stood there, looking after us.

The lights astern grew fainter, drew together into a single blur, and sank into the sea. There were fireworks at Torre del Greco. The course was south a half east for Capri Passage. It was my watch, and the others were busy making sail. They put everything on her, plain sail and kites, and shut down the motor. Then they went to bed, and left the quiet ship to me.

I called Pat at half-past three, and just as I went to sleep I felt the ship heel down, and heard the water growling past the planks, and knew that the night breeze had come.

CHAPTER EIGHTEEN

The Road Again

*

So we took to the road again. It seemed marvellously fresh and untouched, an uncontaminated creation, apart entirely from the world that had so much of human complexity in it, so much red-and-brown intricacy of hopes and fears and little, shifting, emotional distractions. Out there was Creation, simply. A sort of abstract dawn. Other more familiar and saner things formed no part of it; it was, itself, Existence.

The sky was cloudless, of course, and the sea very calm – on the shadow side of the ship, where the light shone under the keel and struck up through the water it was blazing, glaring blue. The dinghy, toddling along astern, pattering over the water, was floating in a pool of strange, thick, gaudy colour like the blue of translucent blue glass.

At night the stars came out and blazed like white fires. They were so clear and vivid that the distances between them were as visible as the distances that separated them from us, who looked up at them: they filled all space. There is less of monotony in life at sea at night, perhaps because there is no expectation that anything will happen. The stars move so fast, and there are always different ones to see, and millions of them. And at night, besides, there is always a sense of a meaning in the world, a feeling of some significance, hidden for the moment, but just on the point of becoming clear.

At our first sunrise we were through Capri Passage. The mainland, a wild, forested, almost uninhabitated portion of Italy, lay twenty miles to the eastward, and Capri itself was behind us. In the interval between the night wind and the day wind there were only scattered breezes lying isolated on the water, with broad lanes of calm between them. We hunted these out with the motor, sailed through, and out on the other side of each, and went chasing after the next. The sea breeze came just before ten o'clock, and we pushed along all day very quietly and contentedly, having it abeam. We heard again the old voices in the rigging, the sound of two women talking, that we had first heard between Ailsa Craig and the Mull of Galloway. The waves went gurgling easily and pleasantly past the ship, not growling, as in rough weather. By nightfall, Capri was gone, and there was only the inland hills in sight, very faint, with clouds on their tops. The sun went down into the sea.

At eleven o'clock, it being my watch, I saw something on the horizon ahead. A red glare of fire. It came unannounced, silent and terrifying, bursting up from the inside of the earth. Stromboli. It blazed up like a flaming hand, hung in space for a moment, and then died in a slow fall of scattered sparks. The name Stromboli, I had been told, should be pronounced with the accent on the first syllable; this gives it a grander sound in the mouth, I think, and makes of it an epithet more in keeping with its quality, a quality of resounding bombast – an eternal melodrama of gnomes. I had seen Stromboli once before, but it was different from my remembrance of it: it blazed once in several minutes only, and not every seventy seconds, as I had thought, and the flame was bigger and more torch-like. I was a little disappointed at this, for the circumstance seemed to take away something of the faithfulness of the mountain; I like to think that it has blazed dutifully since the days of the Romans – a period brief enough in the life of a volcano, to be sure, but long to us, since we see it from the human side. I like to think of the steersmen of the galleys watching for it. At any rate, there is no lighthouse there.

It was gone at daylight, of course, and it was not until late afternoon that we saw the island itself. It was the first land of a group new to us. We were getting somewhere. Ships began to appear – we must have had twenty sailing vessels in sight at once, all bound north, some keeping close to the coast for the land and sea breezes, some standing up offshore past Stromboli on the course that we were on. This was good company. They all came together, as if they had been suddenly released from bad weather in the Straits – as, indeed, they were.

At dark we picked up Cape Vaticano, and during Bill's watch, which was the one with the dawn in it, we rounded Peloro and headed down through the passage, between Scylla and Charybdis.

There was little wind in the Straits, and we ran the greater part of the distance under power. We lay for half the night off the very toe of Italy, placid and breathlessly calm, seeing the trains rumbling along the shore – dim lines of moving lights – and hearing men talking, and a donkey braying, ten miles away.

At midnight the wind came from the north, and we set a course due east, across the Ionian sea for the island of Cephalonia, distant two hundred and twenty miles.

It was a grand wind we had, then. Day and night it held, shifting a point or two backwards or forwards, following the time of day of the sun, exactly in accordance with the rules laid down for it in the Pilot Book. Grand going. The ship was skipping and dancing along. Sparkling blue water, and an empty sky, with no land or ships or clouds or birds in sight. In the afternoon we passed a drifting board – a part of some poor lad's deck load, no doubt, skelped off him in a bora, somewhere up the Adriatic – and I fished it up aboard, and Bill made a seat of it, to use on deck at the tiller. We sighted nothing else. Blue water. This is the place. Breakfast and lunch and dinner and night; hour after hour of sailing. Perhaps we could have managed with a bit more wind, having it on the beam, where it did no harm to us. But even so, we were only twenty-nine hours from land to land.

When Piloto took the helm from Bill, he asked if there was anything for him to watch for.

'Yes,' said Bill. 'A high mountain, on the port bow, at dawn.'

Piloto saw it. Monte Nero, on Cephalonia. It looked to us just as it looked to Odysseus, when he came home from that long Mediterranean cruise of his – Ithaca lies just behind it. That was after he had been shipwrecked and cast up on the beach where the Princess and her maids were playing ball. But we came romping up out of the wine-dark sea, watching for Monte Nero, with a beam wind and a tight ship under us – and saw the mountain of Cephalonia on the port bow, just as he did.

The wind failed near the land, as it is quite likely to do, and we ran all the morning under power. The Gulf of Argostoli opened up, and we could see the island that lies off the entrance of it, a long row island, with a lighthouse at the southern end of it, and a dismal monastery in the centre. On the shores to the north we could see houses among the cypress trees. Greek houses. And we saw a shepherd in a field.

We rounded in to Argostoli harbour. The lighthouse on the point is a circular Doric temple, with a colonnade, and a very small lantern, added like an afterthought, on the roof. The town, the capital of Cephalonia, lay on the other side of the ridge of land where the lighthouse stands. We were very keen to see the town . . . not that it would be so grand, but that it should be there at all.

The harbour opened up. A long quay of yellow stone, very low, and behind it, extending the whole length of the harbour, the town, very neat, very hot, and very quiet. It was Sunday morning.

The first building was a mill, built by the edge of the water, with the word "βέστος" on its end – a thing more startling to see than a Greek sign on Sixth Avenue. After the mill there came an open meadow, and then a large box-like house, built of stone and ivy-covered, with a hip-roof and a flagpole; there were trees in the dooryard, two gate lodges beside the sky-blue gate, and twenty-two windows that looked out across the harbour. We saw at once that this was the residence of the British Consul.

After a further interval there was a church with a statue in the park in front of it, and then the town.

There were several small vessels lying off the quay; little schooners, shaped like gravy-boats, and one, done in the Venetian manner, with broad bowl-like bows, which turned out to be the *Nuevo Pietro* of Rimini. It was just noon when we anchored, and while we were at lunch a boat came alongside with two evil-looking young men in it; they had but two eyes between them, and they spoke in Greek. It was kind of them to do this; we had been looking forward to it. Then they asked us, in French, if we needed any bread. We didn't, and they left us.

About three o'clock, though it was still very hot, we went ashore. The sun was fairly blazing on the white roadway. The air was dry, as if it had been baked. The houses were shuttered tight, and all the shops were closed; the town seemed to be suffocating at the bottom of a pit of white-hot gas that was pouring down on it from the sky.

We walked through to the end of the street, wishing very much that we had a drink, but having no money to buy it. In some of the cafés men were sitting at little round tables – Greek-looking men, who seemed quite at home and unsurprised, and did not even evidence surprise at seeing us. In some of the back streets there were trees and men were playing bowls in the shade. Then we passed through a narrow lane, paved with cobbles, and lined on both sides with closed doors of rough, unpainted, age-furrowed wood, eaten away at the bottoms, and scarred by years – the sort of doors through which desperate adventures emerge into life.

We came to a place which seemed to be a post office, and seeing some men within, through the windows, and thinking that there might be a chance to change some money, we pushed open a door marked "ΕΙΣΟΔΟΣ," and went in. The company present did not speak French, which we tried on the men behind the counter, nor Greek, which they tried on us, but they understood our intention and counted out to us two hundred and thirty drachmæ, for two hundred Italian lire. Then something happened . . . a surprise. I had thought to find surprising things in the island of Cephalonia; I found it surprising enough, indeed, that I should be there myself. But this . . . I wasn't prepared for this. This was too much to guess. All the money was cut in half. Every bill – cut in half.

We turned back at once to the café at the corner, and asked for wine. The boy who brought it had but one eye. We stared at him rudely. This was the third. We wished that we had looked more carefully at the men in the cafés we had passed, and at the bowlers under the trees in the back street. Did the Greeks do things by halves entirely?

The bottle that was brought us bore the name of 'E. A. Toole, Cephalonia,' and while we drank our wine we kept asking one another what the devil it could mean that all the money should be cut in half. We hit upon various explanations, but nothing very reasonable. When the boy brought the bill, which amounted to eight drachmæ, we gave him half of a twenty-five drachma note, and found, by the change which he returned, that it was worth twelve and a half. At first, this seemed natural enough. A moment later, it seemed impossible. We gave the boy a drachma. Perhaps it looked like two, to him. He thanked us politely, but we shall never really know.

We rowed back along the quay to a little stone landing-place and went up the path to the Consul's door.

CHAPTER NINETEEN

The Inviolate Isles

*

THE maid who opened the door was short and dark, with black eyes and smooth-brushed black hair, and she had the round face that is the type of peasant face the world over. We asked for the Consul, and though it was plain that she did not understand the words, she stepped back and motioned us to enter. We were wondering whom we were to see.

The Consul appeared almost at once, having heard voices and footsteps – a small man, rather old and fumbling in his gestures, with an uncertain, far-away look in his eyes. He wore white duck trousers and an ecru pongee coat, and his necktie had slipped down below the fastening of his collar. There he stood, looking as if he were about to scream and dart suddenly out of sight through the doorway behind him. Pat said that we had just entered the harbour and had come to report to him – that being the only excuse we had thought of for our visit – and the Consul, muttering 'No need to report; no need to report,' bowed us into the room.

It was about thirty feet long, and broad and high in proportion, with pale blue walls and bare scrubbed floors like the holystoned decks of a ship, and the ceiling was painted with borders and coloured ornamentation like a room in an Italian house of fifty years ago. There were three windows on the long side, and one at the end, and the white lace curtains that hung before them were bulging airily out with the breeze. The dining table in the centre, of dark polished wood, was enormous; it would have seated sixteen people. A red felt cloth covered it, and there was a vase of flowers in the centre under a fussy old lamp of brass and china and blue glass that hung from a heavy whitewashed beam. At places about the walls some pieces of fine old furniture made spots of darkness in the general whiteness of the room, and over the mantel were two crescent-shaped slabs of wood, of unguessable purpose, studded with brass nails, on either side of an elaborate ebony-cased clock – these things served as reminders, and gave the place an Oriental and exotic air. But just beside them were several framed photographs of long ago cricket teams, with men in striped blazers and small round caps, who looked woodenly out of their remote English background without consciousness of their incongruity.

It was rather bizarre, and yet delightful, and perfect for such a climate – through the open windows we could look across the harbour to the blue slope of the hills, silent and breathless, quivering in the heat of the bright sunshine, with idle water as still as a mirror.

A young man came in. 'This is my son,' the Consul said. He was tall and sunburned, and he had the manner of a man who has been in a great many places. His welcome to us was more demonstrative than the Consul's had been; indeed, the Consul seemed not to have talked in English with anyone for a long time, and was evidently relieved at the son's arrival. We started cigarettes all around, and began to talk.

'. . . The British at one time held this island, you know; they were the ones who built the roads and all the public buildings – as a matter of fact, this house that you're in now was the military hospital at one time; that's why the rooms are so large. There were four wards, you see. My bedroom's as big as this room. Actually. My grandfather came out here in those days, and founded the Ionian Bank, and then when Mr. Gladstone saw fit to give back the islands to Greece – or sold them back, or something – my father was made Consul, and stayed on. My father was born here. Well, so was I, for that matter. . . .

'. . . I'm merely home on leave, you see. I have a job with the League of Nations at Salonika, because I happen to know the languages. You do have to know them out here, as a matter of fact. It's very curious, really. You'll be at a dinner, or something, and the man next you will be talking Russian, and the chap on the other side doesn't know a word of anything but Turkish, and you have to answer a question in Italian, and then translate it across the table into Albanian, or listen to a story in Serb or Rumanian or Bulgar, or something. It's very curious. And not bad fun, I mean to say. Everyone speaks six or seven. . . .

'. . . Perhaps you've heard it. But it seems there were these two beggars, and they were selling brooms. And one chap says, "'ang it all, I don't see 'ow you can sell these bloomin' brooms for a shillin'. I steals the brush, an' I steals the wire, an' I steals the 'andles, and *I* can't sell 'em for a shillin', and mike any money on 'em." And the other chap says, "Ho!" he says. "I steals 'em *ready-made*." . . .

'. . . He'd shot bigger game than ducks, you know. The year before that he'd killed his brother, and he suggested to me that morning that we kill the Crown Prince of Greece, because he was "no good." It seems that this chap and the Prince had scared up a wild boar in the bushes, and the Prince didn't fire, and the boar got away. Of course, he couldn't be sure that the gun was loaded properly, could he? I mean to say; you couldn't blame him, could you? And I had a devil of a time persuading this man not to kill him. He was a fierce-looking old pirate, with enormous moustaches like a buffalo's horns, but a good-natured, harmless old chap, really, when you came to know him. . . .

'. . . There were some holes in the rock – I don't know what to call them, really. They were like pot-holes. In fact, there was a whole series of them, close to the edge of the water. And if you dropped in a bit of straw, or something, it was sucked right down and disappeared. The suction was tremendous. There was a Greek here – I've forgotten his name. But it doesn't matter. This chap had a bright idea, and he connected up a lot of these holes together, and then he cut a channel in the rock from the harbour to this series of holes he'd made, and put a mill-wheel in it. The mill is there now. I dare say you saw it, as you came in; it says "βέστος" on the end of the building. That's the mill. It ran for years, and he used to grind flour in it, but they don't make any flour here any more, and it's been abandoned. There was a constant current into those holes. Curious thing, wasn't it? No one ever understood where the water went to. I mean to say: it simply went down. There was an Italian gunboat over here at one time, and they dumped in any quantity of colouring matter – barrels of it – and watched to see where it would come up. And it never came up. . . .

'. . . That table has a history. It used to belong to the Seaforth Highlanders. . . .

'. . . That's quite all right; he didn't cheat you. Well, you see, it's a very clever scheme, really, if you look at it from the point of view of the Government. They wanted money for the war, and nobody would lend it to them, so they simply cut the notes in half. There's a man's head on one half of the note, if you've noticed, and a crown in a medallion on the other; they simply called in the half with the crown. It's a forced loan. They got half of all the money in circulation, that way, at once. At once. They pay interest on it, of course, and all that sort of thing; it's simply a loan. The man that works for wages – your labourer – is just as well off as he was before; it's where a man had got something saved up – I mean, a little something put by for his old age, sort of thing – he's the man that suffers. He's got only half of what he thought he had. . . .

'. . . Well, see here. If you want to get some wine, come ashore in the morning – say about ten o'clock, if that's all right for you – and we'll go up to my uncle's place and see what it is you want. And then you must come back here and have lunch with us. . . .'

And so, thinking of these things, we went back on

board and sat for a long time after supper talking of life in Cephalonia. A very quiet night, with the stars shining in the water.

I was awakened about six o'clock by the sound of girls' voices. I went to the companion and looked out. It was completely calm, and the sun was just coming up over the rim of Monte Nero. A boat was passing – a big open boat, with an awning set, and a high lateen sail hanging in drooping folds above it. Forward were two men, rowing; they were swarthy lads, very solemn in countenance, and they braced their bare feet on the thwarts as they tugged at great beam-like oars. In the stern sat three nuns, holding black parasols. The body of the boat was filled with girls; they were all in white, with broad flower-trimmed straw hats, and they trailed their hands in the water. They were singing a Greek song, very clear and sweet, with verses that seemed to tell a long story, and an interrupted cadence in a minor tone that seemed to go on forever. I watched them go rippling up the harbour, the tall peak of the sail reflected below them in little detached darting spots of black.

After breakfast we went ashore to the little landing, where the Consul's son was waiting for us. He came out aboard with us to see the ship, and then we rowed back along the shore again to a little wharf near the mill, where we landed and went up to visit the wine factory.

Mr. Toole met us – a small round man, with a brown beard and a roguish twinkle in his eye, who spoke his native English with a Greek accent. He took us in.

A great room like a barn, open-trussed at the top,

with swallows playing in and out between the rafters, filled with rows and rows of big dark casks of wine. A storehouse of treasure, filled with honey-hearted wine. The place seemed very dark, after the brilliant sunshine on the road outside, and cool, so that one felt secluded and sheltered, and quiet, so that one could hear the whirr of the swallow's wings. 'I often wonder what the vinters buy, one half so precious as the stuff they sell.' The precious juice of the grape, treasured away here in big dark casks.

A noble-looking old fellow, whose name was Dmitri, operated a bamboo syphon and brought us samples. First, some of the 1878; Mr. Toole would like us to take some of this, he explained, but it would hardly serve as a table wine, and travel in a small ship, with so much motion, would spoil it. Then, 'to show the difference,' he offered us something that had been made the previous year. The grapes are grown on Monte Nero, and brought down in slow, creaking waggons over the dusty roads, and treaded, ten thousand pounds at a time, in primitive presses of a pattern devised five thousand years ago, which, 'strangely enough, produce a better product than modern machinery.' Nothing is added; the bacillus of fermentation is in the skin of the grapes. It is strained and put in the vats, where it ferments for fifty days. After that, Time works the miracle – it stands in the wood for forty years. The precious juice of the grape.

We looked at the still where cognac was made, and went up to the office above the storeroom, where we were presented to the other two members of the firm – one, who looked like Silenus, rotund and merry; the other, dark and scraggy, speaking only Greek. There were Greek maps on the walls, and Greek account-books scattered about on the high desk, but the books on the shelves were English, and the chairs had come from London. It was quaint and strange: these three elderly gentlemen in their shutter-darkened office, speaking Greek with one another, keeping the accounts of their business in Greek, living off there in Cephalonia, as remote as hermits, with their treasure stored down below them in the great rows of silent casks.

Mr. Toole took his seat at a table in the centre of the room, exactly as if he were a king, holding audience, and we gathered about him in a half-circle, smoking cigarettes and talking, and now and again mentioning the wine we were going to buy, which was, to be sure, a legitimate subject for the meeting, though it was serving us merely as an excuse to be there. It was finally decided that we were to have some of the intermediate grade, old enough to have distinction, and yet not too old to travel. While Dmitri was preparing the little cask we sat below in the courtyard among the presses, under an arbour, with the swallows darting and twittering above our heads. Dmitri rolled the cask down to the landing and took it out aboard, and we watched Piloto heave it up over the rail on deck.

Then we went to the Consul's house to lunch. We sat in the 'long room,' above the dining-room. It had five windows on the forty-five foot side, and two at the end; a grand piano – very large and old-fashioned, more like a harpsichord – was lost in it. There was pleasant old English furniture about, and bookcases at the end of the room ; though there was an atmosphere of bareness about it, produced, perhaps, by the naked, scrubbed boards of the floor, yet one would want nothing different in such a climate, and there was a livable, resourceful feeling about it. A delightful place to live in, satisfying and tranquil and detached. It was impossible to imagine a better way of living, in all the world of possibilities. What did a little loneliness matter, after all?

Yet the younger members of the family felt a sort of resentment. This was simple enough to understand when one considered that there was, for them, a certain necessity in the circumstance, and an obligation, which removed the element of choice, and substituted instead a feeling of predestined fatefulness. The daughter, who had travelled enough to know that the rest of the world truly existed, was staying merely because her father found it pleasant and congenial; she would have been displeased, and perhaps a little disquieted, if she had been told that her English had a slight foreign sound, because then she would have felt that the very processes of her mind were being attacked and altered by her isolation, and her longing to get away a foolish sort of hopelessness. Her cousin had come from Russia five years before to escape the revolution, and was still there. One might say that she was stuck there. During the war the French had kept a cruiser at Argostoli, and she had had the adventure of seeing somebody. But that was over now. She was resigned to it, and merely sighed sorrowfully when it was mentioned, without feeling bitter.

'We have to live here, and so . . .' The Consul, who had lived there for seventy-two years of his own free will, was in a different case.

During lunch it became evident that we were being envied because of our freedom. We had never been to Athens, but now we were going. And then we would return . . . and reach Europe. Our hosts did not think of themselves as in Europe. And yet they were not in the Orient. They were out of the world altogether. They spoke of Paris as something unattainable, something over and done with, like an episode in history. Of London and England they did not speak at all. The Consul spoke enthusiastically of the climate of his islands, of the pleasant coming and going of the seasons, of the mellow breezes that blew upon them from the Adriatic. 'Eternal summer gilds them yet,' he quoted, and then, in a flash of communicated sadness, he felt constrained to add: 'But all, except their sun, is set.'

At times it seems that there is too much senseless gregariousness in the world, too much scampering after a restless excitement that is alike the aim, and the source, of no more than the excitement itself, and at those times it seems that these people are living as every one should live. But at other times it seems that they are condemned to a Purgatory of sun-bitten hills and miserable loneliness.

Well, somehow, we must be satisfied.

We rowed out to the ship and got under way. The breeze was fresh from the north, and we took two short tacks to get out of the harbour. As we passed the Consul's house we dipped the ensign and waved our caps, because we could see two figures leaning on the sill of one of the windows of the 'long room,' one in black, and one in white. But there was no answer to our waving, and when we rounded the light and put the ridge of land between ourselves and them, they were still there, motionless, looking after us.

CHAPTER TWENTY

The Golden Spearhead

★

THE wind fell light and went ahead; we were all night in getting through the passage between Cephalonia and Zante, and it was not until seven in the morning that we were definitely inside, in Greek inland waters. It was very light weather all day, and very hot; we ran the motor, and succeeded in getting as far as Cape Papas by dark. There was a thunderstorm, but without wind; during my watch, I sat on the stern, hanging my feet over the rail to push off the dinghy that kept nosing up under the counter, and watched the lightning go leaping nimbly from cloud to cloud. It was everywhere, in every valley and on the top of every hill, as if signals were being passed to indicate that some great plan of catastrophic destruction were ready for execution. I sat and watched it, and was impressed with the strangeness of the fact that I was in the Gulf of Patras. There was a strange look to the surroundings – for all it was so dark that no details were visible – the hills were different from other hills, the thunderstorm was unreal and vague, and there were no lights on the shore. Strange. Greece, a country far away.

Towards morning the lightning faded and died away, and a breeze came up from the north-east, growing into a smashing wind at sunrise. It was dead ahead, straight down the Gulf. We kept up along the northern shore, past Missolonghi, beating for the Narrows. We passed Patras, which is a vague, scattered, undecided place, with no discoverable character except an air of having been founded during the previous week to meet the needs of some immature 'boom.'

But the aspect of the country was lovely. The cultivated lowlands near the shore, and the valleys, had a fresh and luscious look about them, and the hills, though they were for the most part bare and craggy, were infinitely variable because of the shadows of the clouds that passed across them. 'As long as the shadows of the clouds shall cross the faces of the mountains.' Homer meant those shadows that we saw. Those were the mountains that he had in mind. He was thinking of mountains . . . but *these* mountains. It kept occurring to me that we were now in the place 'where it all happened'; we were in the exact environment of the old Greeks; this deep gulf that let the sea up into the heart of the land, this blue water, these dim headlands, these surrounding hills with the shadows of the clouds passing across their faces–were their world. They discerned a beauty in the world – and were thinking of this; they discerned a beauty in life, and a promise – a promise, indeed, greater than life showed itself capable of fulfilling, since, when they had pushed on to the farthest limit, they somehow failed – and these hills and seas must have come in for their share of the blame for the failure. One looks about at their world, and feels that it was not the principle that failed, but only the Greeks. And there we are.

Through the Narrows, we had a sloop to race with; we were gaining on her, and would have passed her on the next leg, but she stood over across the Gulf and went into a cove. It fell calm at sunset and remained so all night and until afternoon of the following day. Then we got a fair wind. We had a three-piece spinnaker pole, patched up of the boom-crutch, an oar, and a boat-hook; we set it, and carried on till the pole broke, which happened just as an admiring passenger-steamer was passing us. It took overboard our best bucket when it went. We did come charging up the gulf. We passed Parnassus and the Vale of Delphi, and at sunset Melangavi was abeam. We ran the motor all the time; it pushed along in a loose-jointed and excited manner, trying to keep ahead of the moving water.

Before dark we saw a notch in the crest of the line of hills ahead. The lights at the end of the canal are very small ones, and we did not sight them until we were close in. The features of the shore were very difficult to recognise, because the heaps of canal deposit were of various colours and shapes, and, in the dim starlight, looked like hills and fields and woods, which they were not at all. But we made out the two breakwaters, and steered in and anchored, without knowing quite where we were. There were lights on the white building beside the canal entrance, but no one came out to us, as we had expected, and we went to bed.

A coasting schooner came in during the night and anchored near us, and at half-past four in the morning we were awakened by the clatter of her windlass pawls as she hove short. We got up at once, and I rowed Pat ashore to the office. He asked permission to go through the canal, speaking French, and the man in charge granted it, speaking Greek. The understanding was curiously perfect – still, I suppose vessels never come to ask any other question, nor expect any other reply. Bill had the motor going when we got back aboard; we hove up, swung around, and went into the ditch.

It is perfectly straight, cut through the rock as one would cut through a cheese, with straight walls rising nearly vertical on both sides. Behind us, a barquentine was hove to in the offing, standing back and forth to wait for the towboat that was to come through to get her; we could see her square grey sails against the sky as she passed the opening. We set our foresail to help the motor, for there was a draught through the cut, as if some one had left a door open, and went gaily through in defiance of the rules which forbid carrying sail in the canal, and insist also that 'yards shall be braced up, and all boats swung inboard.'

There is always something thrilling in going through. You come out on the other side into something new and different. The experience is especially moving if, as in this case, the passage is an artificial one, for that means that other men, before you, have felt the need you feel, and have devoted their energy to satisfying it – Nero began that passage through the Isthmus of Corinth, and we came out into Salamis Bay.

The town of Posidonia, at the eastern end of the canal, is a primitive little place, surrounded by deposit heaps and the remains of machinery. We were boarded by a canal official in a white uniform, who came alongside in a launch, and made out the necessary papers among the remains of breakfast on the cabin table, while we were drifting out through the entrance under bare poles. He worked very quickly and efficiently, which surprised us, since he was the first Greek official we had seen. The barquentine was still in sight through the cut, on the European side ; her towboat cast off from the quay and went surging through to get her and bring her back into the Orient. We made sail and squared away across the Gulf of Salamis.

The breeze was fresh, directly over the stern, blowing from Mount Parnassus, and we made eight knots. As we came across that bay we felt four thousand years old; we seemed to have been sailing in those waters since the *Argo* set out on that first cruise of history, and when we rounded the headland at the southern point of Salamis, and saw the Acropolis rising above the plains of Attica, we could see the sun shining on the golden spearhead of Athena as plainly as though it were really there.

'. . . I suppose you're an Athenian?' said the dolphin to the man whom he was ferrying across the sea. 'Of course I am!' said the man. 'Then you know the Pireus?' 'Know him, indeed!' said the man. 'He's one of my best friends!' The dolphin threw him off his back and drowned him. Æsop, I suppose, had the story from the dolphin. . . .

Pireus, the port of Athens, six hundred and sixty miles from Santa Lucia.

We sailed into the harbour carrying everything, with the intention of selecting exactly the berth we wanted—near the centre of the town, safe, clean, quiet. The whole margin of the port was lined with ships, and we came close and looked into every open space as we passed, without finding what we wanted. We shortened sail, and began to tack into an arm of the harbour that was crowded with sailing vessels, whose masts we could see over the roofs of the intervening buildings. But this, of course, was too simple to be permissible. A man appeared alongside in a rowboat, shouting 'Pilot! Pilot!' and telling us that we couldn't go where we wanted to go. This had an official sound, and we gave up, and asked the man aboard. We explained to him what it was we wanted, and he nodded rapidly several times, and said that he had the very thing for us. He said that he wanted ten shillings, but we told him he must mean ten drachmæ; after a time, he thought so, too.

He took us to the worst berth in the harbour. It was nearly out to the entrance again, backed up against an iron shed where all the thieving scum of the port gathered to prey on whatever Luck should send them. Luck sent us. They watched us with hungry eyes as we drew near; when it became evident to them that we were actually going to moor in their territory, their joy was lovely to see – they fairly pranced up and down their narrow strip of quay, offering advice, pointing out the methods and processes that seemed to them most to be commended, and holding out their arms to catch our lines. We moored; the pilot rubbed his hands in satisfaction, and the robbers squatted in a long swaying line on the quay wall, their teeth fairly chattering with excitement and eagerness. We pointed them out to Piloto, and, seeing the old bull-fighter's look flash in his eyes, went tranquilly ashore.

It was amusing to see the Greek signs all about us, and we spelled them out as we went, wondering what they meant. But there were some signs in French, and one which read 'Concert John Bull' which hung before the door of a desperate-looking dive of sombre rooms and dingy windows. A low Greek drinking den is a horribly sinister idea. But farther along the street we came upon a Greek who was playing a zither and singing, and we learned what vice could mean. The street was thick with dust, and we were obliged to step down into the worst of it, each moment, to make room for passing waggons, for the sidewalks were piled high with merchandise of every description, as if the place were a supply depôt in war time. Finally, a tram came, and we piled on. We were impressed with the courtesy of the conductor, who had so much to trouble him – for the car was very full – and yet would take the time to be polite to us, who did not understand his language. We were impressed, too, with the cheapness of the fare; it appeared that this tram would take us all the way to Athens for a sum which, because we were unable to compute it, seemed negligible.

We emerged from the waterfront streets and came out into broad squares and parks with trees, very neat and clean, and shining with newness. There was a café, with chairs and tables set out under cool white awnings, and a great range of automobiles drawn up in front of it. The effect on us was immediate. We were parched for aristocracy and high living and splendour; we became too haughty for the crowded tram. Nothing would do for us but to drive to Athens.

Fifty drachmæ was what the driver of the nearest Ford wanted. We questioned this, and the man brought out his tariff sheet, which was written, or rather typewritten, in Greek, and turned out, on examination, not to have Athens on it. A crowd gathered to see what it was all about. We enjoyed this at first, but the fun soon wore off, and we agreed to fifty drachmæ, which we learned later, was the regular price, and might have been accepted in the first place.

The car took us through a complicated maze of side streets – that peculiar wailing buzz of a Ford horn! – some of which were unbelievably shabby and disordered, lined with low white houses, unkempt and left to carelessness, with listless people and dirty little wild-animal children squatting before them, and impeded with scattered boulders and trenches and cañons cut in the baked hard earth by the rain. From this we came out onto a road that skirted Phaleron Bay, with piers and hotels and cafés and bath-houses and gardens, and the blue Ægean rolling in on a broad beach. Everything looked new.

A broad, straight boulevard, lined with trees, led up towards the Acropolis, and we whirled in. We looked for traces of the Long Walls, which we remembered from school days, but we saw only that the Greeks were fond of advertising. Every barn and wall was covered with signs. In Stadium Street a tyre went flat, and we got out and looked about us.

Our first duty was to find a café. Without a café you

can't do anything. We were not long in discovering what we needed; a large, liberal, confident sort of place, facing a plaza, where the whole of Greece moved up and down before us. We could sit back in assured comfort and watch the panorama; we could watch it and laugh at it, and discuss it, and feel ourselves a part of it – and have more coffee. This was our headquarters; this was the place where we were to be found.

Yet it was not at our café, but at a restaurant farther down the street, that we had our most serious conference. That restaurant is clearly before my eyes, and, it seems, will always be so: our table in the corner of the room, beside a door that led out to another part of the hotel; our straw hats and sticks piled on a piano that stood near; the room filled with quiet, unhurried, easy-going Greeks, talking and gesturing; the whole place lighted one-sidedly by the white glare reflected from the sidewalk outside; and we three, our plates pushed back, ash-trays before us, leaning earnestly forward to discuss the most solemn subject that had come before us for many a long day. Nothing less than the end of this cruise.

We were like men who come suddenly to the end of a trail that they have been confidently following for years. We stopped dead, where we were. It is easy to say that we might have known that we couldn't go on forever, but that is exactly what we did not know. It is easy to say that one can't stay at sea forever, but that is exactly what we thought we could do. We felt ourselves possessed of a natural virtue of continuity.

And now we saw that our time was up.

Partly because of the bad weather along the Spanish coast the year before, partly because of our natural unwillingness to move on while there was so much to see and do in or near the delightful harbours where we had stopped, partly because of our failure to realise that the things we must omit couldn't all be in the future – our time was up. Sicily and Sardinia had long ago been taken off our list; Crete and Rhodes and Cyprus didn't know us; Smyrna, the cities of the Cilician Pirates, the 'street of four hundred columns' that was marked on the charts, were tales told by minstrels; the Adriatic was out of it; the whole North Coast of Africa was represented in our minds by a thin line of blue hills on the horizon. Constantinople and the Cyclades were within a hand's breadth of us, and we were within a hand's breadth of missing them. There were other considerations, in the past and in the future, some trivial, some important and insurmountable. The whole made a complication through which we could find no path. There was no help for it. Our time was up.

But it is when your time is shortest that you can do most. We went to Constantinople – we went in a steamer, but we went. And, after our return to Athens, we took a short expedition, under sail, to the Cyclades.

CHAPTER TWENTY-ONE

O Commander of the Faithful

*

THE RETURNING TURK

I AWOKE very early on the morning that was to bring us to Constantinople, expecting to open my eyes on a wonderful scene, but the view through the steamer's porthole was of nothing but a smooth sea, misty, reflecting back the heat of the sun. After a time a sound like brushing aroused me again, and I saw that our Turkish room-mate, who occupied the berth under mine, had gotten up to prepare his suitcase for debarkation, and was standing looking through the porthole while he carefully removed the dust from a new fez. When he stooped I saw a mosque. It was framed in the porthole. The image shimmered in the heat, and seemed like a mirage in the mist that hung before it, dreamlike and unreal, with a character of fairy gold about it. It was less than a quarter of a mile away, standing back among big trees on a hillside, trembling and mysterious, covered with the pale, golden colour of the sunrise. I should not really have been surprised to see it shrink and vanish.

The Turk stood there, holding his fez in his hands, looking out; his bullet head, which was lumpy in contour, and covered with stubby gray bristles, kept interrupting my view of the mosque as he moved. He looked out on it quite complacently. He did not turn his head to see if I was awake and watching it; it did not occur to him that the view through the porthole could be of exotic interest to the stranger who was behind him. To him, it simply meant home. He was thinking – in Turkish – that he was back again. 'Well, here we are,' he was saying. And turned again to his suitcase.

I got up as soon as he left the room. It had been my intention to dress very quickly and rush up on deck with my camera, in enthusiastic eagerness. But the Near East seemed to have caught me, even at the very beginning, and I didn't care to hurry. The mosque would be there for ever. I was in Constantinople, which fact seemed sufficient for the moment.

I came out on deck just as the anchor dropped. Pera, rising up, looked rather like Boston – the buildings were square-cornered, with a great many windows, and higher than the buildings one is used to in Europe. Across on the other side was Stamboul, still dreamlike, half hidden in the haze.

I had always held to a fancy that the Near East was only 'East' in an inferior degree – a weak imitation, and a compromise of the Far East. As if it had tried to be 'Far' and couldn't, or didn't dare. 'Well, not the Far East, you know; only the Near East.' Like counterfeit fox furs. I had thought to find the Near East overlaid and confused by the characteristics of every nation on earth, and without any characteristics of its own.

Someone on the steamer remarked that Rangoon was a city completely characteristic, unsullied by any foreign influence, and entirely Oriental. Perhaps. But I know very well, without ever having been to Rangoon, that there is a ship-chandler there who comes out in a boat to meet incoming steamers, and shouts up, in English, 'Good-morning, Captain; what can I do for you to-day?' and is told, in English, to go to hell. Thus there is a blot on the landscape, and Rangoon is mixed with an adulterating element.

But in the Near East, the quality of mixture is a part of the character. It is not that the Oriental aspect shows through an overlay of Western civilisation – the two civilisations are there together, and have been since the Near East was the Near East – and in consequence of this one is confused and baffled, looking for some fancied reality hidden away underneath, when it is there before his eyes.

The activity of the port was astonishing. Great swarms of Bosphorus caïques were careening and wallowing about under our stern, and under the sterns of all the steamers, in a reckless, abandoned manner, the men in them shouting and shrilly screaming as if they were in a bitter quarrel with everybody, and yet pulling at their oars calmly – calmly, that is, in comparison with the tumult of voices and water that was about them. On the quay were people from everywhere. Through the crowds went army carts, French and English and Italian. There was an air about it. It seemed very natural, and exactly suited to the connotations of the phrase 'in Constantinople, during the siege.' A clattering mixture, bobbing up and down in an atmosphere of hazy golden light, unreal, introspective without being self-conscious, set deep in a background indefinable, yet definitely recognisable, and in it, through it, head and shoulders above it, the Military. Jingling. With cork helmets. The Near East.

We went down the gangway into it. Our Turkish room-mate, with his Italian suit and his Athenian suit-case and his carefully brushed fez, felt in his pocket to make sure than he had his keys, and went steaming energetically up the street.

THE STORY OF THE FIRST MERCHANT AND THE BEADS

In one of the streets that leads up from the Galata Bridge towards Hagia Sophia I stopped to look in the window of a shop. The proprietor at once came out to meet me, bowing and rubbing his hands in anticipatory pleasure, and assured me that he enjoyed having me look at his merchandise, whether or not I found anything that I wanted to buy. This method of business is very distasteful to me, and it is my very attempt at polite avoidance of it, I suppose, that makes me such an easy prey. The merchant's geniality is so obviously counterfeit, and his courteous protestations so plainly insincere, that it seems little short of criminal to see through them. In consequence – as always happens – in fifteen seconds from the time I had stopped at the window, I was in the rear of the shop with the merchant, uncomfortably examining pearl pen-holders and brass bowls and inlaid daggers and ivory elephants and embroidered tablecloths and embossed card-cases. I asked the prices of a few uninteresting bits of rubbish, and quite put the merchant out of countenance by refusing to be either surprised or indignant at his replies.

With a desperate flourish, he placed before me a red glass bowl filled with scarabs, and asked me what I would give for it. I tried to tell him, but the word stuck in my throat. I could not admire the things nor depreciate them. As for the scimitar and the samovar, which were next in order, they may stay where they are and rot into disintegrated dust, before I will argue about them.

From this I was rescued by the sound of the words 'There he is!' uttered in an unfamiliar voice, and looked up to see a doughy-faced young man in a fez who was pointing me out to Bill and Pat.

They came in, and asked me if I had found anything interesting.

'Have you any beads?' Pat asked the merchant.

'Yes, sir. Certainly, sir.' The merchant dug both hands into a drawer under the counter and covered the top of the showcase with beads.

'How much for these?' Pat asked, fishing out a string.

'Ah, that beautiful amber necklace!' cried the merchant, stepping back, holding his head on one side, to admire them as Pat held them up. 'A museum piece, really.'

'How much?'

'Well, sir, to you, thirty pounds.'

Pat dropped the beads with a fine affectation of haughty indignation. 'I'll give you five.'

The merchant spread the necklace out across his palms and gazed at it. 'Museum piece, museum piece,' he murmured, happily.

'They're not real amber,' Pat said.

'Real amber,' said the merchant, quick as an echo, only changing the tone.

'Why, it's the same stuff they have in every shop in Naples.'

'Not like this,' said the merchant, smiling sadly.

'No; better.'

'Listen, my dear sir,' said the merchant. 'I'm a business man.'

'So am I,' said Pat.

The merchant dropped the beads in question and chose some others from the pile. 'Something in beautiful coloured glass, sir?' he asked suavely.

'From Venice,' said Pat. 'I can get you all you want in the Piazza San Marco for sixteen lire each.'

Well, it ended by Pat getting the amber beads, and two strings of glass ones, for eighteen pounds – Turkish pounds.

THE HISTORY OF THE BARBER'S SECOND SON

When we came out of the shop the doughy-faced young man in a fez was waiting for us and followed us up the street.

'Who is this bird?' I asked.

'I don't know,' Bill said. 'He appeared from somewhere and told us you were in that shop. I guess he thinks he's a member of the club.'

Indeed, he clung to us like a lonely puppy, and when I set down my camera case for a moment he picked it up and insisted on carrying it. This, of course, gave him the right to walk with us, instead of a few paces in the rear, as he had been doing, and he began to talk.

'My father was a barber and he never had a great deal of money, but he made up his mind that my brother and me were to have a good education. My father wanted that we should go into business, and as soon as we were through the High School he sent us to the college. My brother studied English because he thought it would be a benefit to him. Of course we spoke French already. And I studied German, because I thought we had so many Germans here and we did so much business with Germany that it would be a benefit to me. And so I spent three years in learning to speak German and then I was for nearly two years working in a Turkish importing house that sold rugs in Germany. And when the war came I was too young, you see. And I wanted to come back here to Constantinople. . . .'

We passed through an ancient gateway at the end of a street and stooped to crawl under a heavy chain that was hung across from one side to the other. We thought it curious, and the Barber's Second Son explained that it was to prevent the passage of automobiles. But there were iron posts three feet high and three feet apart, set across the whole width of the street, and an automobile could not have passed, even if there had been no chain. When this was pointed out to the Barber's Second Son he said that there was a queer kind of Turkish cart, with wheels so high that the body of the cart passed over the tops of the posts. . . . I thought this very ingenious of him, seeing that he had had no time to think. He felt obligated to know everything, and to have some answer ready for anything that we might ask.

'But they told me that I could not go back. So they kept me there in Germany. And I had a letter from my brother in England, and he said in the letter that he was trying to get into the English Army to fight against the Germans because he did not want that they should get Constantinople. And so I told them. . . '

We came to the 'Cistern.' This, he told us, was a huge vaulted and colonnaded hall, under ground, and filled with water; the existence of it had been known for a long time, because of the fact that historical documents mentioned it, but its exact location had been doubtful, even though for a long period of years people had been drawing water from the wells that were pierced down into it. It was accidentally discovered by a man who was enlarging his cellar, and now there is a boat in it, and a curious tourist may row about by torchlight between the elaborately ornamented columns. Houses and streets are built completely across it.

'I told them that I wanted to go back to Constantinople to get into the Turkish Army, and they knew that my brother was on the side of the English, you see, because they find out everything. And they said that they would not let me go because they did not want that I should go in the English Army. And I did not see what I could do then. And I wrote to a friend of my father's here in Constantinople, and he was in the Office of War, you see, and he got the Office of War to send a letter for me to come back to be an officer in the Turkish

Army. It was an order, you see. And so I showed it to them. . . .'

We emerged into a great open space which had once been the Hippodrome of Old Byzantium. On either side of it there was a mosque. One of these mosques was Hagia Sophia.

I think we spent two hours wandering about in that magnificence. We were utterly tired, and it did not seem possible that we should have any enthusiasm left for anything, ever again.

Painfully, dragging our feet, we turned back down the hillside street by which we had come up, and went into Stamboul again, to visit the Bazaars.

'And so I showed it to them and they laughed at me and said that if I was going to go into the Turkish Army it was the same thing to go into the German Army, because they were going to be friends with Turkey. So they made me go into the German Army and I was a Corporal. You see, my brother was in the English Army, and I was supposed to be fighting against him! Only he was stationed at Mitylene, and it was his work to read the letters that were found on the Turkish prisoners that were brought in. And in a place called Krachack . . . . '

The Bazaars are rambling tunnels, joined together in an intricate system of mazes; in the vaults are square openings, through which the slanting sunlight pours down, making dusty prisms in the gloom, and spots of vivid radiance on the floors and walls. There are booths and counters along the sides of the tunnels, and the merchants sit upon them, surrounded by their merchandise, which is heaped and hung about them in dim and cobwebby confusion. The merchandise is fascinating, even though so much of it consists of articles that can be called no more than 'second-hand,' and we tried to restrain one another from buying great quantities of useless junk which would be a satisfaction to us in later years, after all, only because of the fact that we should be able to remember buying it in the Bazaars of Stamboul.

Certainly there is a charm about the place that comes near to compensating for the necessity of doing business in the traditional Oriental way, and I found myself much more willing to argue about prices when the whole place looked so like a den of thieves that buying and selling in the ordinary simple manner seemed effete and ridiculous.

We went afterwards to a rug auction, where there were a great many Turks sitting about an open space, bidding on rugs that were spread before them. We sat on benches beside the door, and the Barber's Second Son translated some of the auctioneer's patter for us, and told us the amount of the bids. He said that this was a very good way to buy rugs – or a very bad way, I have forgotten which.

At the conclusion of all this we went across the tunnel and into a hole in the wall – and it developed that the Barber's Second Son kept a shop in the Bazaars himself! We could not understand the psychology of his bringing us to his own shop after we had been, under his guidance, to all the others, and had neither patience nor money to buy anything. But he blandly spread a handful of rings out on the corner before us, leaned across it, and said:

'And in a place called Krachack I was taken prisoner

myself, by the English, and as soon as I was better of my wound they put me in the headquarters to talk with the Turkish prisoners that were brought in. And so I was able to do something to keep the Germans out of Constantinople after all. But my brother. . . . '

We gathered up our parcels and wearily started out of the shop. But he caught up his fez again and hurried after us, to make sure that we took the right tram. He was a queer fish, altogether. He had plodded about with us for more than six hours, carrying our bundles, acting as guide and interpreter, and speaking for us in the shops. We had bought nothing from his own shop, and had rewarded him with nothing more than one cup of very bad coffee. And yet he remained with us until our tram came, and said:

'But my brother says that he and me were very fortunate, because Turkey was on the wrong side in the war, but we two were separated on opposite sides and so we were on the right side together. And I think so, too.'

THE STORY OF THE SECOND MERCHANT AND THE BRASS BOXES

Pat was so much pleased with his success in the matter of the beads that he fell in with the Oriental manner with great vigour and enjoyment, and I found him in one of the booths in the Bazaars negotiating for a brass box. At first I thought that he was buying it for pure love of argument, but when I looked at the box I was convinced of its charm. The merchant was asking forty pounds for it, and Pat was telling him, with great conviction of manner, that it would cost no more than three dollars on Second Avenue in New York.

'Do you think you can fool a Scotchman?' Pat asked.

The merchant laughed, and said, 'I should not try.'

'But you're trying now,' Pat told him, and bought the box forthwith for twenty-five pounds.

I was so delighted with this that I picked up a smaller box from a table near me, and, in what I intended to sound like a burst of desperate frankness, offered three pounds for it. The merchant was interested in this, and we talked about it for some time, throwing figures back and forth between us, but in the end he let me have the box for the price I had named.

When we returned to the hotel and spread our purchases out on the table for review, I discovered that the box I had bought was plainly marked on the bottom. The price was three pounds.

THE ADVENTURES OF THE COUNTESS AND THE FLOWER GIRL

The scenes in the streets of Pera – which, because it is the 'foreign' quarter, and different from Stamboul, achieves a double strangeness – are immensely fascinating. As we walked along the Grand Rue de Pera in the evening we saw Turkish bankers and veiled ladies and Chinamen and British Tommies and American gobs and Greek porters and French admirals and Italian staff-officers and Armenians and sight-seeing flappers and Arabs and waifs from everywhere. There was a large number of Russians, wandering in the streets because there was nothing else for them to do. Many of them were still in uniform, though some of the officers had fallen so low as to add a civilian hat or jacket to their dwindling equipment, and privates, who had obviously kept their uniforms solely because they had nothing else to wear, had drawn their belts very tight and were trying to sell toys that they had whittled, or coat-hangers, or books of poems, or shoe-strings, and some were disabled, or wore signs around their necks and held tin cups in their hands. Through such scenes we passed on our way to a cabaret where we had been told that we should see the best of the night life of Constantinople.

The restaurant itself was in a basement underneath a theatre, but the ground sloped sharply down from the street at that point, so that the dining-rooms and dancing floor opened on a terrace, before which was a spacious garden. There was a tent for the orchestra at one side, and set about in the gravel paths were tables and chairs; in the centre there was an open space of cement for the professional dancers, facing a simple but ingenious stage, and between the cypress trees at the back there was a view of Asia, across the Bosphorus, on which the moon was shining.

We took our seats at the edge of the terrace and bought some flowers for our table from a girl who was peddling them about among the guests. This girl was an insignificant little thing, and though she spoke English, her attempts at conversation were very halting. We got rid of her by sending her for the waitress.

Although she wore an apron, and took our orders in a

strictly professional manner, the waitress was quite obviously a lady. We had been told, previously, that a great many of the wealthiest and best-born people of Russia had found a precarious sort of refuge in Constantinople, where, though they were entirely without resources, they were demonstrating their right to the title of 'aristocrats' by courageously operating restaurants, or working in shops, and, in general, making a living for themselves by doing work for which they were totally unfitted, by training or by education, to do. This lady was beautiful, with very large dark eyes, and she made graceful and very expressive gestures above the table with fascinatingly pretty hands. During the latter part of our dinner she came and sat with us, and, at our urgent request, told us her story.

Her husband had been a Count, one of the largest estate owners in the vicinity of Moscow, an officer of the Imperial Guard, and a man of great wealth, so that the 'revolutionaries were after him' among the very first. At the time of the catastrophe she was living at their town house in Moscow, together with her husband's mother and her own younger brother, a boy of eleven. A mob of marauders, under pretence of serving a warrant for his arrest, broke into her husband's house, in spite of his protests, and in defiance of the fact that he was armed. He pushed his family behind him, overturned a large library table so that it served in some sort as a barricade, and faced the mob in the doorway with the promise to shoot the first man that crossed the threshold. While the crowd hesitated and seemed to consult together, some one in the rear ranks levelled a rifle and shot the Count through the heart. The marauders then all made a rush together.

She had attempted to reach the revolver that had fallen from her husband's hand, but before she could do so she was caught, nearly choked, and thrown on the floor, while the gang busied themselves in forcing open a desk, in the corner of the room, in which her husband kept his papers. In the confusion, and owing chiefly to the fact that the men had taken the candles from the mantel in order to have light for their search, she had managed to slip away with her brother and made her way to the garden at the rear of the house. Here she had hidden in a cistern, but the boy, as he attempted to follow her, was seen by someone in a rear window, and, not being willing to betray her hiding place, had run to the stables. She never saw him again. The water in the cistern was frozen, but the ice had broken under her weight, and she had been forced to remain in the water up to her knees for nine hours.

The house was wrecked, looted, and partly burned, and she did 'not know what to do.' She went to a friend, also a former army officer, and asked for his help. He promised to find a way to send her out of the country, and, until this should be possible, offered her hiding in his own house. She walked there, through the snow, in evening dress, wearing a soldier's overcoat.

On the third day, the captain came for her, dressed as a peasant, and bringing similar clothing for her, and together they took a train, which, she was told, was to go to Odessa. But the train got no farther than Kharkov, where the captain took her to a hotel that was used as a headquarters by the revolutionaries. 'And there,' she said, 'he had me quite at his mercy.'

Twice she had attempted to escape, but had been brought back, and finally a guard was stationed, day and night, before the door of her room. This was 'fortunate,' for she was able to bribe the man, and, pretending that she was an army nurse, on her way to duty at a hospital in the suburbs of the city, had gotten out to the open road.

Then, by the help of farmers' waggons, by walking, and, towards the end, by joining herself to the straggling trains of refugees, she had managed to reach Odessa. She had offered her services in caring for the sick on a Black Sea steamer, and had been given a passport for Constantinople, but for Constantinople only.

That was three years ago. In April, she had had a letter from the captain, who had sent her papers, and a part of the necessary money, and asked her to join him in Geneva.

We asked her if, considering the circumstances, she would be willing to accept the money and go to him.

'Oh, yes!' she said, eagerly, and then, realising how incredibly inconsistent this must sound, smiling wistfully, looking out at the moonlight on the Bosphorus, she added, 'At first, I wanted to kill myself. But now . . . now . . . I'm . . . Oh, can you understand? I'm fond of him, in spite of everything.'

At this point she was obliged to leave us for a moment, and while she was gone the flower girl returned, with her tray of red roses. She insisted on talking to us. She was a Countess, too.

THE SEVENTH, AND LAST, VOYAGE OF MOHAMMED THE SIXTH

We had confided our passports to a courier whom we had met at the hotel so that he might secure for us an invitation to have tea with the Sultan. This we thought a great honour – and the courier did nothing to lessen the impression – but we learned later that the privilege was open to any one who could convince the authorities that he was not an anarchist or a spy. For myself, I looked forward to the visit with great apprehension, for I was sure that a Connecticut Yankee in the Sultan's Court could hardly fail in committing some breach of Oriental etiquette in the presence of the twenty-four wives to whom we would no doubt be presented. But as we approached the palace I was comforted by the sight of many other foreigners, who, to judge by their dress and manner, were no more familiar than I with the niceties of Court procedure; we were all to be in the same boat, I thought, and by committing our faults together would take away some of the blame for our individual clumsiness.

Just in front of the palace some soldiers were occupied in dragging a man along the street. He was in rags, and very dusty from rolling over and over in the gutter in his efforts to escape being clutched, and now they had him by the collar; he bent his knees in the manner of a devilish child who refuses to walk, and was being scraped along down the hill, shouting and gesticulating, with his tattered coat hoisted up about his ears. Our courier told us that this man was a well-known character, who came every Sunday to speak to the Sultan, and was every Sunday dragged away. 'For of course,' the courier said, 'they would never let him speak with the Sultan.'

We were received very courteously, with deep bows, by several officers in splendid uniforms, and were ushered into a room which commanded a view of the street along which the Sultan was to pass on his way to Prayers. The room was furnished in the style of the French Decadence, with a large and elaborate mirror above an over-fringed mantel, and might have been the musty and tattered parlour of any *pension* in Paris. We saw at once that we were to get no nearer than this to the magnificence of the inner palace, and took our places in the windows to look out into the street below.

Troops were gathering. We had been told that the Sultan went to Prayers at a different mosque each Sunday, and that when it happened that the day's mosque was on the opposite side of the city, the lines of troops, which were continuous along the whole route, made an imposing sight; on this particular Sunday, however, the Sultan had selected a mosque that was hardly more than across the street from the palace, and the military escort was restricted to small companies of each of the sort of troops that were at his disposal. They were very various, in uniforms of white or red or field grey or green, and just under the windows was a splendid line of mounted troops in blue and gold. Bands were stationed at intervals between the companies. A man came out of the mosque and spread a red carpet on the steps. A motor sprinkling cart appeared and watered the roadway. An Officer of the Household walked down between the lines of troops to assure himself that all was ready. On the minaret of the mosque a muezzin, in his black turban and flowing robe, came out and leaned on his elbows on the parapet of the little balcony. At the head of the hill a very dashing cavalry captain, gorgeous in crimson and silver, with a flashing sabre, stood motionless and expectant, facing the palace gate.

It was very quiet; we could hear the faint hooting of the steamer whistles in the Golden Horn, two miles away.

All at once there was a stiffening in all the ranks, a scraping of feet, the noise of palms slapped against the stocks of rifles as the men came to attention; the troopers advanced their lances, with pennants fluttering, and the horses all raised their heads and pricked their ears forward; at the head of the hill the captain's flashing sabre whipped up to the salute.

The Sultan rode alone, in a victoria. He was dressed as any one would be, except that he wore a fez – which, to be sure, is no sort of distinction in Constantinople – and he reminded me faintly of a history teacher that I once had in High School. He looked up at the windows of his palace where the guests were gathered and responded to the salutations.

As he passed each group of soldiers there was a flourish of brassy music from the nearest band, and the men in the ranks, presenting arms, shouted 'Long live the Sultan!' Then the next band crashed out, and the lusty shout was repeated. And behind all this, serving as a background for it, high up in the sky above it, thin and clear and quavering, was the voice of the muezzin calling to Prayers.

THE STORY OF THE DERVISH AND THE RED-HOT SPOON

As soon as the Sultan had vanished into the mosque, and we had been offered coffee and cigarettes by the officers whom he had delegated to receive us, our courier told us that we would be just in time to see the Dervishes.

We drove up over the hill and down again on the other side into an area of desolate bare ground without grass or trees or streets. A few disconsolate houses were scattered about, and the hard, baked ground was strewn with tin cans and old shoes and littered rubbish. We drew up before one of these houses, which was built of wood, and much out of repair, and, after our courier had exchanged a few words with the custodian at the door, went in.

We were late, and the service had already begun. There were a number of other visitors, seated on benches against the wall, behind a wooden barrier that ran along three sides of the room. Above the aisle so formed there was a screened gallery for the women, whom we could hear stirring and shuffling about from time to time behind the lattice. The two windows on the long side of the room were open, and a curious crowd stood on tiptoe outside.

Between the windows there was a niche in the wall, hung with rugs, and decorated – or, at least, so we thought– with swords and daggers of antique pattern. The floor of the room was bare, except that there were mats laid down around its edges, and rugs in the niche. Here sat the priest, a dark, bearded man, with features of the Jewish type; he wore dark robes, and had a green turban. The worshippers were seated cross-legged, or kneeling, in a hollow square, three deep, backed up against the railing; there was no altar – though a small charcoal brazier was standing on the floor in front of the priest – and the congregation did not face towards Mecca, but towards the open space in the centre of the room.

Several men came in during the first ten minutes of our attendance; as each entered, he advanced into the open space and bowed formally to the roomful in general, standing with his feet close together and his hand on his breast, as if in a prescribed posture; a place was then made for him among the rows of worshippers; he knelt, bent forward to touch the floor with his forehead, and began his devotions. If a chorus were proceeding, he joined in with it at that point; if it were a solo recitative, he took his part in the accompaniment.

When we came in, it happened that the chant was in unison; a portion of the Koran, I thought, since there were no repetitions of phrases, and the name of Mohammed occurred often. There was a distinct rhythm, and all kept to it, stressing the syllables in exactly the same way – monotonous, psalm-like cadence, a dreary sing-song, though the pronunciation was careful and distinct, as if the significance were in the words, and not in the sounds.

At the command of the priest, who struck the floor before him with his hand to emphasise the words, the chant stopped, dying away in a low, meaningless rumble of sound, as though it were abandoned reluctantly. Without a pause, the priest began the next phase; he started a low moan, carefully pitched and musical; it was taken up by one man after another until the whole room shook with it, a level, steady tone like the hum of machinery, without variation or break, because no two men paused for breath at the same instant. At the sign from the priest, one of the men began a chant alone, starting on a note an octave above the moaning, and returning at the beginning and end of every sentence to this keynote. He was a young man, and very earnest. He had a thin, ascetic face, very pale; his eyes were closed and his head thrown back; he trembled with intensity, and his sharp, wavering voice cut through the monotone like the note of an oboe above a muted orchestra. It was tremendously effective, because of its very evident sincerity, and there was a queer, unaccountable quality in it, as if secret and mysterious forces were at work close at hand under the surface of life. Moreover, the spell must have been particularly powerful to those who took part in it, for the young man's voice was passionate in its fervour, and the droning, because it permitted no variation of pitch or force, must have required a difficult restraint.

This continued for half an hour, and then the priest stopped it, and began repeating 'Allah is very great and He is our God,' striking the floor with his open palm to mark the cadence. The crowd took it up. Now it was the sound that was important, and not the words; the same phrase, over and over, until all sense of its beginning and ending was lost, and one heard only the maddening beat of the accented syllables. The previous chant had put the men in a state of coma, nearly, without will or thought or consciousness, but this drove them to frenzy. All kept the time. Some moved their hands convulsively; some swayed their bodies from side to side with a rapid, swinging motion; some nodded their heads with a frantic, machine-like impetuosity; some provided a secondary rhythm with their gasps to catch the breath. They did not see nor feel nor think nor hear; it was as if they would go on forever and forever. There was an appalling sense of *possession* about it, and it was frightful to see.

After a time the priest himself dropped out and tended the fire in the brazier.

One man threw up his hands and called on the name of Allah. It was not a prayer; it was a cry of agony. His hands were raised in a pitiful gesture of suffering. He beat his thighs and howled. A young boy behind him sobbed and wept; the tears rolled down his cheeks. Near him, a man of fanatical, demon-haunted aspect nodded his head more and more violently until his body was moving in a terrible abandoned tossing that actually lifted him from the floor and sent him bouncing madly, on his knees, out across the open space in the centre of the room. His great mop of black hair flung up and down. His eyes were closed. He did not know that he was moving, probably. The priest's assistant moved the brazier to one side lest he should fling himself into the fire. But he hopped more and more to the right, until he had made nearly a half circle, and then stopped. No one watched him. Indeed, no one saw him.

These men were caught in the grip of something terrible. The priest drove them, urging them on with shouts, beating on the floor to mark the time – it was as if he was pushing them forward into the reach of a cruel and fiery-eyed Deity who demanded all that their strength could give in revenge for their sins against Him. They could not escape. They believed, and they were inevitably caught. They could not plead, they could not go back; they were swept in by their own faith, and there could be no thought of mercy.

The phase that followed this was worse. No words were pronounced, but only a rhythmical groaning. They expressed every shade of fear and helpless anguish; they were seized by a desperate sort of panic, as though they could not crowd out sounds to express their contrition and their sense of sin. They were a gathering of corpses, lifeless, yet horribly animated, with souls that had gone elsewhere and pointed back at the sorrowful sacrifices that they had left behind.

The priest turned and rummaged in the niche behind him; he brought out various swords and daggers, a mallet, a broad hoop of wood, and three long iron spikes with balls of the size of a man's fist on their ends and little hanging chains like scourges. He arranged these things carefully on the floor before him. He got up from his place and disrobed, standing back in the niche behind a cloak which two others held up to cover him. When he emerged again, his clothing was rolled up so as to leave a naked strip about his waist. He stirred up the fire in the brazier. Then, shouting to the others to be yet more frantic, he began his penance.

He beat himself over the head with the flat of a sword,

keeping time to the groaning; he drove daggers into his flesh, twisting the points in, first, and then striking the hilts with the hoop; he forced one of the sharp spokes into his abdomen, and then into his head above the eye. His frenzy was very elaborate and carefully calculated to be harmless, and he kept looking up at the visitors to see if they were impressed. He was an obvious old fake.

But no hint of his insincerity reached the worshippers, and the men who helped him were infinitely careful that the imaginary blood should be wiped away from the gashes he had cut, and they drew out the daggers as tenderly, and with expressions as solicitous and horrified, as if the points had really been driven three inches into his bowels, instead of being merely caught in the creases which he made in his flesh by bending nearly double. He was the driver. He had started it, and built it up. He had played upon the terror of the others, and had made them afraid of this God who lived in their own minds. Really, it was pitiful to see. The illusion vanished. The earnestness of the congregation became a mere object of commiseration, instead of an evidence of the moving power of an Idea. Before, I had felt the utter reality of this God. Now, the whole scheme was plainly a man-made scheme.

In the very midst of it, the man who had cried on the name of Allah advanced and took from the priest an iron spoon which had been heating in the brazier. The priest slapped it quickly against his palm and blew on it several times before relinquishing it, for it was red when it first came from the fire. The man kissed the handle. Then he lapped the bowl with his tongue. He did this perhaps twenty times, walking about the room. It hissed when his tongue touched it. There was no timidity in his manner, nor did he once glance aside to see how the audience was taking it. He was doing penance for his sins.

Two young men came forward. The priest took one of the iron spikes and held it up for the penitent to kiss. Then he thrust the point of it through the young man's cheek, from the inside of the mouth, holding two fingers against the face without, as one would do if he were sticking a blunt instrument through a hanging curtain. The flesh bulged between his fingers as he pushed. Then he led the boy across and drove the projecting point of the spike into the wood of one of the posts that supported the gallery, striking the ball on the end with the mallet. There the boy stood, rather terrified. All the frenzy was gone from him. His eyes had a curious look, as if he could not understand why it was not more painful. There he stood, waiting. The other boy was treated in the same manner, but he stood in such a position that I could not see his face.

We came away then.

For hours we thought of it. And we kept speaking of the priest. . . .

THE STORY OF THE FISHERMAN AND THE DEMON

We came out of Phaleron Bay under all plain sail, and stood east along the coast of Attica, bound on an expedition to the Cyclades. Without the Cyclades, we should have felt that we hadn't been in the East at all ; without a visit to the Isles of Greece, the Ægean would have been no more than a highway for us. The thousand ships, the Persian transports, and the sea-fights, Ceyx and Halcyone, the Argo and the Golden Fleece, without the Cyclades, become no more than phrases in a book. There are so few Sacred Islands now – in fact, there are none at all.

The wind was offshore, in general, and it performed some amazing evolutions: we had vessels on four sides of us, each with a different breeze, and once we ran down to, and *passed*, a boat running west before the wind, while we were before the wind heading east. There were streaks of calm and lanes of wind weaving in and out in all directions, except, of course, that they did not actually cross. It would have made pretty racing weather, and a clever helmsman, by watching the colours of the water and the run of the waves, might have followed a lane of fair wind right through the fleet, or alternately reached and run while keeping one steady course.

Along towards the end of the coast there is an island with a narrow passage between it and the main; we were afraid that the wind would drop at sunset, though it blew so strongly then, and thought it best to put into Port Collona for the night; for this plan it would shorten our course to pass inside the island. The wind came ahead through the passage, and blew in knock-down squalls; the cat's-paws went scurrying over the water in quick fans of white, and the spray was whipped up and driven like fine snow. I had never seen this before, in such tiny squalls; it happens in cyclones, but here it was restricted to separate areas of a few acres each.

We stood offshore for a time, after getting through the passage, and then reached in for the harbour, and anchored off the beach. The wind did not go down with the sun, but blew strong and squally all night. A windy spot, Port Collona.

The port was a lonely place. A few scattered houses along the shore, a little schooner, five or six rowboats drawn up on the sands, and the wind singing down off the coast under the stars.

In the morning we rowed ashore to the point and went up the hill to see the temple. Part way up the slope we passed through a ruined street of little huts, the quarters, I suppose, of the priests and custodians. It was a remote and solitary place for men to spend their lives; but the supply ships for Athens were often wrecked on the cape, and to protect them from this disaster a temple was necessary on the hill, and men to tend the shrine. There the temple stood, on the crest of the cape, looking out to sea. There was something very moving about it: golden yellow marble shafts against the blue sky, with the sun-bitten, stony ground below and the wine-dark Ægean spread behind, the wind humming cleanly through the ruin, and the God of the Place departed. It was deserted and abandoned; the ruin seemed to indicate the fact that this was finished, completed, no longer useful. The men who had had the first idea were dead. But what had become of the Spirit? Where is Posidon now? We – we came long afterward, and stood beside the deserted altar;

the idea was known to us, but the vital strength of it had been lost. It has passed through too many minds. The Athenian supply ships, in these days, round the cape under their own power, without the need of it.

We put in a reef and got away, carrying the smallest jib. The wind was strong, from the north; we made the water fly, and the coast of Kuthnos – which was where we were bound – came rolling up to meet us.

The Cyclades, from a distance, are as lovely as all the connotations of the name imply, but as we came nearer this quality faded, for there are no trees on the hillsides, and hardly any grass, but only bare brown rock and a dark and scraggy sort of heather. The thought of the Cyclades is stirring. But the islands are no more than islands, set in a salty sea.

The shores were high, with bold cliffs of naked rock, and on the western coast, three or four miles down from the northern end of the island, was the harbour of Merika. We reached in on the port tack. On the southern side was a very small and very white chapel, built on a projecting bit of artificial land, with a retaining wall to keep it from slipping into the sea. At the head of the harbour, on the level valley bottom, was a village of seven houses. In some manner or other the place escaped a look of dreariness. It is incredibly quiet and remote, but the peaceful aspect of it is uppermost, and it has an air of monastic seclusion and tranquillity and security about it. If a man should want to escape from the world, he might go to Merika, where, no doubt, he would discover that escape was not what he wanted. But he could live there. People do live there.

With the glasses, I could see some children playing on the beach, with chickens and goats and pigs around them, and in front of one of the houses, which had a stone terrace built out before its door, appeared a group of five or six men, watching us. They all shouted together – the sound reached us as a confused wailing – and flapped their arms up and down to indicate that we should let go everything. We dropped anchor, and they seemed satisfied.

After lunch Bill and I went ashore to look for the ruined fortress, which, according to the Pilot Book, lies on a hill to the northward of the village. We took the shore road that wound around the shoulder of the nearest hill and were followed by a man and two boys and a dog, who dropped behind when we started up the hot slope of the second hill. We found no ruins on the summit, or on any other summit. The road dropped again to a sandy valley similar to the one in which Merika stands, where there was one solitary house. There was a pleasant beach, with cool clear water flowing in, and Bill went swimming while I sat and played in the sand. Knowing that there were the ruins of an ancient city within a mile of us, we admitted that it would be foolish not to see them; yet it was very hot, and a mile is a long distance. Besides, it would be very easy to let on that we had seen the ruins, and we could describe them, without fear of contradiction, as accurately as if we had climbed all over them.

As we started back we met a little girl with a water-jar,

who came singing down the hill on her way to bring home the goats; she stopped when she caught sight of us, brushing aside her hair to stare at us, but as soon as we had passed she took up her song again, and did not look back. The goats were waiting for her in the corner of the nearest field. When we came over the last hill we saw the *Caltha* riding lonely at anchor, and the level sunlight shining on her side, and on the white wall of the little chapel.

As we were passing the house with the terrace, I turned back to ask Bill if he thought we might safely consider the place a public café, for there was an official air about the house, and I had seen some men sitting about an iron table before the door. But I was interrupted in my question by the woman of the house, who nodded to me through the kitchen window, and beckoned me, with a saucepan which she happened to have in her hand, to come in. We went up.

There were six or seven men there, a boy or two, a dog, a cat, and three young pigs. Our reception was extraordinary. One of the men – a ragged, desperate-looking, hairy scoundrel – set down his wine bottle, brushed aside the gesticulating arms of his companions, and came forward to offer his hand.

'Goddam,' he said. ''Scuse me; all drunk.'

He grinned at us – a red-eyed, genial leer – and waved his hand, in explanation, in the general direction of the others, who grinned also, and spoke in Greek.

'Where did you learn English ?' we asked him.

'San Francisco,' he answered. ''Scuse me. Like Hell. All drunk.'

He introduced us to the company. Each man rose from his seat, shook hands, and sat down again; the boys, who were not presented, sat and stared. Instead of mentioning names, which, obviously, would have been superfluous under the circumstances, our host pronounced the word 'Drunk' as he handed each man forward.

He had been in San Francisco for five years, but it was ten years ago, and most of his English had escaped him, except for a few of the more useful words. He managed to convey to us his conviction that 'America great country Goddam,' but that here in the Cyclades, 'Business rotten like Hell.' In California, he had been a labourer – gestures indicated this fact – but here he was a fisherman, as they all were – as for them, they were drunk. Which was plain to see.

They were very talkative and friendly. They teased the cat for us until it yelled; they kicked the dog about between their feet, saying that he was a low Turko hound, and deserved bad treatment – they indicated that if we wanted to take him, as a gift, and drown him, they would be pleased to assist and cheer. They told us over and over again that the English and the Americans were 'ηαλά' but the French 'very bad.' They made remarks about their King in explanation of this opinion, but the idea was lost on us, even when it had been translated into English.

They brought out wine and coffee and dried fish and tomatoes and pickled roe and fried eggs and bread and cheese, which they set out on a cloth-covered box before us, and prepared for us with their own personal pocket knives – fishermen's knives, black and gummed with guts and gurry. They laughed uproariously over nothing and spilled wine and cuffed one another over the head in crude playfulness, and had a good time. They asked us to take their picture, in a group, which, though it was so nearly dark, we did, after waiting for one more man, whom they felt they could not do without, and whom they summoned from the other end of the village by shouting all together. This man was sober, and he wrote his name in a note-book for us, so that we should know where to send the picture. When we rose to go they would let us pay for nothing. We shook hands all around, five or six times, exchanging 'ηαλά' and 'Goddam,' and parted with the utmost geniality. Our host staggered after us to the edge of the terrace, called "scuse me, boys,' and exploded in unquenchable mirth.

On board, Pat had been watching us through the glasses, and having seen the farewell demonstration, wanted to know what it was all about. While we were at dinner we heard the splash of oars alongside, and the sound of voices. Our friends from shore had sent us gifts – two bottles of wine, and some apples, tied up in a cloth. They came aboard, and climbed clumsily down the companion, blinking in the lamplight. Our man from San Francisco was first, and he was followed by a schooner captain – a filthy, weather-battered old buccaneer, who was interested in nothing but ships, and talked of nothing else. We made room for them, and they sat down uneasily. A third man followed them – a younger drunkard with buck teeth, who kept grinning and saying 'ηαλά.' We offered them something to drink, but they preferred tea, which they accepted, and inhaled noisily while they talked. They insisted on making cigarettes for us. They were horrible to look at, bullet-headed and degenerate, and the cabin stank of them, but they were offering us the freedom of their city with all their hearts.

When it came time for them to leave, the man from San Francisco lingered behind the others and sought about in his mind for some elusive thought that he wanted to express. Plainly, he had something to tell us. The others were up on deck, and called to him to come, but he shook them off with a gesture, and stood there, looking at us in a puzzled, embarrassed manner, his head a little on one side, his tongue in his cheek. All at once he stretched out his hand.

'Good night,' he said. 'Sleep good, boys. Don't be afraid.'

CHAPTER TWENTY-TWO

Back West

★

We left Phaleron Bay in the afternoon of the fifth of July. The breeze was light, and it was very hot. Indeed, for weeks we had been living in pyjamas, day and night, dressing only for the period between the hours of seven and midnight, which are the hours that custom and habit have declared tolerable. The sun went down behind Mount Parnassus, which appropriately marked the way. Olympus, we had not seen. But we had been under the shadow of it. There was a decree against us, a 'Greek fate,' long delayed, but now inexorably active. We were bound back west.

It seemed strange that the *Caltha* should be bound across the Gulf of Salamis again. It seemed strange to have our sea routine back, our freedom. It seemed strange that we should be going west. And yet this was the first time in more than a year that we had set out on any road of any considerable length, that is – which we had travelled before. And so it seemed familiar, too. We knew exactly what was before us: the canal, the Corinthian Jinx, the passage inside Cephalonia, the Ionian Sea, the Straits, the West Coast. We thought to find nothing new. Except that the weather is always new.

In the morning, while we were coming into the harbour of Posidonia, Bill began tinkering with the motor. It had a sprained wrist, he explained, and other imaginary complications of a more psychological nature, and it would be wise to run it as little as possible. This was in accord with our wishes and intentions. If it would take us through the canal, we should ask nothing else of it, ever.

We swung into the channel, when our turn came, and started. But after a quarter of a mile the motor stopped. Bill did everything to it that the limits of time allowed, but it sat and stared at him. The ship swung across the ditch, with the bowsprit scraping along the wall on one side, and the mizzen boom dragging on the other. The current was carrying us, but we got some lines ashore, and stopped, just as a canal official came running. It pleased us to assume that his profanity was directed at our motor, and we added our curses to his. But the motor did not start. A towboat was coming behind us, and we passed her a line. At the western end, where she dropped us to pick up a liner that was waiting to go east, we made sail and stood off down the Gulf. We covered the motor's face. It died young; it could not be said to have really lived.

It was a long, slow journey down the Gulf of Corinth to the sea. I remember nights of stars and glassy water, when we spent the whole period from dark to dawn opposite some lonely light on the shore. I remember sitting at the table in the cabin, with the thermometer at a hundred and six, and the square of sunlight through the skylight resting perfectly immovable on the floor beside me. I remember the mountains hanging in the air, breathless, writhing in the heat, as if they had been projected on a film of oil, as if they were images in a bed of coals. I remember the sea, baking hot, as if there were a fire beneath it. Hours and hours of stillness. And a man appearing now and again in the cabin door, his face burned nearly black, his eyes looking very white and startled, mopping his brow, waving his hat before his face. 'Any wind?' 'No. No wind. Not a breath.'

This was the Corinthian Jinx. We had no object in life but to escape from it. Once let us get out into the Ionian sea, we said, where our good norther is blowing, and all will be well. And down off Missolonghi we did find a breeze – a smashing, rollicking wind that put life in the sky and cooled the air and moved the mountains, and sent us through the passage to sea, out of sight of Cephalonia. But our good north wind was not there.

We were becalmed. We were seven days in covering that two hundred and twenty miles from Cephalonia to the Straits. For two whole days we had a barque in sight on the horizon. The breakfast eggshells were in sight beside us all day long. At evening on the fourth day we saw Mount Ætna, when the sun set behind it. In the morning it was gone. From time to time we had strange squalls. There would be an uneasy heave in the sea, coming from the northwest; then there would be a humming noise in the air, and a strip of feathery white on the horizon; then it would blow. We would shorten sail, and go lashing off to the westward, laying over, throwing spray, with the wind screaming. There would be no clouds, no rain, nothing that could be called a storm – only clear skies and bright water in the sunshine, and this crazy whistling wind, going nowhere, out of nothing. In an hour it would drop flat again, and we would idly float. At sunset, Mount Ætna would show on the horizon.

And the world would turn round, and the sun would rise again, and there would be no land in sight.

At the sixth sunset we made out the mountains of the mainland, and during that night we crept up to the toe of Italy again, and lay drifting off the beaches to the eastward of Capo del Armi, with the same donkey braying in the midnight stillness, and the same patient train shuffling along the shore.

Mercifully, there was a breeze in the Straits, and we came through with less delay, even though we stopped at Messina for bread, than when we had come through bound east under power. We sailed through the very centre of Charybdis, and skirted the edge of Scylla. The ancients dreaded these monsters, though it seemed to me, who have been in the Bay of Fundy, that they were insignificant. Perhaps we did not see them under their worst conditions, for the currents are very erratic, and alter like the whims of maidenhood; perhaps a galley, with five banks of rattling oars, is reason enough for helplessness. Yet the big steamers went through carefully, taking care to follow exactly the rules laid down for them in the Books. The *Caltha* passed twice between the monsters, and twice passed the Mount of Circe. But what songs the Sirens sang!

The day on which we started up the coast of Italy, bound for Genoa, marked a year from the day on which we had left Paul Jones' mooring on the Clyde.

We made bets on the probable time of our arrival in Genoa, but no one guessed the truth: we were seventeen days in making five hundred miles. How we did it,

I don't know. We kept in close to the coast, so as to have the benefit of the land and sea breezes – which did not come. We lay rolling in the heavy ground swell, without a whisper of wind, for many days and nights. Once we had a sharp north-easter, and sprung our topmast. We crossed Naples Bay, between Capri and Ischia, in a night of wind. Off Argentario – Argentario, in Italy! – we ran for ten hours, with a spinnaker set, before a smashing southerly, which was the only fair wind we had in a passage of twenty-seven days. But for the most part we fanned along, in incredible slowness, and counted progress by days, rather than by hours or miles. Nine miles from Genoa – so close that we could distinguish the flags on the ships in the harbour – we lay immovable for thirteen hours. Then a light north-easter found us, and we got in.

The port of Genoa is crowded always, and just now it is crowded with idle ships. We found a berth that pleased us in the centre of a group of idle lighters. In a clumsy shanty built on the deck of one of them, lives Angelo, a watchman. It is reported of Angelo that he owns the lighters, and that they bring him in seven thousand lire a day – when they work. It is reported, too, that he has rich vineyards in the interior, and is immensely wealthy. But he lives in a shanty, as watchman, with a boy to help him – a commentary on wealth, for though there are many rich men who try to buy from life things that life will not sell, there are some few, like Angelo, who do not try. Perhaps he lacks imagination. Perhaps he has always wanted a shanty on a lighter. At any rate, there Angelo is, with Pedro, whom he gives five lire a day, and a package of cigarettes.

Pedro is from Montevideo ; a young, stalwart lad, who has had trouble in his time. He had run away to sea when he was even younger, on a voyage to Australia; he had made two trips to New York – where he did not go ashore – and several short passages in the Mediterranean. On one of these last he suffered the misfortune to miss his ship – he was seeing the town, probably, and the captain sailed without him. Because he did not have his papers with him – what sailor goes ashore expecting to stay? – he spent two months in jail. From which emerging he looked for a home-bound ship, or a job – and found Angelo.

Piloto told us this. He came back to the ship one afternoon, after a visit to the lighter, and said that Pedro wanted to work his passage with us.

'Does he know where we're going?' Pat asked.

'He say no matter. So long go away from Genoa.'

'But we're going to Marseille. Does he speak any French?'

'Litty.'

'But suppose he can't find a job in Marseille?'

'No can fine job in Genoa. Ally same.'

'And he wants to work his way?'

'Say yes. Say no want money. Suppose stop Marseille ; all finish Pedro. No ask nothing. Suppose no get ship, go Barcelona.'

'How will he get to Barcelona?'

'Doan no. Suppose feet.'

'Did you tell him we were going to Marseille?'

'Say doan no. Say no stop Genoa. He say me all right.'

'Is he a good man?'

'Doan no. I just now see. Maybe yes, maybe no.'

'You think he's honest?'

'Yes, I think.'

'Well, don't say anything to him just now. When we're ready to go, if you think he's a good man, we'll take him.'

'Ah, no, Mr. Pass. No. Suppose you like, you say Pedro. You no like, no go. I say nothing.'

We watched Pedro, after this. Once or twice, when Piloto wanted to spend an evening ashore, Pedro came aboard and did duty as watchman. A stocky lad, hardly more than nineteen years old, with big hands and a hearty, simple face; he sat patiently on the fore hatch, in the starlight, singing *Torna a Surriento* in a baritone voice of singularly pleasing quality – sang of Sorrento, but dreamed of the River Plate. He spoke often of his mother, in Montevideo. He wanted to get home. We took him with us, and gave him a start along his road.

In Genoa, Bill had to leave us. For the last time, Piloto rowed him ashore in the dinghy. I met him later at the station, and saw him take the express for Torino, Modena, Paris, Havre . . . New York. 'Genoa the Magnificent.' I never knew anybody who didn't have unhappy associations with it.

CHAPTER TWENTY-THREE

In Which We Make an End

★

You know what the Riviera is like, and I will not trouble you with any dissertation on it. For us, on this occasion, the setting of the Riviera had a special significance: we were ending our voyage there, and were on our last passage. Yet perhaps it was not so special, either. For it seems to me that no one can go to the Riviera, ever, under any circumstances, and not be poignantly aware of the fragile barrier that separates joy from sorrow. There are beginnings there, and endings . . . and the loveliness of the environment adds a pain to both.

We stopped in at Antibes, with the intention of having the ship hauled out and cleaned, for she had not been scrubbed and painted since it was done at Gibraltar; she was foul with weed and barnacles, and moved through the water like an ox-cart. But the railway at Antibes had not sufficient depth of water for us, and we went on to Cannes, where the ship rested for ten days on the beach, and we, deprived of our most obvious resource – our ability to move on – and shut up in towns which were 'out of season,' and therefore held no more than the spark of life – we found great difficulty in finding anything to do. We saw more, and worse, moving-pictures than were ever before crowded into so short an interval of time, and we sat longer, and more quietly, in cafés along promenades than had ever before been done by animate objects.

When at last we were launched, a mistral was blowing.

We waited for two days for it to be finished, and then set sail for Marseille.

The first night out from Cannes we spent in Agay Road; at sunset of the second day we passed Cape Camaret and entered Hyères Islands Sound. The wind had hauled steadily, all through the day, following the sun; in the morning we had it on the port quarter, and now, after it had swung all through the compass, through west, we had it on the starboard beam. It blew fresh, and we went gaily. At eleven o'clock, when I came on deck to take the helm from Pat, he had just picked up the red light that lies halfway through the Sound. I passed this, and soon afterwards picked up three lights ahead: the one to the southward was a big double flash, and showed over land – long before I could see the light itself I watched the long bands of radiance from it, whipping across the sky, – in the centre was an occulting light, and to the northwards, also over the land, was a dim yellow gleam that flashed three times. One of these marked the way out of the Sound. It was a dark night, very clear, and the lights seemed close. I lashed the tiller and went below to look at the Light List.

I sat at the table in the cabin, under the yellow lamplight, and opened the book. Everybody aboard was asleep. The water babbled against the planks, the ropes creaked, and the blocks were talking softly. A dark night, full of stars, inside the Hyères Islands, with three lights in sight ahead, and the voyage nearly ended. . . .

It was the central light – the occulting one – that marked the passage. I went up on deck again. For a few moments I could see nothing; then the light appeared again, right over the bowsprit; I had set her for it, when I went down, and she was still holding for it. It lies on a small island off the coast, and as soon as we were through the narrow strait I called Piloto, and turned in.

The breeze lasted till dawn, and then dropped, and we were all day in drifting from Toulon to Ciotat.

At dark we picked up Planier Island light. It was twenty miles away, a sharp white electric spark, close down on the water. There was nothing else in sight in the whole world, except a dull smudge of smoke that hung over the cape where we were to alter our course for Chateau d'If, and the stars, which were doubled below us in the glassy water. It was my watch from eleven till two, again, and when I went down I told Piloto to call me when we got near the land. The breeze was all up off the water, and the big topsail was doing all the work; we slipped along without a sound. It would be daylight before we got in.

Just after three o'clock I was called. Chateau d'If light was close aboard, and the land was all about us. The breeze was just the same; I could see the stars slipping along behind the rocks on the tops of the islands, and the reflections of them swooping and darting off away from us in the ripples that we spread from our bows. By four o'clock it began to get light in the east, and the silhouette of Notre Dame de la Garde was standing up very sharp and black on the summit of the hill. It rose out of the murk. The whole lower shore was hidden in a pall of smoke from the ships in the port.

As we came close, we had company; several steamers – which are able to make plans always to arrive by daylight – came through the Canoubier passage behind us, and we reached up for the harbour entrance through a fleet of several hundred fishing boats. A perfect babble of sound came across the water, a steady hum of voices, such as one hears in a crowded café. Indeed, we were in town, then.

I made out the transbordeur bridge, through the smoke, against the sunrise, and steered in. As soon as the end of the outer mole was abeam I called Piloto and Pedro on deck and sent them to stand by the headsail sheets, for the wind was blowing directly out of the Vieux Port, and we should have to beat in. The entrance is very narrow, with the high walls of forts on both sides; the motor boats were all about us, going and coming as thick as taxicabs; we were carrying everything, for the wind caught only the upper canvas.

Just as we were in the narrowest part, standing across, two ships came out: a big brigantine, under sail, and a great ugly-looking steamer, in charge of two tugs. The brigantine was ahead, with the first of the steamer's towboats panting along just under her stern; the steamer filled up the whole opening, and most of the sky as well. We crossed the brigantine's bow, almost under her bowsprit – there were men at work on her fo'c's'le head, catting an anchor, and they stopped to look down at us. Once across there was no more than fifty feet of space left for us between the steamer and the walls of the fort. The gentle breeze was blowing down this lane. The motor boats were all about us. I backed the foresail, and eased up along the walls of the fort, hardly moving through the water, so as to gain time for the steamer to pass, and yet not dead still, so as to keep steerage way.

With a rush, the sun came up over the city. The bridge was across the very top of the sky, and the two ships towered up, big and black, against the glare. The transbordeur went rumbling across, loaded with carts and women with fish baskets and workmen for the port. All about us the city was waking up for the day. It was as if we had come to view a special spectacle which could not start until we came.

As soon as we were abreast of the second towboat, which was hanging to the steamer's stern to keep her from swinging, I backed the jib, too, and swung over on to the other tack. We passed just clear of the towboat, and in ten seconds we were close up against the fort on the other side – a high grey wall, with crumbling loopholes. We came about again and cut in front of the transbordeur, which was on the return trip. Piloto and Pedro were crouched on deck, forward, holding the sheets, ready to let fly and haul at the word. We ducked under the bowsprits of big square-riggers and schooners, and scraped across the chains of steamers – in and out, taking a longer tack wherever the space between the ships permitted it. So we came into the Vieux Port. Ahead, along the open path of wavering grey water, I could see the trams coming and going up and down the Cannebière.

Halfway in, on the south-eastern side, we found a berth that pleased us, and rounded up beside a big schooner yacht. The anchor dropped.

This was on Friday, the twenty-second of September, five thousand fifty-one miles from Gourock, on the Clyde.

A week later we paid off Piloto and sent him back to Cartagena. As for Pedro, we bought him a ticket for Barcelona, gave him some money, and told Piloto to see that he did nothing foolish before he got to Spain, for we were apprehensive that he might stumble on just the chance he wanted, and, in his dumbness, make some simple remark about the jail in Genoa, or his lost papers, that would spoil his luck. But nothing of this apprehension reached Pedro; he was grateful and jubilant; he could see Montevideo, and his mother, from where he stood.

Then we set about selling the ship. In the course of time, there appeared three prospective buyers; a meeting was held in the office of one of them, where Pat opened their bids. While this was going on, I sat in our café, waiting for the news, staring at the wall and smoking endless cigarettes.

I tried to think what it would be like to travel on a ticket. I made vague plans for last errands, and for the transfer of baggage. I wondered if life at home was still going on – as before, or differently. I thought of the silhouette of Notre Dame de la Garde against the dawn, that morning which seemed so long ago, when we came into the Vieux Port. I thought of that dark night inside the Hyères Islands. I thought of Bill, leaving us in Genoa and of how I came back to the ship after he had gone, wondering why everything seemed so different. I thought of the long road up the west coast of Italy, and the calms in the Ionian sea, and the Corinthian Jinx. I thought of the Cyclades, and Constantinople, and the Canal, and the big house at Cephalonia. I thought of the Straits, and Stromboli, of Napoli and Santa Lucia, and of that first distant mountain of Italy, rising out of the summer sea. I thought of the blow off Asinara, when we ran into Bonifacio, and of Palma, with that strange far-away atmosphere of detachment that there is about it, making it seem like a dream. I thought of Granada, and the bull-fight, and of those long days on the road to El Dorado, when we fought for every inch of progress along the dreary flint coast of Spain. I thought of the sunrise behind the Rock, and the crossing of the Bay, and that golden morning at Penzance. I thought of that black night off the Longships in the big seas, and the Skerries, and Albert Dock, and Ailsa Craig, and Paul Jones' Yard. I thought of that evening when I sat on the sawhorse in the garret, when Pat came in and said that he wanted to go on a cruise. I thought of this book, and of how I should feel when I came to write of that hour I spent in the café on the Cannebière, smoking endless cigarettes, staring at the wall.

Then Pat came, and told me. The ship was sold.

The new owner sent his valet aboard, on the following morning, to act as watchman. He sat disconsolately on the forehatch, playing with his cap, and wondering what he should do if the ship should begin to sink under him. Our trunks were on the quay. I was below, packing a suitcase, looking vaguely about me for something I had forgotten, and seeing nothing, I believe, that I shall ever forget. I was touched by that same sort of incredulity that we had felt when we sat for the first time in that cabin; then, I had not been able to believe that I was starting, just as I could not believe that I was leaving now. Then I heard a step on deck, and the sound of some one talking with the valet. Talking Italian. A voice I had often heard, in Genoa, singing *Torna a Surriento.* I went up, and there was Pedro.

We sat on the hatch, and talked.

'What happened?' I asked him.

Well, he had gone to Barcelona. All day, with Piloto, he had looked for work, and had found nothing; there were no foreign ships in Barcelona, he said, but only Spanish coasters, which, even if they had needed him, would have gotten him nowhere. In the evening Piloto had taken the train for Cartagena. He had seen him go. And then he had gone to sleep on a bench in a park – in front of a police station, I suspect, seeing how guilelessly Pedro went through the world – at any rate, he was aroused at dawn by a policeman, who wanted to know about everything. Where were his papers? He showed what he had. Ha! A sailor? Where was his ship? He had no ship – as yet. Oh! Ah! As yet. Well, where had he come from? Marseille. Good. Back to Marseille.

The policeman took him by the arm as far as the station, where he was turned over to a special guard, charged with conducting him as far as the border. It had been suggested to him that he try Bordeaux. But Pedro was not in an experimental mood. Besides, Bordeaux was in France, too, wasn't it? No; France was France. And he was not being sent to Genoa, which reassured him, I suppose, and kept him from jumping out of the window of the train. So – in short – here he was.

I asked him how he had gotten from the border to Marseille.

He smiled, held up one dusty boot, and slapped it lustily.

Back there in Montevideo, when he was fifteen years old, and had run away to sea, he wanted to see the world, I suppose . . .

Pat came back, and we gave Pedro some money, telling him that he must not fail to find a job before it was gone. He nodded.

Pedro and the valet helped us to load our trunks into two taxicabs. Pat had a Rénault; I was in a Ford. As we started, just before the bow of a little freight steamer from Constanza cut off my view, I looked back at the *Caltha*.

We went scuttling through the dock-side streets in a cloud of hanging dust, to the steamer.

Printed in Guernsey by the Star and Gazette Co., Ltd.

A LIST OF VOLUMES ISSUED IN
THE TRAVELLERS' LIBRARY

3s. 6d. net each

JONATHAN CAPE LTD.
THIRTY BEDFORD SQUARE LONDON

THE TRAVELLERS' LIBRARY

*

A series of books in all branches of literature designed for the pocket, or for the small house where shelf space is scarce. Though the volumes measure only 7 inches by $4\frac{3}{4}$ inches, the page is arranged so that the margins are not unreasonably curtailed nor legibility sacrificed. The books are of a uniform thickness irrespective of the number of pages, and the paper, specially manufactured for the series, is remarkably opaque, even when it is thinnest.

A semi-flexible form of binding has been adopted, as a safeguard against the damage inevitably associated with hasty packing. The cloth is of a particularly attractive shade of blue and has the author's name stamped in gold on the back. Each volume costs 3s. 6d. net (postage 3d.).

*

1. CAN SUCH THINGS BE? A volume of Stories by Ambrose Bierce

¶ 'Bierce never wastes a word, never coins a too startling phrase; he secures his final effect, a cold thrill of fear, by a simple, yet subtle, realism. No anthology of short stories, limited to a score or so, would be complete without an example of his unique artistry.' *Morning Post*

2 THE BLACK DOG. A volume of Stories by A. E. Coppard

¶ 'Mr. Coppard is a born story-teller. The book is filled with a variety of delightful stuff: no one who is interested in good writing in general, and good short stories in particular, should miss it.' *Spectator*

3. THE AUTOBIOGRAPHY of a SUPER-TRAMP by W. H. Davies. With a preface by G. Bernard Shaw

¶ Printed as it was written, it is worth reading for its literary style alone. The author tells us with inimitable quiet modesty of how he begged and stole his way across America and through England and Wales until his travelling days were cut short by losing his right foot while attempting to 'jump' a train.

4. BABBITT A Novel
by Sinclair Lewis

¶ 'One of the greatest novels I have read for a long time.' *H. G. Wells* '*Babbitt* is a triumph.' *Hugh Walpole* 'His work has that something extra, over and above, which makes the work of art, and it is signed in every line with the unique personality of the author.' *Rebecca West*

5. THE CRAFT OF FICTION
by Percy Lubbock

¶ 'No more substantial or more charming volume of criticism has been published in our time.' *Observer*
'To say that this is the best book on the subject is probably true; but it is more to the point to say that it is the only one.'
Times Literary Supplement

6. EARLHAM
by Percy Lubbock

¶ 'The book seems too intimate to be reviewed. We want to be allowed to read it, and to dream over it, and keep silence about it. His judgment is perfect, his humour is true and ready; his touch light and prim; his prose is exact and clean and full of music.' *Times*

7. WIDE SEAS & MANY LANDS A Personal Narrative
by Arthur Mason.
With an Introduction by MAURICE BARING

¶ 'This is an extremely entertaining, and at the same time, moving book. We are in the presence of a born writer. We read with the same mixture of amazement and delight that fills us throughout a Conrad novel.' *New Statesman*

8. SELECTED PREJUDICES A book of Essays
by H. L. Mencken

¶ 'He is exactly the kind of man we are needing, an iconoclast, a scoffer at ideals, a critic with whips and scorpions who does not hesitate to deal with literary, social and political humbugs in the one slashing fashion.' *English Review*

*

9. THE MIND IN THE MAKING An Essay
by James Harvey Robinson

¶ 'For me, I think James Harvey Robinson is going to be almost as important as was Huxley in my adolescence, and William James in later years. It is a cardinal book. I question whether in the long run people may not come to it, as making a new initiative into the world's thought and methods.' *From the Introduction by* H. G. WELLS

10. THE WAY OF ALL FLESH A Novel
by Samuel Butler

¶ 'It drives one almost to despair of English Literature when one sees so extraordinary a study of English life as Butler's posthumous *Way of All Flesh* making so little impression. Really, the English do not deserve to have great men.' *George Bernard Shaw*

11. EREWHON A Satire
by Samuel Butler

¶ 'To lash the age, to ridicule vain pretension, to expose hypocrisy, to deride humbug in education, politics and religion, are tasks beyond most men's powers; but occasionally, very occasionally, a bit of genuine satire secures for itself more than a passing nod of recognition. *Erewhon* is such a satire. . . . The best of its kind since *Gulliver's Travels*.' *Augustine Birrell*

12. EREWHON REVISITED A Satire
by Samuel Butler

¶ 'He waged a sleepless war with the mental torpor of the prosperous, complacent England around him; a Swift with the soul of music in him, and completely sane; a liberator of humanity operating with the wit and malice and coolness of Mephistopheles.' *Manchester Guardian*

13. ADAM AND EVE AND PINCH ME Stories
by A. E. Coppard

¶ Mr. Coppard's implicit theme is the closeness of the spiritual world to the material; the strange, communicative sympathy which strikes through two temperaments and suddenly makes them one. He deals with those sudden impulses under which secrecy is broken down for a moment, and personality revealed as under a flash of spiritual lightning.

14. DUBLINERS A volume of Stories
by James Joyce

¶ A collection of fifteen short stories by the author of *Ulysses*. They are all of them brave, relentless, and sympathetic pictures of Dublin life; realistic, perhaps, but not crude; analytical, but not repugnant. No modern writer has greater significance than Mr. Joyce, whose conception and practice of the short story is certainly unique and certainly vital.

15. DOG AND DUCK
by Arthur Machen

¶ 'As a literary artist, Mr. Arthur Machen has few living equals, and that is very far indeed from being his only, or even his greatest, claim on the suffrages of English readers.' *Sunday Times*

16. KAI LUNG'S GOLDEN HOURS
by Ernest Bramah

¶ 'It is worthy of its forerunner. There is the same plan, exactitude, working-out and achievement; and therefore complete satisfaction in the reading.' *From the Preface by* HILAIRE BELLOC

17. ANGELS & MINISTERS, AND OTHER PLAYS
by Laurence Housman

Imaginary portraits of political characters done in dialogue—Queen Victoria, Disraeli, Gladstone, Parnell, Joseph Chamberlain, and Woodrow Wilson.

¶ 'It is all so good that one is tempted to congratulate Mr. Housman on a true masterpiece.' *Times*

18. THE WALLET OF KAI LUNG
by Ernest Bramah

¶ 'Something worth doing and done. . . . It was a thing intended, wrought out, completed and established. Therefore it was destined to endure, and, what is more important, it was a success.' *Hilaire Belloc*

19. TWILIGHT IN ITALY
by D. H. Lawrence

¶ This volume of travel vignettes in North Italy was first published in 1916. Since then Mr. Lawrence has increased the number of his admirers year by year. In *Twilight in Italy* they will find all the freshness and vigour of outlook which they have come to expect from its author.

20. THE DREAM A Novel
by H. G. Wells

¶ 'It is the richest, most generous and absorbing thing that Mr. Wells has given us for years and years.' *Daily News*

'I find this book as close to being magnificent as any book that I have ever read. It is full of inspiration and life.' *Daily Graphic*

21. ROMAN PICTURES
by Percy Lubbock

¶ Pictures of life as it is lived—or has been or might be lived—among the pilgrims and colonists in Rome of more or less English speech.

'A book of whimsical originality and exquisite workmanship, and worthy of one of the best prose writers of our time.' *Sunday Times*

22. CLORINDA WALKS IN HEAVEN
by A. E. Coppard

¶ 'Genius is a hard-ridden word, and has been put by critics at many puny ditches, but Mr. Coppard sets up a fence worthy of its mettle. He shows that in hands like his the English language is as alive as ever, and that there are still infinite possibilities in the short story.' *Outlook*

23. MARIUS THE EPICUREAN
by Walter Pater

¶ Walter Pater was at the same time a scholar of wide sympathies and a master of the English language. In this, his best known work, he describes with rare delicacy of feeling and insight the religious and philosophic tendencies of the Roman Empire at the time of Antoninus Pius as they affected the mind and life of the story's hero.

24. THE WHITE SHIP Stories
by Aino Kallas

With an Introduction by JOHN GALSWORTHY

¶ 'The writer has an extraordinary sense of atmosphere.'
Times Literary Supplement

'Stories told convincingly and well, with a keen perceptive for natural beauty.' *Nation*

25. MULTITUDE AND SOLITUDE A Novel
by John Masefield

¶ 'As well conceived and done, as rich in observation of the world, as profound where it needs to be profound, as any novel of recent writing.' *Outlook*

'This is no common book. It is a book which not merely touches vital things. It is vital.' *Daily News*

26. SPRING SOWING Stories
by Liam O'Flaherty

¶ 'Nothing seems to escape Mr. O'Flaherty's eye; his brain turns all things to drama; and his vocabulary is like a river in spate. *Spring Sowing* is a book to buy, or to borrow, or, yes, to steal.' *Bookman*

27. WILLIAM A Novel
by E. H. Young

¶ 'An extraordinary good book, penetrating and beautiful.'
Allan Monkhouse

'All its characters are very real and alive, and William himself is a masterpiece.' *May Sinclair*

28. THE COUNTRY OF THE POINTED FIRS
by Sarah Orne Jewett

¶ 'The young student of American literature in the far distant future will take up this book and say "a masterpiece!" as proudly as if he had made it. It will be a message in a universal language—the one message that even the scythe of Time spares.'
From the Preface by WILLA CATHER

29. GRECIAN ITALY
by Henry James Forman

¶ 'It has been said that if you were shown Taormina in a vision you would not believe it. If the reader has been in Grecian Italy before he reads this book, the magic of its pages will revive old memories and induce a severe attack of nostalgia.' *From the Preface by* H. FESTING JONES

30. WUTHERING HEIGHTS
by Emily Brontë

¶ 'It is a very great book. You may read this grim story of lost and thwarted human creatures on a moor at any age and come under its sway.' *From the Introduction by* ROSE MACAULAY

31. ON A CHINESE SCREEN
by W. Somerset Maugham

¶ A collection of sketches of life in China. Mr. Somerset Maugham writes with equal certainty and vigour whether his characters are Chinese or European. There is a tenderness and humour about the whole book which makes the reader turn eagerly to the next page for more.

32. A FARMER'S LIFE
by George Bourne

¶ The life story of a tenant-farmer of fifty years ago in which the author of *The Betteswiorth Book* and *The Memoirs of a Surrey Labourer* draws on his memory for a picture of the every-day life of his immediate forebears, the Smiths, farmers and handicraft men, who lived and died on the border of Surrey and Hampshire.

33. TWO PLAYS. *The Cherry Orchard & The Sea Gull*
by Anton Tchekoff. Translated by George Calderon

¶ Tchekoff had that fine comedic spirit which relishes the incongruity between the actual disorder of the world with the underlying order. He habitually mingled tragedy (which is life seen close at hand) with comedy (which is life seen at a distance). His plays are tragedies with the texture of comedy.

34. THE MONK AND THE HANGMAN'S DAUGHTER

by Ambrose Bierce

¶ About half this volume is taken up by *The Monk and the Hangman's Daughter* and the other half by *Fantastic Fables*. The first is a beautiful but very grim story and the second is as weird a collection of fables as it is possible to imagine.

35. CAPTAIN MARGARET A Novel

by John Masefield

¶ 'His style is crisp, curt and vigorous. He has the Stevensonian sea-swagger, the Stevensonian sense of beauty and poetic spirit. Mr. Masefield's descriptions ring true and his characters carry conviction.' *The Observer*

36. BLUE WATER

by Arthur Sturges Hildebrand

¶ This book gives the real feeling of life on a small cruising yacht; the nights on deck with the sails against the sky, long fights with head winds by mountainous coasts to safety in forlorn little island ports, and constant adventure free from care.

Ready Shortly.

37. STORIES FROM DE MAUPASSANT

Translated by Elizabeth Martindale

¶ 'His "story" engrosses the non-critical, it holds the critical too at the first reading. . . . That is the real test of art, and it is because of the inobtrusiveness of this workmanship, that for once the critic and the reader may join hands without awaiting the verdict of posterity.' *From the Introduction by* FORD MADOX FORD

38. WHILE THE BILLY BOILS First Series

by Henry Lawson

¶ These stories are written by the O. Henry of Australia. They tell of men and dogs, of cities and plains, of gullies and ridges, of sorrow and happiness, and of the fundamental goodness that is hidden in the most unpromising of human soil.

39. WHILE THE BILLY BOILS Second Series
by Henry Lawson

¶ Mr. Lawson has the uncanny knack of making the people he writes about almost violently alive. Whether he tells of jackeroos, bush children or drovers' wives, each one lingers in the memory long after we have closed the book.

41. IN MOROCCO
by Edith Wharton

¶ Morocco is a land of mists and mysteries, of trailing silver veils through which minarets, mighty towers, hot palm groves and Atlas snows peer and disappear at the will of the Atlantic cloud-drifts.

42. GLEANINGS IN BUDDHA-FIELDS
by Lafcadio Hearn

¶ A book which is readable from first page to last, and is full of suggestive thought, the essays on Japanese religious belief calling for special praise for the earnest spirit in which the subject is approached.

43. OUT OF THE EAST
by Lafcadio Hearn

¶ Mr. Hearn has written many books about Japan; he is saturated with the essence of its beauty, and in this book the light and colour and movement of that land drips from his pen in every delicately conceived and finely written sentence.

Ready Shortly.

44. KWAIDAN
by Lafcadio Hearn

¶ The marvellous tales which Mr. Hearn has told in this volume illustrate the wonder-living tendency of the Japanese. The stories are of goblins, fairies and sprites, with here and there an adventure into the field of unveiled supernaturalism.

Ready Shortly.

45. THE CONQUERED (A Story of the Gauls under Cæsar)
by Naomi Mitchison

¶ 'With *The Conquered* Mrs. Mitchison establishes herself as the best, if not the only, English historical novelist now writing. It seems to me in many respects the most attractive and poignant historical novel I have ever read.' *New Statesman*

46. WHEN THE BOUGH BREAKS (Stories of the time when Rome was crumbling to ruin)
by Naomi Mitchison

¶ 'Interesting, delightful, and fresh as morning dew. The connossieur in short stories will turn to some pages in this volume again and again with renewed relish.' *Times Literary Supplement*

*

The following additional volumes in the series will be issued shortly.

47. THE FLYING BO'SUN
by Arthur Mason (with an Introduction by Edwin Muir)

48. LATER DAYS: Recollections
by W. H. Davies (Author of *The Autobiography of a Super-Tramp*)

49. IN THE MIDST OF LIFE: Stories
by Ambrose Bierce

50. IN DEFENCE OF WOMEN
by H. L. Mencken

51. VIENNESE MEDLEY: A Novel
by Edith O'Shaughnessy

52. PRECIOUS BANE: A Novel
by Mary Webb

53. THE INFAMOUS JOHN FRIEND: A Novel
by Mrs. R. S. Garnett

✿